Corporate Community Involvement

Corporate Social Responsibility Series

Series Editors:
Professor Güler Aras, Yıldız Technical University, Istanbul, Turkey
Professor David Crowther, De Montfort University, Leicester, UK

Presenting applied research from an academic perspective on all aspects of corporate social responsibility, this global interdisciplinary series includes books for all those with an interest in ethics and governance, corporate behaviour and citizenship, regulation, protest, globalisation, responsible marketing, social reporting and sustainability.

Recent titles in this series:

Human Dignity and Managerial Responsibility
Edited by Ana Maria Davila Gomez and David Crowther
ISBN: 978-1-4094-2311-9

Regulating Multinationals in Developing Countries
Edwin Mujih
ISBN: 978-1-4094-4463-3

Managing Responsibly
Edited by Jane Buckingham and Venkataraman Nilakant
ISBN: 978-1-4094-2745-2

Territories of Social Responsibility
Edited by Patricia Almeida Ashley and David Crowther
ISBN: 978-1-4094-4852-5

Auditor Independence
Ismail Adelopo
ISBN: 978-1-4094-3470-2

The Balanced Company
Edited by Inger Jensen, John Damm Scheuer and Jacob Dahl Rendtorff
ISBN: 978-1-4094-4559-3

Corporate Community Involvement

A Visible Face of CSR in Practice

BİLGE UYAN-ATAY
Yıldız Technical University and Bahçeşehir University, Turkey

Routledge
Taylor & Francis Group

LONDON AND NEW YORK

First published in paperback 2024

First published 2013 by Gower Publishing

Published 2016 by Routledge
4 Park Square, Milton Park, Abingdon, Oxon OX14 4RN

and by Routledge
605 Third Avenue, New York, NY 10158

Routledge is an imprint of the Taylor & Francis Group, an informa business

Publisher's Note
The publisher has gone to great lengths to ensure the quality of this reprint but points out that some imperfections in the original copies may be apparent.

Gower Applied Business Research
Our programme provides leaders, practitioners, scholars and researchers with thought provoking, cutting edge books that combine conceptual insights, interdisciplinary rigour and practical relevance in key areas of business and management.

British Library Cataloguing in Publication Data
A catalogue record for this book is available from the British Library.

Library of Congress Cataloging-in-Publication Data
Library of Congress data has been applied for.

ISBN: 978-1-4724-1244-7 (hbk)
ISBN: 978-1-03-283701-7 (pbk)
ISBN: 978-1-315-57427-1 (ebk)

DOI: 10.4324/9781315574271

Contents

List of Figures

List of Tables

Preface

Recognition that corporations are embedded within societies is playing an increasingly significant role in shaping strategic decision making in modern business organisations. Corporate community involvement (CCI) is becoming an increasingly salient aspect of corporate social responsibility (CSR) and encompasses a diverse range of activities from philanthropic giving and employee volunteerism to cause-related marketing (CRM) and sponsorship, and supports a range of community needs from education and welfare to cultural and artistic development. As such it provides an ideal focus for exploring the economic, strategic, cultural and institutional influences on CCI.

This book presents the first systematic analysis of CCI behaviours in Turkey. Turkey, as a secular, developing, largely Muslim country with a growing economy, provides a comparative research context that is culturally, economically and institutionally distinct from other environments within which CCI has been studied. The economic and historical roots of Turkey combined with its unique geography have resulted in considerable diversity in its economic, social and cultural dimensions. The ever-growing participation of Turkey in international agreements as well as its involvement in social and cultural campaigns has played an important role in increasing awareness and consciousness of CSR and other associated issues throughout the country. This situation draws the attention of the researchers in order to capture the CSR situation of the country. The aim of this book is to elicit how these specific dimensions impact upon CCI decision making and the choice of activities undertaken. A model has been developed based on the application of the behavioural theory of the firm. The model engenders the studies which aim to explain the situation of CCI in an institutional, cultural and national context and through the CCI model, it is expected that the multicultural and complex characteristics of the CCI phenomenon can be understood. By this way the multicultural factors on CCI behaviours and the choice of CCI decision making has been studied.

This book focuses on the CCI activities of the largest corporate givers. Today, private corporations are increasing in size and in many cases the resulting higher profile is attracting growing public pressure to consider their societal involvement. Moreover, with globalisation of the economy has come an increase in the scale of the social impact of businesses. As a consequence of these developments, the number of ways companies invest in the community has increased, for these are seen as means of managing relationships with stakeholders. This book is aimed at investigating the nature of these activities as one visible aspect of CSR, namely, corporate CCI.

Today, firms would appear to want their CCI projects to make a continuous and therefore sustainable contribution, with many of these projects being embedded in their core competencies and being related to long-term strategic development. This book shows that it is apparent that companies can have different motivations (strategic to philanthropic) for engaging in the same form of CCI. Additionally, this book indicates that all the forms of CCI are interconnected and hence aims to shed light on why firms choose one or multiple types of CCI, which types of firms prefer which aspects of CCI as well as the motivations for participating in CCI at all.

Bilge Uyan-Atay

List of Abbreviations

AKP	Justice and Development Party
B2B	Business to Business
CAF	Charities Aid Foundation
CCC	Corporate Community Contributions
CCI	Corporate Community Involvement
CECP	Committee Encouraging Corporate Philanthropy
CRM	Cause-Related Marketing
CSR	Corporate Social Responsibility
DEİK	Foreign Economic Relations Board
DOHAYKO	Helping Street Animals in Turkey
EHDHK	Homeless Animals and Nature Protection Association
EU	European Union
GDP	Gross Domestic Product
GRI	Global Reporting Initiatives
HR	Human Resources
HRM	Human Resources Management
ICCA	Institute for Corporate Culture Affairs
IKSV	Istanbul Foundation for Culture and Arts
IMF	International Monetary Fund
IT	Information Technology
MNEs	Multinational Enterprises
NGOs	Non-Governmental Organisations
OECD	Organisation for Economic Co-operation and Development
OLS	Ordinary Least Squares
OSGD	Private Sector Volunteer Association (Özel Sektör Gönüllüleri Derneği)
PR	Public Relations
R&D	Research and Development
ROA	Return on Assets
ROS	Return on Sales
SME	Small and Medium Enterprise

TEGV	Educational Volunteers Foundation of Turkey
TEMA	The Turkish Foundation for Combatting Soil Erosion, for Reforestation and the Protection of Natural Habitats
THKD	Turkey Animal Protection Association
TKYD	Corporate Governance Association of Turkey
TOG	Community Volunteers Foundation
TUİK	Turkish Statistical Institute
TUSEV	Turkey Third Sector Foundation
UN	United Nations
UNDP	United Nations Development Programme
UNESCO	United Nations Educational Scientific and Cultural Organisations
UNISEF	Unite for Children
VIF	Variance Inflation Factors
WBCSD	The World Business Council for Sustainable Development

Introduction to Corporate Community Involvement

This book focuses on the corporate community involvement (CCI) activities of the largest corporate givers in Turkey compared with other countries. Today, private corporations are increasing in size and in many cases the resulting higher profile is attracting growing public pressure to consider their societal involvement. Moreover, with globalisation of the economy has come an increase in the scale of the social impact of businesses. As a consequence of these developments, the number of ways companies invest in the community has increased, for these are seen as means of managing relationships with stakeholders. This book is aimed at investigating the nature of these activities as one visible aspect of corporate social responsibility (CSR), namely, CCI.

1.1 Defining Corporate Community Involvement

CCI has been defined as 'the way in which a company shares its resources with the communities that it impacts upon. It encompasses all forms of company support for the community, including charitable donations, community projects, employer supported volunteering, sponsorships, cause-related marketing and gifts-in-kind' (CAF, 2007). There has recently been increasing output of academic articles investigating this phenomenon, driven by awareness of the considerable amounts involved in donations by companies to communities. For example, the largest 100 UK firms collectively contributed approximately £1.3 billion to the voluntary sector in 2008 (CAF, 2009), which is more than three times what they gave in 2001, and the proportion of pre-tax profits donated by the largest companies has quadrupled since the late 1980s (Smith and Locke, 2007). Moreover, according to the most recent research by the Committee Encouraging Corporate Philanthropy (CECP, 2009), entitled

'Giving in Number', the top 137 American companies, including 55 companies in the Fortune 100, gave $11.25 billion in cash and products in 2008.

Further, increasingly, many leading corporations are allocating significant amounts of time and resources to the support of community involvement projects. These projects encompass a variety of forms, such as: corporate support for developing education and healthcare systems, involvement in culture and arts programmes, helping elderly people, and organising programmes for the society in which they are located, repairing local schools and hospital buildings as well as developing nationwide programmes in developing and undeveloped countries. To date, cash giving has been the most common form of corporate community activity. Regarding this, in 2006, *Business Week*, in order to shed light on corporate philanthropy's biggest givers, surveyed companies in Standard & Poor's 500 stock index to assess the amount spent on philanthropic activities. The results showed that 190 companies out of the 200 that responded reported numbers reflecting cash gifts, whereas only 125 provided values for gifts in-kind, such as products and services.

Nonetheless, it has been also observed that firms, in addition to their cash donations, are increasingly becoming involved in their society using employees, non-profit organisations and clients' sources. For example, Deloitte found another way to recruit college students every year that involved building a CCI idea into their business strategy – they introduced the Alternative Spring Break, bringing together students from countries across the globe so as to provide them with the opportunity to join Deloitte professionals in delivering collaborative works for the benefit of society. The potential recruits were thus able to experience the company's culture first hand. The outcomes were so effective that the traditional recruitment process was abandoned and replaced by recruits being identified through this procedure (www.deloitte.com/us/asb, 2007). In sum, this company has intentionally incorporated community involvement into their business plan, seeing it as a powerful tool for change that can enhance their performance.

Today, firms would appear to want their CCI projects to make a continuous and therefore sustainable contribution, with many of these projects being embedded in their core competencies and being related to long-term strategic development. Further, a survey conducted by McKinsey in 2007 (McKinsey Report, 2007) suggests that consumers' growing expectations of firms taking societal responsibility makes corporate philanthropy more important than ever. However, many respondents to this survey clearly expressed the opinion that companies are not meeting social goals or stakeholder expectations very effectively. It also emerged in this report that companies that are doing well are taking a more strategic approach, such as enhancing the company's reputation or brand, or pursuing more concrete business goals, such as gaining information on potential markets.

Often companies target the areas where government provision remains insufficient, hence acting as key providers of aid to civil society. For example, Novartis supports local communities by engaging in volunteerism and philanthropic activities through their foundation. That is, the Novartis Foundation for Sustainable Development collaborates with various forces in society at the local level to secure basic needs and to improve the health and living conditions of the world's poorest people. Similarly, Johnson & Johnson supports community-based programmes that are aimed at improving health and well-being. To this end, the company listens to the opinions of their community partners so as to identify the most suitable areas for investment, such as helping mothers and infants to survive childbirth. They also support doctors, nurses and local leaders as they work to provide the best medical care for their people as well as educating communities on how to reduce their risk of infection from preventable diseases.

Many companies pioneer in specific chosen areas and invest consistently in these, with education being key amongst them. For example, IBM, seeing this as their number one social priority, has developed projects on school reform and talent under its corporate citizenship and corporate affairs programmes. In particular, their efforts are focused on preparing the next generation of leaders and workers through the Reinventing Education Program in the US and 12 other countries, in which they have invested $75 million. They have also extended their educational work to the KidSmart Early Learning Program, which puts technology in the hands of the youngest students through the science and technology adventures on the TryScience Web site (www.tryscience.org), whilst maintaining their long-standing support for universities and colleges as well as for adult literacy. Regarding their literacy endeavours, IBM's Reading Companion initiative employs innovative speech recognition technologies to reach children as well as adults in search of improved reading competency. Similarly, Unilever developed a hand-washing awareness programme called Lifebuoy and, by working with partners in government and non-government organisations (NGOs), this became the largest private hygiene education initiative in the world. However, by promoting their own product in this campaign it can be seen that engaging in community projects benefits the company as well as society. In general this raises the issue of whether companies engage in CCI for reputational reasons and/or if they see it as a means for selling more goods or services, a matter returned to later.

In sum, there has been tremendous growth in CCI projects of all sizes in recent years, spurred on by organisations such as the UK charity Business in the Community which provides a crucial source of information aimed at motivating businesses and the Government to engage in such activities. A report written by the CEO of Deloitte in 2009 states that CCI can help to: build customer relationships, improve staff recruitment and retention, motivate a company's employees and to achieve a company's strategic goals, whilst at the same time having a positive impact on the community in terms of beneficial social change and strengthened relationships with community groups. In fact, the projects incorporated into some companies' strategic implementation are now so extensive in some cases that they are having a profound impact on community development.

1.2 The Reason for Investigating Turkey

This book examines the CCI activities of firms through analysis of leading companies situated in Turkey. The economic and historical roots of Turkey combined with its unique geography have resulted in considerable diversity in its economic, social and cultural dimensions. The general research aim is to elicit how these specific dimensions impact upon CCI decision making and the choice of activities undertaken.

A review of Turkey's history reveals that a corporate culture of paying attention to the needs of society and allocating resources for their fulfilment dates back to the Ottoman Empire. Regarding this, the concept of a 'foundation', as initially shaped under the Ottoman Empire, consisted of an institutionalised charity approach in the fields of education, health, and social security (Bikmen, 2003). As a legacy from those days, many conglomerate family businesses in Turkey still own a foundation, which they use to channel their social contributions (Bugra, 1994). Moreover, much of the wider society in Turkey perceives socially responsible behaviour by companies, corporate donations and charity activities as a part of this 'foundation culture' and believes that firms should conduct charity work so as to increase the welfare of the society in which they are located.

By 1980, Turkey realised that it would not be possible to provide for sustainable development, given its legacy of high inflation, economic crises and military interventions in the preceding era, but recognised the need to make significant changes to ensure a stable economy. Hence, from this time onwards work was undertaken to reduce the state's role in the economy, liberalise the markets and compete with the economies of developed countries (Ararat and Ugur, 2003). Increases in exports, liberalisation of import regulations, growth of foreign capital investment, flexibility in the exchange rate policy and privatisation were among the most important components of the reforms launched during this period. In 2001, the country went through a serious economic crisis which led to a significant devaluation of its currency and caused thousands of people to become unemployed, particularly in the banking sector, as well as leading to hundreds of small and medium-sized companies going bankrupt (Akyüz and Boratav, 2003). These consequences of the crisis revealed the need for improved institutional governance and, above all, the importance of taking serious steps in terms of transparency and accountability.

After 2001, a stability programme was put into practice under the supervision of the International Monetary Fund (IMF) and the accompanying structural reforms resulted in Turkey reaching a high level of annual economic growth between 2001 and 2005. For instance, in 2005 the gross national product increased by 7.5 per cent (TUIK, 2008). As for industrial production, the years following the 2001 crisis witnessed a considerable increase in the production and capacity utilisation rates. Moreover, after a quick post-crisis recovery process the inflation rate dropped rapidly as well as the Turkish Lira gaining value, and all of these developments were viewed positively at the international level. The opening of accession negotiations with the European Union (EU) and recognition of Turkey as a success story by the IMF reflect this positive evolution. Subsequently, despite the global crisis that emerged in 2008, its stable inflation and growth rates observed over the last five years have created a favourable environment for companies to continue to deal with social issues.

The ever-growing participation of Turkey in international agreements as well as its involvement in social and cultural campaigns has played an important role in increasing awareness and consciousness of CSR and other associated issues throughout the country. The proliferation of such developments has affected civil society, the business world, the state and other social stakeholder groups. Moreover, the recent alignment of Turkish legislation on associations and foundations with the 'EU acquis' has also accelerated the positive evolution of civil society organisations, by generating a more appropriate environment in the country for civil participation. In sum, Turkey's historical culture in relation to the foundations, its growing voice in the international arena and its economic evolution has allowed the business community to be effective in terms of its contributions to society.

1.3 The Relationship between Corporate Community Involvement and Corporate Social Responsibility

Generally, CCI activities are seen as a part of the broader CSR strategy and thus, they are often managed in CSR departments (CAF, 2007), but some CCI activities are not embedded in the CSR programmes within firms. Therefore, the extent to which CCI can be considered as a part of CSR strategy is addressed next as along with an exploration of the definitions of CSR.

In the extant literature, there are a variety of definitions of CSR and the relation of CCI to CSR can be seen to be divided into two main camps. The first view is that CCI is simply a part of CSR and, therefore, any such activity should be incorporated into the overall CSR strategy. The second stance that arises in the literature is that the definition of CSR only covers part of the definition of CCI, because CSR does not embrace all forms of CCI activities. Which definition of CSR relates to which of these two assumptions will be examined in detail below.

Firstly, under the lens that the relationship between the CSR and CCI is one where the latter should be considered as a part of the former, both Carroll (1979; 1991) and the European Commission (2007) have provided CSR definitions that support this view. Carroll (1979) defined CSR by developing a conceptual model which describes the essential aspects of CSR, where economic responsibility is a part of a company's social responsibility, and he also added legal, ethical and discretionary responsibilities as components of the latter. Similarly, the European Commission (2007) sees CSR as follows: 'A concept whereby companies integrate social and environmental concerns in their business operations and in their interaction with their stakeholders on a voluntary basis.' That is, this definition emphasises that: (1) CSR covers social and environmental issues; (2) CSR is not or should not be separate from business strategy and operations, for it is about integrating social and environmental concerns into the business strategy and operations; (3) CSR is a voluntary concept; and (4) an important aspect of CSR is how enterprises interact with their internal and external stakeholders (employees, customers, neighbours, NGOs, public authorities, and so on). It is apparent that the definitions put forward by Carroll (1979) and the European Commission (2007) embrace all forms of CCI, which can be carried out for pure philanthropic, strategic philanthropic or commercial purposes.

However, in other literature the definitions of CSR do not embrace the entire meaning of CCI. The reason for this is that some authors (Aupperle et al., 1985; McWilliams and Siegel, 2000; Burke and Logsdon, 2006) have found evidence that CSR may not be associated with the economic responsibility of the firm. An example of this was a study by McWilliams and Siegel (2000), which investigated the relationship between CSR and financial performance. According to these scholars, if this relationship has a positive correlation, additional investment in CSR should be made in order to maximise profits, but if a negative or neutral correlation is found, this means that investment in CSR has little or no impact on performance. Their empirical analysis revealed that CSR has a neutral impact on financial performance, thus refuting its being linked to the economic responsibility of the firm. That is, McWilliams and Siegel's findings support the second perspective that a part of CSR embraces a part of CCI.

The reason for this can be explained as follows. As has been discussed, CCI has economic and commercial purposes, such as increasing the profit levels of the company, but, according to McWilliams et al. (1999), CSR cannot be carried out for economic purposes, because it has no affect on the financial performance of a firm. Thus, under this lens its definition cannot embrace some forms of CCI, such as sponsorship, but it can embrace pure philanthropic forms, such as creating foundations or cash giving. Therefore, according to McWilliams et al.'s (1999) perspective, the concepts of CSR and CCI are distinct in terms of the purposes of the activity for the firm.

In sum, how the various definitions of CSR embrace the various parts of CCI has been discussed. Regarding this, some of these definitions cover all forms of CCI, whilst others do not. The two different perspectives on CSR have arisen from the ongoing debate about the relationship between it and the economic performance of the firm, that is, whether it is positive, negative or neutral.

1.4 Overview of the Book

There are nine chapters covering the three phases mentioned in this introduction. Chapter 2 contains a literature review on CCI, which has four elements. First, the meaning of CCI is examined in detail and how the relevant literature for the literature review was selected is presented. Second, in order to gain an understanding of how the existing literature has been conceptualised, the extant theories/approaches found in the existing CCI literature are outlined. Third, methodological approaches employed in the extant empirical literature on CCI are identified and critically examined. Fourth, a summary of the prior work is given at the end of the chapter in order to illustrate where the gaps are to be found.

In Chapter 3, the conceptual model to be applied in the empirical chapters is devised, which serves to assess the CCI behaviours of the companies studied and to ascertain how they can be differentiated from each other in terms of their CCI activities. As explained above, the behavioural theory of the firm is drawn upon to show how its core concepts can be used to establish the determinants of CCI in this model. Finally, drawing on the literature there is an explanation regarding how and why these determinants affect CCI decision making.

In Chapter 4 the methodology is presented, which contains discussion on such matters as the research paradigm, sampling strategy, data collection process and the subsequent analysis. This serves as a foundation for the following four empirical results chapters (Chapters 5 to 8).

Chapter 5 is the first empirical one and presents the descriptive data collected from a CCI questionnaire. In order to enrich understanding of the context, this chapter also contains discussion on the important facets of Turkey's cultural, economic and legislative environment. Finally, the survey findings and their implications for management policy are synthesised in order to address the research questions presented above.

Chapter 6 provides additional information on the Turkish environment, and discussion as to whether the culture, economic conditions and standard of living are having an affect on the decisions on CCI activities. In particular, how companies manage their CCI activities and their preferences for involvement are investigated. More specifically, the enquiry involves using the aforementioned survey to assess how organisational structure can shape managerial understanding of CSR departmentalisation and how this in turn influences CCI activities. Subsequently, the findings are presented and conclusions drawn as well as there being further comparative analysis using the findings of extant studies.

Chapter 7 contains survey outcomes regarding the determinants of scale and composition of CCI activities in which firms become involved in Turkey. First, based on the conceptual framework developed in Chapter 3, testable hypotheses are developed deploying three variables taken from the behavioural theory of the firm, which are viewed as being the most likely to affect CCI decisions. Moreover, how these three variables affect such decisions is examined. Finally, the results obtained for this chapter are discussed and the theoretical and practical implications considered.

Chapter 8 contains the findings of qualitative case studies conducted in four large companies situated in Turkey. First, there is an explanation of the CCI process that involves summarising these firms' decision-making processes under the key categories identified by the survey. Second, drawing upon the case study findings, the outcomes from the qualitative questionnaire analysis are revisited to provide further insights into these. Third, the results obtained for this chapter are discussed and how far these results are consistent with the underpinning constructs of the behavioural theory of the firm are examined.

Chapter 9 concludes the book and its main aim is to address the research questions put forward in this introductory chapter. To this end there is a synthesised view of the findings from Chapters 5, 6, 7 and 8 that involves drawing together the results and insights from these distinct examinations, discussing the findings and assessing the implications for theory and management practice. The chapter also evaluates the limitations of the research and proposes future lines of enquiry.

2

What the Existing Studies on Corporate Community Involvement Tell Us

Corporate community involvement (CCI) has been defined as 'the way in which a company shares its resources with the communities that it impacts upon. It encompasses all forms of company support for the community, including charitable donations, community projects, employer supported volunteering, sponsorships, cause-related marketing and gifts-in-kind' (CAF, 2007). This definition from the Charities Aid Foundation (CAF) is a good starting point for developing a more comprehensive one as it encompasses all manifestations of the phenomenon. Moreover, examining the characteristics of CCI will provide an understanding of the kind of activities that firms consider as being their CCI activities.

2.1 Understanding the Term 'Corporate Community Involvement'

From the CAF definition, it is clear that CCI is complex, covering a wide variety of behaviours that involve particular corporate resource commitments and motivations and which relate to a broad range of social issues and causes. However, this definition fails to address a number of issues, including: (1) the kind of resources that firms give to communities; (2) the purposes for taking up CCI and (3) which department of the firm undertakes CCI activities. In order to explore these topics, the four following key issues are addressed through examination of the existing literature: the resources that are deployed in CCI; firm preference when engaging in CCI activities; the reasons for becoming engaged; and ways in which companies carry out their CCI activities.

Regarding the particular resources that are deployed in CCI, Hess et al. (2002) have suggested that it can entail the use of a significant part of a firm's resources and can include the firm's products, services, money, employee time and talent. In addition, they divided a firm's resources into three segments – physical, organisational and human capital – in order to explain how firms collect necessary supplies and deliver them to those in need. Smith (1994) also pointed out that sometimes companies donate to non-profit-making organisations through offering managerial advice or technological/communications support. Moreover, Burke et al. (1986) distinguished two ways of giving – cash donations and non-cash donations – and argued that which is provided is dependent on firm resources and their attitudes to CCI.

The areas in which companies make donations has been investigated in various studies in the existing literature. Navarro (1988) identified contributions by firms financing a broad range of activities, including health and welfare services, education and research, culture and the arts, and various civic activities. Moreover, Rigaud (1991) pointed out that companies' donations mostly involved 'social and humanitarian causes and issues' (p.57). Regarding these, the Committee Encouraging Corporate Philanthropy (CECP, 2007) identified health and social services, education, community and economic development, and the natural environment. Brammer and Millington (2003) cited a whole host of causes – education, the arts, medical research, disability, sickness, economic devaluation/regeneration, the environment, children/youth, the elderly, politics, religion and sport.

The reason for engaging in CCI activities is also discussed in the extant literature. With respect to this, Haley (1991) defined CCI and its purpose as 'necessitated investments, social currency, and social responsibility efforts which managers use to influence society and various stakeholders'. Similarly, Moore (1995) argued that involvement in CCI offers real strategic benefits to participating businesses through enhanced corporate reputation. Moreover, Smith (1994) claimed that companies develop giving strategies in order to increase their name recognition among consumers, boost employee productivity, reduce research and development (R&D) costs, overcome regulatory obstacles, foster synergy among business units and gain a competitive edge. Porter and Kramer (2002) suggested that CCI is used to increase company visibility, improve employee morale and also to create social impact. However, Bright (2006) contended that an organisation's philanthropic activities are usually well-intentioned and not merely for instrumental gains. In sum, the previous explanations for participating in CCI activities can be summarised as follows: commercial motivation, altruistic motivation, local community support, employee commitment or the personal motivation of the manager.

Prior research on how CCI is implemented falls into two categories, the first being concerned with what types of giving there are and the second focused on how these types of giving are undertaken and under which departments within the companies. In relation to these considerations, there has been a large number of studies discussing CCI by classifying the types, as identified above (for example, Yankey, 1996; Korngold and Voudouris, 1996; Porter and Kramer, 1999; 2002; Hamil, 1999; Smith, 1996; Wymer and Samu, 2003). However, the extant literature has tended to focus on corporate philanthropy, corporate sponsorship, corporate volunteerism and cause-related marketing (CRM). Additionally, a few studies have investigated which department generates the decision to participate in CCI. Regarding this, Brammer and Millington (2003) elicited that firms manage their CCI through their CSR department, marketing/public relations (PR) department or their central administrative functions. Further, Smith (1994) stressed that companies fund CCI not only from philanthropy budgets, but also from business units, such as marketing and human resources (HR), whilst Porter and Kramer (1999) discussed the fact that although CCI is often handled by the corporation directly sometimes it is organised through a company foundation.

Drawing on the above discussion, the following broad definition of CCI is put forward as that which underpins this research endeavour.

> *CCI is the giving behaviour of companies to their communities and their environment formulating and implementing the company's, non-profit organisation's or other institutions' resources for altruistic and commercial purposes. The decision to give might be taken by a firm's central administrative functions, CSR or marketing/PR departments. Contributions can embrace a broad range of areas such as the environment, education, health/care, sports, arts, culture, politics, and religion. CCI can take the form of corporate philanthropy, CRM, corporate sponsorship, gifts-in-kind, community projects, corporate volunteerism programmes, employee volunteerism, and collaboration with non-profit, government or other institutions.*

2.2 Forms of Corporate Community Involvement

In this section the focus is on four manifestations of CCI: corporate philanthropy, corporate sponsorship, CRM and corporate volunteerism that were identified from the literature search process. More specifically, these forms of CCI are defined and their differences discussed, and it will emerge that each is usually incorporated with other forms of CCI.

2.2.1 CORPORATE PHILANTHROPY

Corporate philanthropy was defined by Himmelstein (1997) as 'the act of corporations donating some of their profits to nonprofit organisations in education, the arts, social services, environment and public policy'. Moreover, corporate philanthropy is widely accepted as being one of the most visible ways that a business can help a community (Wulfson, 2001). Further investigations into corporate philanthropy have shown that by the early 1980s, many CEOs had begun linking their involvement with social causes to the company's strategic behaviour (Wulfson, 2001; Saiia et al., 2003). This researcher posits that cash giving is the distinctive aspect of this type CCI when compared with the other forms and thus, is used in this book to identify articles on corporate philanthropy, irrespective of whether they are driven by commercial or benevolent motivation.

In general, because corporate philanthropy is defined as the amount of cash donated it is easier to measure the amount given than with the other forms of CCI and hence it has received a significant amount of attention from researchers. Although, on face value, the level of corporate philanthropy refers to the total amount of money donated by companies, scholars have used a variety of measures to investigate this. That is, apart from the actual amount of cash given (£/$m) (Levy and Shatto, 1978; Arupalam and Stoneman, 1995; Adams and Hardwick, 1998; Boatsman and Gupta, 2001; Brammer and Millington, 2004a; Gan, 2006; Brown et al., 2006), they have also used: the contribution ratio (Johnson, 1966; Levy and Shatto, 1978; Fry et al., 1982); the firm's giving to sales ratio (Navarro, 1988); total cash plus in-kind contributions (Buchholtz et al., 1999); the generosity ratio (Campbell et al., 2002); cash payouts (Bartkus et al., 2002; Seifert et al., 2004); cash donations plus charity receipts (Seifert et al., 2003); and the ratio of corporate charitable contributions to turnover (Brammer and Millington, 2004b).

Other notable studies have included dependent variables other than the amount donated. For instance, Wokutch and Spencer (1987) measured the perpetual CSR rating as a dependent variable in order to find the effect of philanthropic activity on organisational performance, whilst Campbell et al. (1999) investigated why some companies give to charity and others do not, and defined a firm's giving behaviour as a dependent variable. Further, Saiia et al. (2003) set out to prove that corporate philanthropy has become part of company strategy using the measure of belief in strategic philanthropy as the dependent variable. Brammer and Millington (2005: p.517), when researching the factors that affect the expenditure and participation decision, specified two dependent variables, 'the participation decision' and 'the level of charitable donations made by the firm normalized by firm size as measured by the level of total sales'. These articles will also be explained in this subsection, even though they do not define corporate philanthropy in terms of cash donation as they provide important information about the scope of corporate philanthropy.

Turning to the independent variables in the prior empirical research and first considering size, a firm's assets are the variable most commonly used to measure this. Moreover, regarding this, the total value of assets has been shown to be associated with the contribution ratio (Johnson, 1966; Levy and Shatto, 1978; Brammer and Millington, 2004b); cash donations (Levy and Shatto, 1978; Adams and Hardwick, 1998; Brammer and Millington 2004a; Gan, 2006; Brown et al., 2006; Amato and Amato, 2007); cash payouts (Bartkus et al., 2002; Seifert et al., 2004); the firm's giving behaviour (Campbell et al., 1999) and the expenditure and participation decision (Brammer and Millington, 2005). Navarro (1988) contended that the benefits of corporate contributions are likely to accrue to labour rather than capital and that as a result employee numbers should be accepted as another variable used to measure size. In relation to this, the employee variable has been defined as labour intensity (Navarro, 1988) or the number of staff employed by the firm (Arupalam and Stoneman, 1995; Brown et al., 2006) and has been investigated in terms of its association with the total amount of cash donated by each company (Navarro, 1988; Arupalam and Stoneman, 1995; Brown et al., 2006). Firm sales have also been used for measuring size (Buchholtz et al., 1999; Campbell et al., 1999) and using these Campbell et al. (1999) found that size has no significant effect on a company's giving behaviour, in contrast to the rest of the research on this matter.

Company characteristics variables have been defined as corporate behaviour (Wokutch and Spencer, 1987), membership (Campbell et al., 2002), the company name (Gan, 2006) or the firm's internalisation (Brammer et al., 2009). Wokutch and Spencer (1987), using Lehman's behavioural model, classified organisations on the basis of their involvement in different types of activities and found that, out of four categories, only two, named Saints and Cynics/Repenters, made high contributions. Moreover, Campbell et al. (2002) elicited that PerCent Club members make higher charitable contributions than non-PerCent Club members. Gan (2006) counted the number of mentions of a company's name in court cases or the news and found this to have a positive impact on giving. Brammer et al. (2009) extended the studies on corporate philanthropy by investigating the influence on charitable giving exerted by a firm's international business environment and determined that an environment where negative social issues exist influences the corporate charitable giving of companies' subsidiaries.

A wide range of the literature has addressed corporate philanthropy through the nature of the ownership and managerial structure of a company and the various variables adopted have included: shareholder value (Adams and Hardwick, 1998; Bartkus et al., 2002; Brammer and Millington, 2005; Brown et al., 2006); managerial preferences (Levy and Shatto, 1978; Navarro, 1988; Buchholtz et al., 1999; Campbell et al., 1999; Saiia et al., 2003; Brammer and Millington, 2005; Brown, et al., 2006); board size (Brown et al., 2006; Bartkus et al., 2002); the existence of blockholders (Seifert, et al., 2004; Bartkus et al., 2002); and pressure from stakeholders (Brammer and Millington, 2004a). At first there was no support for the view that there is a link between discretionary donations and a company's ownership structure (Adams and Hardwick, 1998; Bartkus et al., 2002). However, later on Brammer and Millington (2004b and 2005) determined that among givers, firms with more highly concentrated shareholdings donate proportionally more than those with more diluted holdings. Further, Brown et al. (2006) found that giving enhances stakeholder value, which could explain the earlier finding that there is a significant relationship between concentrated shareholding and charitable giving.

Many researchers have highlighted the fact that managerial preferences, their level of discretion and values significantly influence the giving decision (Levy and Shatto, 1978; Buchholtz et al., 1999; Campbell et al., 1999; Saiia et al., 2003; Brown et al., 2006). Regarding this, Brammer and Millington (2005) discovered that the amount of a director's remuneration is negatively related to the likelihood that a business is involved in corporate giving. This finding is consistent with the study by Navarro (1988), which found that corporate donations and executive pay act as substitutes for one another in some firms. Other important findings indicate that the existence of a large board (Bartkus et al., 2002;

Brown et al., 2006), as well as external and internal stakeholder preferences, significantly affect charitable giving. However, Seifert et al. (2004) and Bartkus et al. (2002) elicited that blockholders limit corporate philanthropy. In sum, there has been substantial evidence from the research that the ownership and managerial structure of the company affects the decision regarding corporate philanthropic giving.

Most of the articles on corporate philanthropy have sought to elicit whether there is a correlation between it and a company's financial resources. Here, the focus is on the results of these studies rather than the proxies used to represent financial resources. The findings from the literature, in general, support the fact that the current tax-deductible status of contributions has led to firms treating these as ordinary business expenses (Johnson, 1966; Navarro, 1988; Arupalam and Stoneman, 1995; Boatsman and Gupta, 2001; Brammer and Millington, 2005). Advertising has also emerged as having a positive relation with corporate donation (Navarro, 1988; Levy and Shatto, 1978; Fry et al., 1982; Boatsman and Gupta, 2001; Brammer and Millington, 2005; Brown et al., 2006). Moreover, earlier studies found that the existence of a free rider problem amongst employees in a firm (Navarro, 1988) diminishes the levels of donations. Such studies have used also firm leverage as a variable to identify the extent of corporate resource constraints (Adams and Hardwick, 1998; Brammer and Millington 2004b; 2005).

Another stream in the literature relates to cash resource availability. In relation to this, an early study was carried out by Buchholtz et al. (1999), measuring firm resources as return on sales (ROS), return on assets (ROA) and organisational slack and it emerged that the level of these firm resources is positively related to philanthropy. Other studies have also found a positive relationship between the availability of a firm's cash resources and cash donations (Seifert et al., 2003; 2004; Gan, 2006), but no significant relationship between corporate philanthropy and a firm's financial performance has been elicited (Seifert et al., 2003; 2004; Brammer and Millington 2004a). The results of extant studies also indicate that among givers the rate of giving is positively related to corporate profitability (Navarro, 1988; Adams and Hardwick, 1998), managerial utility (Boatsman and Gupta, 2001) and R&D intensity (Brammer and Millington, 2005) and negatively related to firm indebtedness (Brown et al., 2006). Brammer and Millington (2004b) determined that during the early period of corporate charitable donation the amount given was significantly positively correlated with profits, but this relationship weakened during the 1990s as firms became increasingly responsive to stakeholder influences.

Industry is another important factor determining corporate philanthropy and has been investigated in studies regarding it from two perspectives. The first relates to determining the proclivities regarding the issue of different industries and the second to finding which industry type is most generous. In relation to the latter, some researchers have investigated which sectors donate the most, but the findings have been inconclusive. For example, Johnson (1966) investigated the years between 1954 and 1958 and elicited that manufacturing, construction, trade and service industries made the highest contributions. However, other scholars have found different sectors to be the largest donors, such as: finance and retail industries between the years 1979 to 1986 (Arupalam and Stoneman, 1995); service and utility industrial groups or the year 1994 (Adams and Hardwick, 1998); and firms which produce industrial commodities, firms in an industry with significant environmental or social costs and a consumer focus, and firms in the pharmaceutical and defence industries between 1989–1990 and 1998–1999, respectively (Brammer and Millington, 2004b).

Other studies have chosen specific industries to test their research hypotheses. For instance, Buchholtz et al. (1999) chose food and services as well as software industries, because they are populated with many mid-size firms. In relation to this they contended that these industries comprise groups of firms with very different business practices, capital structures and product markets and therefore would provide an excellent environment in which to test their hypotheses. Campbell et al. (1999) categorised food firms either as givers or non-givers after asking them whether they had donated surplus food to any local charity so as to link the outcomes with the main type of product sold. Brammer and Millington (2004a) expressed the view that industry conditions may have a significant impact on the delegation by management of corporate donations and in order to prove this they looked at companies operating in consumer goods, high-wage and regulated industries. Clearly, these industrial effects on corporate philanthropy need to be borne in mind.

2.2.2 CORPORATE SPONSORSHIP

The other focal forms of CCI can be carried out through either the cash or non-cash resources of the company and sponsorship is one of these. This was defined by the executives of the Royal Philharmonic Orchestra (1974) as 'the donation or loan of resources (people, money, material, etc.) by private individuals or organisations to other individuals or organisations engaged in the provision of those public goods and services designed to improve the quality of life'.

Another definition provided by the Economist Intelligence Unit in its 1980 report on sponsorship is more comprehensive and states that: 'A sponsor makes a contribution in cash or in kind – which may or may not include services and expertise – to an activity which is in some measure a leisure pursuit, either a sport or within the broad definition of the arts.' Gardner and Shuman (1987) suggested that sponsorship is an important component of the promotion mix, which they defined as investments in causes or events to support corporate or marketing objectives. Moreover, Quester and Thompson (2001) found that sponsorship effectiveness is directly related to the degree to which sponsors are willing to maximise their investment by spending on additional advertising and promotional activities, which emphasises the fact that companies donating their resources to good causes also need to promote them.

The extant literature on sponsorship comprises a large number of academic articles, many of which were identified by the scholars who authored the two studies that are recognised as being the definitive international meta-reviews on the subject (Cornwell and Maignan, 1998; Wallisser, 2003).[1] That is, these two papers encompass the relevant studies conducted between 1983 and 2001 and between them cover a total of 233 articles, some of which are empirical, whilst others are more conceptual in their approach. As the contributions of the conceptual articles have already been addressed above in this literature review, in the following subsection the empirical studies are considered. Moreover, as there is no single extant meta-review of the literature for the years after 2001 until the present date, other relevant papers that pertain to this period are examined.

With respect to the two meta-studies, Cornwell and Maignan (1998) adopted four research streams: managerial aspects of sponsorship, measurement of sponsorship effects, strategic use of sponsorship and legal/ethical considerations in sponsorship. Subsequently, Walliser (2003) complemented this work with additional studies that were published in Europe prior to 1996 and extended the earlier review by analysing sponsorship articles for the period from 1996 to 2001. Walliser (2003) used the basic research streams suggested by Cornwell and Maignan (1998), but owing to the large number of studies involved, articles focusing on legal and ethical aspects were omitted from his review.

Cornwell and Maignan (1998) revealed that research on the management of sponsorship activities has considered: audience considerations (Gardner

---

1   These two studies are litereture reviews and the following references formed part of these studies.

and Shuman, 1987; Polonsky et al., 1995); objectives (Otker, 1988; Marshall and Cook, 1992; Mount and Niro, 1995); budgets (West, 1990); organisational structure and personnel requirements (Abratt et al., 1987; Armstrong, 1988; Witcher et al., 1991; Marshall and Cook, 1992). In response to this, Walliser (2003) offered the finding that more recent research has examined it from a network perspective (Farrelly et al., 2006; Erickson and Kushner, 1999) and has also focused on effective ways to control sponsorship outcomes (Hermanns, 1987; 1991; Hermanns and Glogger, 1995). Both reviews have accepted that all these dimensions vary according to the type of company engaging in the sponsorship (for example, industrial or consumer firms) and the type of sponsorship undertaken (for example, sports or arts). However, Cornwell and Maignan (1998) stated that the research on managerial aspects of sponsorship was very descriptive but also fairly piecemeal and thus more holistic evaluations were required; a suggestion that was backed up by Walliser (2003).

The effects of sponsorship and how the authors of existing articles measured these effects form a central feature in the two reviews, reflecting the fact that it is significant in the literature in this domain. Cornwell and Maignan (1998) identified three measurement methods, namely; exposure-based (Hulks, 1980; Ensor, 1987; Pham, 1991; Sparks, 1995), tracking measures (McDonald, 1991; Cuneen and Hannan, 1993; Pope and Voges, 1995; Stotlar, 1993) and experiments (Pham, 1991). Regarding these, Walliser (2003) reported that tracking techniques are mostly frequently used to evaluate sponsorship effects, whereas there are few studies regarding the use of experiments. Further, Cornwell and Maignan (1998) pointed out that exposure-based methods can be carried out by monitoring the quantity and nature of the media coverage obtained for a sponsored event and estimating direct and indirect audiences. However, they noted that according to Pham (1991) these methods are restricted to providing information about the commercial effects of sponsorship. Moreover, Cornwell and Maignan (1998) explained that tracking techniques are used to evaluate the awareness, familiarity and preferences engendered by sponsorship, by drawing on consumer surveys. Additionally, Walliser (2003) focused on articles which measured awareness (for example, Renner and Tischler, 1997; Olivier and Kraak, 1997; McDaniel, 1999), image (for example, Giannelloni, 1993; Didellon-Carsana, 1998) and purchase intention (for example, Daneshvary and Schwer, 2000). In sum, Cornwell and Maignan (1998) found that studies regarding the effectiveness of sponsorship have yielded inconsistent findings and that there was a pressing need for well-designed experiments that can shed light on consumers' perceptions of and reactions to using sponsorship as a stimulus.

Turning to the strategic use of sponsorship, Cornwell and Maignan (1998) and Walliser (2003) reported that there are a few articles which have specifically addressed this matter (for example, Otker, 1988; Cornwell, 1995; Hoek et al., 1997). Cornwell and Maignan (1998) indicated that the literature regarding this focused on counter-strategies, in particular ambush marketing (Sandler and Shani, 1989; Cornwell, 1995; Meenaghan, 1994; 1995; Retsky, 1996). Moreover, some suggest that there is a need to examine the strategic use of sponsorship and how it can be integrated into the overall communication strategy. In the review by Walliser (2003), some of the focus of literature is on the strategic analysis of sponsorship activities (Lopez et. al., 1994), and the integration of sponsorship into the marketing mix (Piquet, 1998). Furthermore, the literature produced after 1995 gives more information on counter-strategies (Doust, 1997; Hoek et al., 1997; Meenaghan, 1996; 1998a; Payne, 1998; Shani and Sandler, 1998). In sum, most of the articles dating from between 1989 and 1998 have studied counter-strategies rather than examining the strategic use of sponsorship and its integration into an overall communication strategy.

The legal and ethical considerations in sponsorship are only addressed in Cornwell and Maignan's (1998) work and not in that of Walliser (2003). Regarding these, various legal questions have been explored, such as: the taxation of sponsorship fees (Wise and Miles, 1993); the use of sponsorship in the promotion of socially desirable products and behaviours (Ledwith, 1984); and the power of the sponsor over those sponsored and the activity (Beck, 1990). In the meta-review, some of the potential negative effects of sponsorship were discussed, but the paucity of research on this was noted. Consequently, Cornwell and Maignan (1998) argued the case for carrying out longitudinal studies in order to be able to elicit whether the nature of sports and cultural activities positively affects sponsor perceptions over time.

In order to make some observations regarding more recent scholarly outputs regarding sponsorship, a total of 32 articles published in the period from 2001 have been reviewed. It emerges that after 2001, these publications have tended to examine specific areas such as: sports (Lachowetz et al., 2003; Hickman et al, 2005; Chadwick and Thwaites, 2005; Miloch and Lambrecht, 2006); the arts (Chong, 2003); or other cultural organisations (Apostolopoulou and Papadimitriou, 2004). Moreover, as a proxy for a measurement of the effectiveness of sponsorship, the majority of these articles have attempted to gauge: sponsorship awareness (Tripodi et al., 2003; Pitts and Slattery, 2004; Grohs et al., 2004; Venkataramani et al., 2006; Miloch and Lambrecht, 2006); customer attitudes (Sneath et al., 2005; Christensen, 2006); or return on investment (Priutt et al., 2004). Furthermore, the literature of this period has examined: company managers' and owners' perceptions of sponsorship (Farrelly and Quester, 2003; Priutt et al., 2004); the effect of sponsorship on employee attitudes (Hickman et al., 2005); and the integration of sponsorship into company strategies (Cliffe and Motion, 2005; Kloppenborg et al., 2006). Some of the works have investigated sponsorship in different forms of media, such as the internet (Drennan and Cornwell, 2004; Rodgers, 2004) and television (Masterson, 2005). However, only one article from the literature pertains to the conducting of a comparative study (Shen, 2004).

In sum, in this subsection papers on sponsorship covering three different periods of time have been reviewed. The first period encompasses the studies carried out prior to 1988 and these were covered in the literature review by Cornwell and Maignan (1998). These authors recommended that sponsorship-related literature needs more in-depth investigation, particularly with respect to measuring its impact and examining the different types. The literature pertaining to the second time period has been examined by drawing on the work of Walliser (2003), who reviewed the major studies between 1998 and 2001. This author's overall conclusion is that there is a pressing need for scholars to generate better insights regarding sponsorship perceptions amongst the end users and that there should be better understanding of international perspectives. Regarding the last time period, from 2001 to date, more researchers have looked at different types of sponsorship, such as internet sponsorship (for example, Rodgers, 2004), TV sponsorship (for example, Masterson, 2005) and sports sponsorship (for example, Hickman et al., 2005). Further, the majority of these more recent articles have studied consumer awareness, attitudes and perception (for example, Grohs et al., 2004; Venkataramani et al., 2006; Miloch and Lambrecht, 2006; Ladik et al., 2007; Sirgy et al., 2008; Bennett et al., 2009; Tsiotsou and Alexandris, 2009). Moreover, a significant theme addressed in these papers is the fit between the sponsor and the activity being sponsored (Masterson, 2005; Poon and Prendergast, 2006; Garry et al., 2008; Copetti et al., 2009; Madill and O'Reilly, 2010). However, in some cases, such as that of the sponsoring of the Olympic Games, serious consideration of strategic or brand-related initiatives regarding the companies' sponsorship decisions is lacking (Papadimitriou et al., 2008). Consequently, issues such as brand fit, the effects of sponsorship,and the issues arising from new environments such as the media, as well as robust international comparisons, still appear to need further enquiry by researchers.

2.2.3 CAUSE-RELATED MARKETING

The earliest and most detailed definition of CRM was given by Varadarajan and Menon (1988), as being 'the process of formulating and implementing marketing activities that are characterised by an offer from the firm to contribute a specified amount to a designated cause when customers engage in revenue-providing exchanges that satisfy organisational and individual objectives'. According to File and Prince (1998), CRM has become a key element underpinning the marketing strategies of many companies and is considered as an effective way to attract new business segments. Berglind and Nakata (2005) stated that 'marketing a product, service, brand, or company by tying it in with a social cause is the essence of CRM'. Moreover, CRM is accepted as a joint venture between a corporation and a non-profit group to market products or services through a public association (Yankey, 1996; Austin 2003; Hajjat, 2003) for the purposes of being a good corporate citizen, helping the community, motivating staff and communicating the essence of the company's mission (William and Endacott, 2004). Finally, as with the other forms of CCI, CRM can contain dual purposes – benevolence and commerce.

Most of the extant studies on CRM have investigated its impact on consumer choice and their ability to understand these campaigns (Smith and Alcorn, 1991; Ross et al., 1992; Holmes and Kilbane, 1993; Drumwright, 1996; Webb and Mohr, 1998; Strahilevitz and Myers, 1998; Barone et al., 2000; Olsen et al., 2003; Broderick et al., 2003; García et al., 2003; Hajjat, 2003; Strahilevitz, 2003; Basil and Herr, 2003; Pracejus and Olsen, 2004; Pracejus et al., 2004; Hamlin and Wilson, 2004; Vaidyanathan and Aggarwal, 2005; Trimble and Rifon, 2006; Grau et al., 2007). In addition, File and Prince (1998) considered the motivations of firms for undertaking CRM. However, the effect of CRM on the perception of consumers constitutes the majority of this subsection, that is, the focus here is on what previous studies have found about the effectiveness of CRM campaigns in terms of their impact on consumer choice.

CRM has been accepted as the most creative and cost-effective product marketing strategy that has emerged in years (Smith and Alcorn, 1991). Consistent with this, File and Prince (1998) argued that many companies engage in CRM campaigns for the purpose of enhancing the image of their company and, more specifically, this is often undertaken to promote specific products and services through association with a non-profit organisation. According to Nowak and Clarke (2003), there are several factors that potentially contribute to the success of a CRM campaign, such as the sponsor's product quality, fair pricing, customer traits, the reputation of the associated non-profit organisation and the sponsor's reputation, shared values, good communication and the drawing up of specific terms that protect both parties' assets and clearly outline each party's responsibilities. In general, companies achieve successful CRM campaigns when they receive positive returns from their consumers.

The discussion of the potential impact of CRM campaigns on consumer choice has constituted an important element in the extant CRM-related literature. A number of studies have elicited that most consumers view CRM favourably and that consequently these campaigns positively affect purchase decisions (Smith and Alcorn, 1991; Ross et al., 1992; Holmes and Kilbane, 1993; Strahilevitz and Myers, 1998; Barone et al., 2000; Strahilevitz, 2003; Hajjat, 2003; Broderick et al., 2003; Pracejus and Olsen, 2004; Pracejus et al., 2004; Hamlin and Wilson, 2004; Vaidyanathan and Aggarwal, 2005; Trimble and Rifon, 2006; Grau et al., 2007). However, in spite of the widespread adoption of CRM many scholars contend that the success of CRM campaigns depends on the circumstances in which they are launched. That is, they are more likely to be successful when: a company arranges them for the benefit of a local charity (Smith and Alcorn, 1991; Ross et al., 1991); the money is given to treat a disease or to support disaster relief (Ross et al., 1991); the targeted consumers have children (Ross et al., 1992); the product falls into the luxury category (Strahilevitz and Myers, 1998); a large amount of money is given to charity (Ross et al., 1991; Hajjat, 2003); and finally, when vivid rather than pallid messages are conveyed (Baghi et al., 2009). Moreover, Hoek and Gendal (2008) considered whether respondents who had previously purchased brands linked to worthy causes became more responsive to CRM and elicited that the choice behaviour of such individuals was virtually identical to that of those who had not purchased a brand promoting a cause. Further, a recent study investigated the involvement of employees in the development of CRM strategies (Liu et al. 2010), viewing CRM as a way of achieving success with corporate social performance strategies by raising company legitimacy in the eyes of its stakeholders. The results showed that, first, the extent of employee participation in CRM decisions varies significantly across firms, second, larger CRM campaigns tend to be managed centrally with relatively less employee participation than smaller ones, and third, firms offering financial services are more likely to make CRM decisions centrally with relatively less employee participation, than firms in the retail service sector.

Other work has indicated that the success of CRM campaigns is related to factors such as: gender (Ross et al., 1991); high involvement (Hajjat, 2003; Broderick et al., 2003); the ethical nature of the firm (Strahilevitz, 2003); good fit

(Pracejus and Olsen, 2004; Hamlin and Wilson, 2004); and psychological factors (Youn and Kim, 2008). More specifically, Ross et al. (1991) reported that women have more favourable attitudes towards a firm's CRM applications than men, whilst Hajjat (2003) noted that if consumers are highly involved with the cause and if the expectations of those consumers are met by the CRM conditions (for example, size of the donation), then the company will receive a positive consumer response. Moreover, Strahilevitz (2003) concluded that when firms are perceived to be ethical by their consumers, their CRM campaigns affect their image positively and Pracejus and Olsen (2004) reported that brand and cause fit substantially affect consumer involvement in CRM campaigns. This point was supported by Hamlin and Wilson (2004), who elicited that where companies can achieve a good fit between the CRM campaign, the company image and the products and brands, their consumers' perceptions can be positively affected. Further, Youn and Kim (2008) noted the importance of several other psychographic factors including interpersonal trust, religious beliefs, social networks, external locus of control and advertising scepticism, all of which they found had positive relationships with consumer attitudes regarding CRM. Moreover, Trimble and Rifon (2006) found that compatibility between the sponsor and the cause potentially creates positive consumer perceptions, depending on the individual characteristics of the consumers. Another research study elicited that it was vitally important to persuade customers to participate in a firm's CRM campaigns (Vaidyanathan and Aggarwal, 2005). More specifically, these scholars found that getting young people involved in raising money for people in need positively develops their self-esteem and consequently fosters the development of positive perceptions on the part of these youngsters towards CRM campaigns.

The potential negative impact of CRM campaigns on consumers' perceptions has also been addressed in the literature (Polonsky and Wood, 2001; Webb and Mohr, 1998; Garcia et al., 2003; Basil and Herr, 2003; Olsen et al., 2003). More specifically, Webb and Mohr (1998) discovered that half of their study sample expressed a negative attitude towards CRM campaigns, because consumers often became suspicious about commercial objectives being merged with social objectives. Moreover, Polonsky and Wood (2001) reported that CRM campaigns can be seen as 'over commercialization' of firm activities that are purported to be for the benefit of society. Some empirical research has shown that there can be negative outcomes from a CRM campaign. For example, García et al. (2003) found that attitudes of consumers towards Pepsi worsened after the firm held a CRM campaign in Spain, because consumers still held negative perceptions regarding the ethical nature of the Pepsi corporation. Negative outcomes were also reported by Olsen et al. (2003), who found that firms deciding to express the size of their donations as a percentage of profit caused confusion in the mind of consumers. Finally, Basil and Herr (2003) noted that a negative fit between a company and charity or a negative perception of a company may put CRM campaigns into the 'dangerous donation' category, whereby the public see the activities as opportunistic.

In sum, most of the extant CRM studies have focused on the effects of CRM campaigns regarding consumer perceptions. Some of these have emphasised those factors that can positively affect the decision by consumers to participate, whilst others have looked at reasons why CRM campaigns can negatively affect the perceptions of potential consumers and the image of a company.

2.2.4 CORPORATE VOLUNTEERISM AND MULTIPLE FORMS OF CORPORATE COMMUNITY INVOLVEMENT

Corporate volunteerism was defined by Wild (1993) as any formal organised company support for employees and retirees who wish to volunteer their time and skills in service to the community (Peterson, 2004). Regarding this, Yankey (1996) pointed out that many non-profit organisations need more people to implement their promised programmes. According to Gilder et al. (2005), employee volunteering has positive effects on attitudes and behaviour towards the organisation, and further, Bussell and Forbes (2001) emphasised that altruism must be the main motive for corporate volunteerism. Peterson (2004) went on to consider the motivations behind corporate volunteerism and identified the following: the perceived necessity of contributing to society, the desire to interact with others, matching a cause with individual beliefs, receiving indirect rewards, such as publicity, goodwill and status; and receiving tangible benefits, such as prizes, free passes and awards offering exclusive privileges.

Despite the prominent position of CCI in the literature, there are relatively few empirical studies that have investigated multiple forms of corporate giving all together. The earliest of the empirical work on multiple forms of corporate giving was by Burke et al., (1986), who investigated the nature of corporate involvement on the part of San Francisco Bay Area companies. More specifically, they examined these companies according to their size, age and the location of their headquarters and found that firms that were very large and old tended to make higher contributions than their counterparts. Moreover, they elicited that CEO opinions played an important part and that most CEOs were relatively satisfied with the overall level of their community involvement programmes. The role of the CEO in corporate giving has also been examined more recently by Dennis et al. (2007) and they found that firms with CEOs who strongly believe that philanthropy should be an important component of their self-identity give to a larger extent than those with CEOs who do not. The outcomes of another study by Besser (1999), focusing on local communities, revealed that older businesses and those with more employees are significantly more likely to be committed to and provide support and leadership to the community. In addition, the author found strong evidence for the idea that community support is good for business, especially in small town settings.

Other empirical studies on multiple forms of corporate giving have focused on the perspectives of groups of people, such as stakeholders (Brammer and Millington, 2003), shareholders (Clarke, 1997) and CEOs (Clarke, 1997; Werber and Carter, 2002). Regarding this, Clarke (1997) investigated the degree to which shareholders are consulted and elicited that if CCI represents a normal business cost, CEOs usually prefer not to share their strategies in relation to it with the shareholders. Werber and Carter (2002) probed the connection between CEO membership of different non-profit organisations and corporate giving to foundations, finding that when CEOs are not on such a board, the connection is lessened, but is not eliminated all together. Moreover, from their study it emerged that foundation giving may be partially explained by CEO affiliation to such entities. From a different perspective, Brammer and Millington (2003) evidenced that the CCI decision is affected by stakeholder preference, firm structure and industry type. Moreover, recently the active role of employees in relation to CCI efforts has been found to be an important determinant (Van der Voort et al., 2009).

Although, as explained above, the majority of the extant empirical literature on CCI has considered the US or UK scenarios, there has been some focus elsewhere, such as the Netherlands (Meijer et al., 2006; Van der Voort, 2009), Norway (Brønn, 2006), Australia (Madden et al., 2006) and China (Zhang et al., 2009). Meijer et al. (2006) investigated CCI in the Netherlands, examining corporate giving and corporate sponsorship activities separately at the national level. Their survey covered how much companies gave (in money or in kind), what the goals of giving were and what the managers' motivations were for donating. In a different vein, Madden et al. (2006) focused on small to medium sized enterprise (SME) community involvement and their findings suggest that these have a preference for avoiding cash gifts when supporting local causes and would therefore benefit from the development of guidelines and templates describing best practice. Nonetheless, Brønn (2006) examined a Ronald

McDonald community involvement initiative in Norway and fleshed out the difficulties faced by this multinational firm in its efforts to do something good for a local community outside its home country. That is, the attempts to build a Ronald McDonald House met much resistance and many barriers were erected by political parties, doctors and academics. More recently, Zhang et al. (2009) researched whether the amount given in charity and the likelihood of a firm's response to catastrophic events relates to ownership type. They found that the extent of corporate contributions for state-owned firms following a disaster is less than that for private firms.

Regarding the few studies that have looked at cross-country differences in CCI activities (Bennett, 1998; Brammer and Pavelin, 2005), Bennett (1998) discovered that European businesses generally adopt commercial orientations towards corporate giving. This was supported by the results from a study by Keller and Aaker (1998), which showed that community involvement has a lesser effect on society than marketing activities that demonstrate product innovation and environmental concern. Regarding the comparison of commercial approaches to CCI, according to Bennett (1998), French and German firms seemingly adopt these more than UK ones in their corporate philanthropy management. Brammer and Pavelin (2005) looked for the patterns in corporate community contributions (CCC) in the UK and the US and established that there are significant differences between the two countries, which they attributed to the different stakeholder environment.

Table 2.1   The differences between the forms of CCI

Forms of CCI	Resource Involved	Where Managed in Firm	Intent/ Purpose	The Degree of Awareness of Society
Corporate Philanthropy	Money	Various	Benevolent and strategic	Low/medium
Corporate Sponsorship	Money Gifts-in-kind Employees	Marketing	Increase consumer demand Brand awareness	Medium/high
CRM	Money coming from consumer purchases	Marketing	Enhance image Promote specific products Motivate staff Be a good corporate citizen	High
Corporate Volunteerism	Employees	HR	Increase employee motivation	Low
Multiple Forms	Employees Money Gifts-in-kind	Various	Cost effective giving Supporting local communities	Low

Table 2.2   Conceptualisations of CCI

	Theories/Approaches that Consider CCI to be to a Firm's Benefit	Theories/Approaches that Consider CCI Activities to be an 'Ought to Do' Action	Theory/Approach that Considers CCI to be an Activity that Causes Conflict
Organisational Level	Instrumental motivations for CCI (instrumental stakeholder theory, resource dependence theory) Institutional perspective (institutional theory)	Normative motivations for CCI (normative stakeholder theory, altruistic motives)	
Individual Level			Individual motivations for CCI (agency theory)

The discussion above has pinpointed the main differences between corporate philanthropy, corporate sponsorship, CRM, corporate volunteerism and multiple forms of CCI, and has shown that these rest on variations in purpose, departmental location, the resources involved and the degree of awareness of society. Table 2.1 summarises the key differences between the forms of CCI with respect to these issues.

2.3 Conceptualisation of Corporate Community Involvement

In Table 2.2, the ways in which CCI has been conceptualised are presented according to three approaches. In addition, the literature on CCI are grouped into four categories acting at either the organisational or individual level: instrumental motivations for CCI, the institutional perspective, the normative motivations for CCI and individual motivations for CCI, each of these is now examined in turn.

2.3.1 INSTRUMENTAL MOTIVATIONS FOR CORPORATE COMMUNITY INVOLVEMENT

The articles coming under the instrumental perspective consider CCI as a strategy that provides the firm with some economic and social gain contributing to profit and utility maximisation. Moreover, this literature highlights a variety of processes through which CCI might deliver instrumental benefits, such as the profitability of sales, product and service development, advertising, the actions of competitors, and the attitude of prospective and/or existing customers. Additionally, under the resource dependence and instrumental stakeholder theory lenses, it has been argued that companies engage in CCI activities in order to respond to the demands made by their stakeholders (Pfeffer and Salancik, 1978; Adams and Hardwick, 1998).

The articles that adopt resource dependence theory investigate CCI activities in an organisation as an answer to pressures from the internal and external environment. Pfeffer and Salancik (1978) illustrated several phenomena that come within the resource dependence perspective, one of which relates to charitable donations. Under this lens, companies make donations to communities in order to receive critical resources, which help to increase the value of the firm. That is, the companies, in making donations, can increase revenues, reduce costs or receive critical resources from key suppliers (Pfeffer and Salancik, 1978; Barney, 1991). Seifert et al. (2004) investigated the financial correlates of corporate philanthropy and concluded that resource dependence theory provides the theoretical foundations for strategic philanthropy. They argued that some types of giving, such as corporate philanthropy, can provide benefits to the firm (that is, contribute to competitive advantage, influence the firm's brand name or reputation, improve employee productivity by allowing workers to select local charity recipients). In sum, proponents of resource dependence theory see CCI activities in an organisation as an answer to pressures from the company's internal and external environments and mostly are of the opinion that these CCI activities help organisations to access stability and legitimacy in the marketplace.

Turning to the aspect of stakeholder theory in relation to instrumental motivation, it is argued that companies please their stakeholders by carrying out CCI activities in order to obtain financial and utility benefits. That is, under this optic organisations shape their CCI activities according to stakeholder preferences and attitudes. Moreover, the extant literature in this domain suggests that the stakeholder environment affects CCI activities (Adams and Hardwick, 1998; Brammer and Millington, 2003; 2004a) in that the decision to contribute funds to charities and community projects appears to indicate that managers are seeking to improve customer and/or investor goodwill. In turn, the development of goodwill among the various stakeholders enables companies to broaden their strategic options in the future (Adams and Hardwick, 1998). Furthermore, Brammer and Millington (2004a) suggested that corporate charitable contributions play a significant role in the process of stakeholder management by enabling managers to demonstrate their commitment to a social agenda, thus reducing the risk of adverse reactions by internal and external stakeholders. In sum, under this lens the preferences and expectations of stakeholders shape the way in which companies understand their environment, in that their response in terms of CCI is rooted in a strategy aimed at gaining financial and utility benefits.

With regards to the articles on sponsorship and CRM, many of these have treated CCI as a marketing strategy that serves to develop ideas concerning how the company can combine its giving purposes with its marketing operations. Moreover, much of the extant literature has proposed that CRM and sponsorship reflect marketing attitudes towards company giving (for example, File and Prince, 1998; Hajjat, 2003; Basil and Herr, 2003; O'Hagan and Harvey, 2000; Cornwell and Maignan, 1998). More specifically, companies, through their CRM and sponsorship activities, aim to increase their ability to shape their corporate image, increase awareness, gain competitive advantage and create a communication tool with society for showing their concern about their environment (Meenaghan, 1983; Pope and Voges, 1999).

Many articles that address corporate philanthropy (for example, Navarro, 1988; Arupalam and Stoneman, 1995; Saiia et al., 2003) consider instrumental motives for this. In one such study, Johnson (1966: p.489) found that there was evidence of there being 'the traditional profit motive' for engaging in philanthropic activities. Later on, Navarro (1988) developed a formal economic model portraying the contribution process in which, because corporate contributions are considered tax deductible, companies orient themselves to make such contributions. The other studies in this area have also pointed out positive correlations between charitable donations, turnover and profitability of the firm (Arupalam and Stoneman, 1995), or with tax rates (Boatsman and Gupta, 2001). In the literature regarding sponsorship, some authors have examined it as a business investment strategy that aims to earn direct profit (for example, Calderón-Martínez et al., 2005; Farrelly and Quester, 2005). That is, these researchers set out to find whether there is any correlation between sponsorship activities and profit maximisation.

2.3.2 INSTITUTIONAL PERSPECTIVE

Proponents of the institutional perspective of CCI suggest that organisations mirror societal conventions, traditions and values (Selznick, 1957). Matten and Moon (2004) pointed out that a country's formal and informal organisations agree that CSR, and by inference CCI as a part of this, is in their interest and so many of them have included them in their overall strategies. Moreover, the economic actors set rules, forms and practices regarding the nature of the CCI. As a consequence, the literature adopting this stance considers the ways in which the national and cultural environment and competitors' behaviours influence the CCI behaviours within the firm (Brammer and Pavelin, 2005; Gan, 2006).

Early works sought to explain institutionalisation which resolved social dilemmas via social structure (Zucker, 1988) and deemed domain, form and criteria as three general aspects of organisational operations that govern values and norms (Hinings and Greenwood, 1988). However, prescient academics observed that this early institutional theory permitted only isomorphism and stability and, thus, it was insufficient to guide change in organisations. (Greenwood and Hinings, 1996). Consequently, DiMaggio and Powell (1991) introduced neo-institutional theory to explain change in organisations. Further, Greenwood and Hinings (1996) in their work argued that neo-institutional theory should emphasise cognition rather than the values and moral frames pertaining to institutional theory. Under this lens, Oliver (1991) identified the different strategic responses that organisations enact as a result of institutional pressure. Later, Oliver (1992) introduced the notion of deinstitutionalisation as a way of explaining the discontinuity of an institutionalised organisational activity or practice having earlier argued that the internal features of an organisation interact with political, functional and social pressures that leads to change. In general, the author explained the notion of change as the possibility of breaking down old institutionalised practices and adopting new ones.

Proponents of institutional theory contend that organisations attempt to obtain stability and legitimacy through their philanthropic activities (Sharfman, 1994). Regarding this, according to Sharfman (1994), US firms during the Second World War used philanthropy to establish a strong presence by supporting social community services. Moreover, in his study he drew upon institutional theory to examine the evolution of corporate philanthropy from its illegal origins to the time when it became both legal and the expected behaviour on the part of businesses. Another contribution of the institutional perspective to CCI studies is its ability to shed light on how environmental discrepancies can shape CCI behaviours. With regards to this, a number of studies have illustrated how the institutional context can lead to differences in such behaviours (Bennett, 1998; Burke et al., 1986; Brammer and Pavelin, 2005). The most recent research has also provided evidence that institutional norms and conditions influence companies to act socially responsibly (Campbell,

2007) and that institutional forces are influential factors in determining the nature and level of their social practices (Marquis et al., 2007). To sum up, studies under the perspective of institutional theory have revealed how firms can obtain legitimacy and increase the possibility of survival by carrying out CCI activities.

2.3.3 NORMATIVE MOTIVATIONS FOR CORPORATE COMMUNITY INVOLVEMENT

The articles that are discussed under normative motivations consider CCI activities as an 'ought to do' action and the theorists covered have focused on the benefits that such activities can provide to the recipients rather than the giver, and draw upon normative stakeholder theory and altruistic theory to explain this.

The normative view of stakeholder theory takes the Kantian view that business ethics demand that the organisation should take stakeholders into account, not because of the profit maximisation purpose, but because this fulfils its duty to each stakeholder (Campbell and Craig, 2005). In Brammer and Millington's (2003) study, under the normative stakeholder perspective it is proposed that businesses have to respond to stakeholder pressure without waiting for any benefits, because they need to show that they are congruent with their stakeholders. In other words, the normative stakeholder perspective views CCI activities as activities that the firms should do in order to be commensurate with their environment (Brammer and Millington, 2003). Moreover, whereas stakeholder theory can account for how stakeholders influence CCI behaviours, the normative perspective considers CCI to be a behaviour that companies must undertake.

The definition of altruism given in the study by Burlingame and Frishkoff (1996) is that altruism is 'unselfish regard for the welfare of others'. In its purest sense, this means that the donor has no knowledge of the beneficiary and receives no external recognition for contributions. Altruistic motivation for companies has also been defined by Moir and Taffler (2004: p.151) as 'doing what is right for society instead of the company considering their own business interest'. However, the altruistic motive in CCI activities has been considered in very few studies (Campbell et al., 1999; Moir and Taffler, 2004) and a reason for this can be found in Drucker's (1984) article, where he argued that this cannot be the criterion by which corporate giving is evaluated, because firms always see their giving activities as business opportunities. This position was also supported by Moir and Taffler (2004) after they examined whether business support for the arts has any altruistic motive or not and found no evidence that this was the case. A contrasting finding was found in a study by Campbell et al. (1999), which investigated the food sector, where it was elicited that altruism is present. Having arrived at this outcome, they posited that this may be motivated by a feeling of social responsibility obligations.

2.3.4 INDIVIDUAL MOTIVATIONS FOR CORPORATE COMMUNITY INVOLVEMENT

The individual motive refers to seeing CCI from the perspective of individual management and this focuses on individual opinions (for example, principal/ agent) about CCI behaviours. The articles which contain this perspective use the agency theory, which proffers that the owners of a business (the principals) are linked by a contractual agreement with managers (the agents) to perform some service on their behalf, which involves delegating some decision-making authority to the agent (Jensen and Meckling, 1976; Fama, 1980). However, agency problems arise when the principal and the agent have different utility functions as these may compromise the agent's ability to make objective decisions that clearly benefit the principal (profit maximisation) (Werber and Carter, 2002). Consequently, agency theorists argue that shareholder interests require protection by the separation of the board chair and the CEO (Donaldson and Davis, 1991). This divergence of interest has led supporters of agency theory to specify certain mechanisms for reducing agency loss (Eisenhardt, 1989), which can minimise agency costs as well as ensuring agent–principal interest alignment (Davis et al., 1997). Nonetheless, in the view of some scholars these mechanisms are not sufficient to solve manager–principal divergence of interest and agency problems still occur (Jones, 1995). That is, according to Jones (1995) there are two problems that occur under agency theory. First, the agent and the principal have conflicting goals, and second, the two have different propensities for accepting risk. This author also put forward two reasons for agent failure: moral hazard and adverse selection (ibid), where in the case of moral hazard, there is a lack of effort on the part of the agent and in the case of adverse selection the agent does not behave in the manner preferred by the principal.

Some studies on CCI have elaborated upon the implications of agency problems. Regarding this, in the case of corporate philanthropy, agents (executives in charge of philanthropic decisions) might neglect their duties to principals (shareholders) by spending shareholders' dollars for reasons of self-interest (Seifert et al., 2003). Moreover, according to the extant literature on CCI, agency theory determines CEO influence on corporate foundation giving in that opportunism may influence charitable giving and thus, this represents a potential agency problem (Werber and Carter, 2002). Further, as philanthropic contributions by managers can be perceived as unnecessary by shareholders, corporate governance can serve as an effective means to curtail agency problems emanating from excessive managerial discretion by aligning managerial interests with owner interests (Bartkus et al., 2002). Moreover, in the case of sponsorship, it has been proven that conflict between principal and agent disappears if there is trust and commitment between them (Farrelly and Quester, 2003) and if there is also a healthy return on shareholder investment (Pruitt et al., 2004).

2.4 Research Agenda

The previous subsections have provided a comprehensive insight into the nature of the extant research on CCI, both conceptually and empirically. Drawing on this, in this section, an agenda for this book on CCI is established.

Firstly, it can be observed from the extant body of work that there has been a rise in the use of the various forms of CCI in the business environment and it is apparent that companies can have different motivations for engaging in the same form of CCI. Given these factors, and the fact that most of the academic articles on CCI have investigated the different forms independently of each other, one aim of this research endeavour is to probe the phenomenon from a holistic perspective. Moreover, as Table 2.1 indicates, all the forms of CCI are interconnected and hence, further research goals are to shed light on why firms choose one or multiple types of CCI, which types of firms prefer which aspects of CCI as well as the motivations for participating in CCI at all.

Secondly, it has emerged that prior studies regarding multiple forms of corporate giving and philanthropy have been heavily skewed towards the US and the UK, although there has been some research on the matter in other Western contexts, such as: Canada, Australia, New Zealand and European countries, mainly focusing on CRM and sponsorship, but few insights on CCI have been gained that relate to the rest of the world. Providing understanding regarding activities in other countries with different cultural and institutional climates will allow for more comprehensive and reliable theory in the field to be developed. To this end, Turkey is chosen as the focal country in this work as it represents a country with such a different climate, when compared with those countries previously researched. In particular, as explained in Chapter 1, its tradition of having the foundation structure for corporate giving is expected to provide rich insights into CCI in other contexts.

Thirdly, the predominance in the extant literature of the quantitative methodological approach has been highlighted. Moreover, and perhaps as a consequence of this, most of the studies on CCI have used secondary data rather primary sources. Further regarding this, research on the US and Western European countries has usually been able to use indices that measure corporate social responsiveness, which makes it easier to find the data that can be processed through quantitative methods. However, in the case of Turkey and other non-Western nations, such data is often not available and, hence, it is necessary to devise a method that enables researchers to collect primary data, if robust comparisons across the world are to be achievable. Therefore, this is a further aim of this particular study. That is, the intention is to collect data for both quantitative and qualitative analysis, which will increase the robustness of the outcomes. In addition, because a qualitative approach in the form of case studies is employed here this will help to redress the aforementioned skewing of the prior research towards quantitative methods. In particular, there has been a lack of qualitative investigation into non-cash and multiple forms of CCI corporate philanthropy, whereas CRM has received substantial attention under this lens (Walliser, 2003).

Finally, as a result of previous studies on CCI mainly focusing on one aspect, as pointed out above, scholars have usually drawn upon a single theory, such as the stakeholder or institutional theory, to arrive at their conclusions. This has meant that no comprehensive theoretical conceptualisation of CCI as a whole has been formed and, consequently, by considering multiple theoretical stances in this book, this researcher has the goal of contributing to this theoretical gap in the literature. That is, by carrying out a holistic study of CCI, as is the case here, this allows for a synthesis of the available theories into a single all-embracing conceptualisation of the phenomenon.

In sum, these four themes underpin this research endeavour. A conceptual model of CCI will be developed in the next chapter in order to determine a holistic perspective of CCI decision making and the choice of the CCI behaviours within the confines of the behavioural theory of the firm. Additionally, in accordance with the second, third and fourth themes, this researcher proposes to examine CCI activities in Turkey within this holistic perspective, and both primary and secondary data are deployed through a mixed methods research strategy.

3

The Model of Corporate Community Involvement Behaviours

Cyert and March (1963), both economists, developed the behavioural theory of the firm out of frustration with the behavioural abstraction associated with neo-classical economics. As expressed by Weintraub (2002), neo-classical economics is characterised by three fundamental assumptions: there is perfect rationality of economic actors; individuals act for utility maximisation and firms act for profit maximisation; and people act on the basis of full and relevant information. There has been much debate in the literature surrounding the theory, not least regarding whether these assumptions reflect real human behaviour. In relation to this, Maital and Maital (1984) stated that neo-classical economists tend to portray economic man 'as a biological–psychological miracle, born fully formed' (p.65) and Etzioni (2010) wrote that neoclassical economics considers people as 'optimisers'.

3.1 The Behavioural Theory of the Firm: A Theory for Developing a Model of Corporate Community Involvement

Under the behavioural theory of the firm lens the key assumptions contrast with those of neo-classical economics, which are considered unrealistic. That is, instead of the perfect rationality, profit maximisation and trying to achieve optimal benefit assumptions, the proponents of behavioural theory argue that there is bounded rationality, satisficing as a rule of decision making and unresolved conflict about organisational goals (Bromiley, 2005; Shen and Chen, 2009). This bounded rationality is down to the fact that individuals are limited by the information as well as having limited cognitive skills (Gigerenzer and

Selten, 2002) and they have to make decisions by paying sequential attention within a very limited period of time. Regarding satisficing, the assumption is that individuals within firms aim to meet criteria for adequacy rather than optimising, as purported in the neo-classical approach. Finally, unresolved conflict about organisational goals refers to the condition that every party in the coalition considers their own benefit instead of coming together to serve one purpose.

Further assumptions in the behavioural theory of the firm relate to organisational structure, managerial behaviour, and internal resources allocation. First, it is proposed that organisational structure is composed of a coalition of individuals who are not united with a single outlook, making varying demands. The classification of the different members of the coalition can be characterised by an organisation chart, which delineates their functions and this can indicate their level of importance within the firm. Secondly, the supporters of the theory assume managers are decision makers who are rationally bound and, instead of seeking optimal allocation of resources, need to predict and attempt to manipulate their external environment as well as spending sufficient time and energy solving the problems that exist in relation to the coalition inside the firm. Moreover, these problems are solved on a sequential basis and more problems can be solved if there are enough slack resources. Thirdly, the management of internal resources allocation depends on using these resources effectively and under the theory the effective usage of these resources is attributed to four factors: the resources are allocated according to their hierarchical priority amongst the coalition, if there is a problem, the resources are used in response to the threat, industrial structure determines how these resources have to be allocated and companies, according to their past performance, know what kind of resources and how much of them should be allocated to specific places.

The behavioural theory of the firm has been widely cited and applied in business management research and has been used to analyse many different research topics, such as: innovation (Nohria and Gulati, 1996; Geiger and Cashen, 2002; Chen and Miller, 2007); strategic management (Baum et al., 2005); strategic planning (Anderson, 1982); corporate governance (Wei and Chen, 2009); organisational learning (Levinthal and March, 1981); and organisational social strategy (Bowen, 2007). The theory has also been used for studies that investigate firms' economic decisions related to price and output (Inselbag, 1973; Prietula and Watson, 2006) and thus, its widespread employment demonstrates its effectiveness in studying human behaviour within firms.

Turning to the process of decision making in the modern firm, in terms of goals, expectations and choice-making procedures (Donaldson and Preston, 1995), firstly, the assumption under the theory is that the nature of the goals depends on past goals, past performance and the past performance of other comparable organisations. Moreover, some goals are identified by subunits within the organisation and the process of goal identification is dynamic, whereby these can change with the arrival or departure of firm participants. Secondly, expectations in the decision making are shaped by the available information being manipulated by different members of the coalition within the organisation with different perspectives. Thirdly, the aforementioned ways in which organisational goals are chosen and expectations manipulated govern the organisational choice. Moreover, under this theoretical lens three factors are considered as leading to organisational choices – the choice is given as a response to a problem, the choice depends on the available information that is manipulated by the expectations and the choice is influenced by the standard decision rules that are shaped according to the past performance of the firm as well as the availability of organisational slack resources.

Regarding the relational aspect of the behavioural theory of a firm, the four concepts identified are: quasi resolution of conflict, uncertainty avoidance, problemistic search and organisational learning. Quasi resolution occurs when some of the coalition members in the company have different goals and, in order to overcome this difficulty, allocating the goals to subunits has been advised (Cyert and March, 1963), which allows each to pursue their own specific ones unhindered by any opposition. That is, decentralisation of the goals, thus ensuring local rationality, should be the action taken for effective performance under these circumstances. In relation to uncertainty avoidance, this is considered to be a feature of organisational decision making that has to take both the internal and external environments into account at the same time. More specifically, such factors as the behaviour of the market, the deliveries of suppliers, the attitude of shareholders and the future actions of governmental agencies all need to be taken into account in the decision-making process. According to the theory there are two ways to avoid uncertainty: solving a problem that occurs immediately rather than developing a long-term strategy, and trying to avoid problems that are perceived as threatening to create risky situations for the firm by understanding the institutional climate of the external environment. Problemistic search refers to the fact that firms are reactive to problems occurring rather than proactive in aiming to avoid these in the first place. Organisational learning relates to companies learning from previous experience and, hence, they adapt their behaviour over time. That is, the goals of the organisations are changeable because, based on their past experience, these will shift when they choose to review, periodically, the decision-making process.

3.2 Developing a Conceptual Model of Corporate Community Involvement

Drawing on the behavioural theory of the firm, a conceptual model for processes involved in corporate community involvement (CCI) decision making is constructed. According to the theory, it is at the managerial level that decisions are made and this assumption is accepted here in relation to CCI. Further, for this research model it is accepted that managers possess only bounded rationality, solve problems on a sequential basis, identify slack resources to meet various coalitions' internal requirements, take actions to meet the expectations of the internal and external environment and predict internal and external threats and opportunities. Moreover, in the case of CCI it is reasonable to suggest that the coalitions identified under behaviour theory, both external and internal, are stakeholders, as discussed in Chapter 2, but they have not been explicitly mentioned by its proponents. Further, it is posited by this researcher that, when making CCI decisions, managers have to take into account uncertainty emanating from the complex interplay between the internal and external environments by following the prescribed procedures identified above in the discussion on the behavioural theory of a firm. However, in this researcher's opinion, although some effective strategies for managing uncertainty have been put forward under this lens, the aspect of the institutional climate, as raised in the literature review, has not been specifically probed. That is, it is posited here that without managers understanding the nature of the institutional constellations in which they are embedded, effective CCI behaviours are more difficult to pursue to a firm's advantage.

In sum, it is put forward here that the CCI decision process can be effectively researched using the behavioural theory of the firm to devise a conceptual model. However, the explicit introduction of stakeholder pressures and the institutional climate, as other factors in such a configuration, will provide greater robustness in any subsequent analysis aimed at testing the CCI model. In the following subsections, stakeholder (termed coalitions under behaviour theory) pressures, institutional factors (referring to the uncertainty avoidance concept of behavioural theory) and resource availability are considered in turn so as to create the CCI model that will subsequently be operationalised in Chapter 7.

3.2.1 STAKEHOLDER PRESSURES

Regarding stakeholder pressures, which are considered here as the first determinant of the model of CCI decision making, as explained above, under the behaviour theory of the firm, these comprise groups of individuals belonging to coalitions within and without the organisation, all of which can have different goals. Where the goals are conflicting this situation has to be resolved if the firm is to function effectively. According to the quasi resolution of conflict assumption under behavioural theory, stakeholders gain managerial attention when managers are faced with a problem and have to decide whether to meet their demands in part or in full as a solution (Bowen, 2007). In other words, under this lens stakeholders are seen as stimuli for the process of problemistic search within the organisation, whereby the firm decides how to respond reactively to a challenge. Logically, within this perspective firms will not proactively look for solutions and, hence, are unlikely to engage in new CCI. In contrast, where there is pressure, firms have to evaluate how important this is in relation to threats to its legitimacy and develop solutions that are within their available resources. Moreover, because these pressures can come from various types of stakeholders exhibiting conflicting goals, as discussed above, this results in the choice of CCI behaviours being contested. As explained previously, behavioural theorists have put forward a number of suggestions for dealing with such situations, including sequential attention to goals, acceptable decision rules and problemistic search. Therefore, as illustrated in Figure 3.1, stakeholders, in terms of their pressure on the firm to undertake CCI activities, become the first variable that affects managerial decision making in relation to whether to engage with CCI and in what form.

Freeman (1984) defined the 'scope of stakeholder' as any group of individuals who can affect or is affected by the achievement of the organisation's objectives. That is, this can include a wide range of coalitions, such as managers, workers, stockholders, suppliers, customers, lawyers, tax collectors, regulatory agencies and so on. Much of the existing literature aimed at understanding the stakeholder environment has tended to focus on who they are, what they want and how they are going to get it (Frooman, 1999). That is, it has been argued in prior research that the firm needs to, firstly, to identify its stakeholders, secondly, elicit its stakeholder's preferences, and thirdly, find out how to satisfy these (ibid). In addition to this, a study by Mitchell et al. (2007) stressed the importance of companies recognising the hierarchy of stakeholder salience in their decision making in relation to community. Moreover, Agle et al. (1999) highlighted the influence of CEO values in CCI decision making whereby they can put pressure on managers to favour certain stakeholder groups' wishes over others, and they classified the salient ones as urgent, powerful or legitimate.

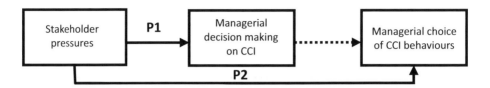

Figure 3.1   CCI as a response to stakeholder pressures

Returning to the idea of the relationship between stakeholder pressure in CCI decision making and consequent CCI behaviours, these relationships have already been probed in the existing studies (for example, Brammer and Millington, 2003; Moir and Taffler, 2004; Meijer el al., 2006). Brammer and Millington (2003) demonstrated that the stakeholder groups in a particular industry put pressure on a company's decision making in a similar way and they have a tendency to opt for the same types of CCI at the sector level. A similar outcome can be found in a study by Déniz and Oberty (2004), where they concluded that the manufacturing industry has specific stakeholder characteristics and these characteristics affect companies' CCI behaviours. The importance of stakeholders can also be seen in work by Wei-Skillern (2004), which illustrated how in recent years the Shell Company has been investigating ways to respond to their stakeholders' expectations. That is, the company re-examined and reviewed its organisational structure and subsequently restructured, having recognised its poor financial performance relative to its competitors in the industry. More specifically, at the time Shell was experiencing intense protests from Greenpeace, consumer boycotts, attacks on service stations in Germany – that is, strong stakeholder concerns about the environment. As a consequence, the company collected information from audiences, employees, shareholders and the general public, and the resulting management strategy that was implemented was heavily influenced by these stakeholder pressures. In sum, the previous studies on stakeholders have shown that the companies that want to participate in CCI activities have to consider the pressures arising from the stakeholder environment.

Having elicited the importance of stakeholder pressure in the CCI decision-making process, the issue arises as to what are the perspectives of the managers under these pressures and how do they address them? The managerial function, when faced with CCI decision making and awareness of the stakeholder environment, has been considered in the extant literature (Kotter and Heskett, 1992; Donaldson and Preston, 1995; Campbell and Craig, 2005). Regarding this,

Kotter and Heskett (1992) contended that managers care strongly that they take into account the interests of those people who have a stake in the business. This is particularly important, for when Donaldson and Preston (1995) investigated three aspects of the stakeholder theory – descriptive accuracy, instrumental power and normative validity – they elicited that the manager is crucial in the exercising of instrumental power. Similarly, Watkins (2000) pointed out that managers find themselves in a position between a tool and its implementation. Consequently, Harrison and Freeman (1999) suggested that managers should devise strategies, which provide a high return for their stakeholders and which will make their organisations competitive in the world economy. From the above discussion, the following propositions are formulated:

> *Proposition 1: Stakeholder pressures have an affect on the managerial decision making as to whether and with how much to invest in CCI.*

> *Proposition 2: After the managers have made the decision to undertake CCI, the managerial choice, regarding its form, is also affected by stakeholder pressures.*

3.2.2 INSTITUTIONAL CLIMATE

The institutional climate is proposed as the second determinant for the CCI model. As explained above, proponents of the behavioural theory claim that understanding the institutional climate is a solution for overcoming uncertainties. That is, according to the theory the external environment can create uncertainty and each organisation must find its own way to overcome this situation. In the case of CCI, these uncertainties can be classified as, for example, the reaction of the community towards a firm's CCI behaviours, how CCI behaviours are considered by the market, how can CCI behaviours be made suitable for the cultural values and norms of the people. Behavioural theorists propose that by following regular procedures and pursuing a policy of reacting to feedback, rather than forecasting the environment, the uncertainty can be addressed effectively. Accordingly, it is posited that CCI decision uncertainties can be solved by understanding the regular procedures of the institutional environment, looking at the past experience of the reaction of the communities, adopting the rules of current institutional bodies and replicating past successful CCI behaviours of competitors.

In the literature many studies have sought to explain what constitutes the institutional climate through examining the process of institutionalisation.

For example, Hinings and Greenwood (1988) defined domain, form and criteria for evaluation as three general aspects of organisational operations that show institutionalisation in a set of values and norms. They claimed business organisations can operate in a wide variety of environments carrying out many different tasks, and they do so as a matter of choice. Moreover, according to Powell (1988), organisational environments are shaped by the external environmental influence on their structure and strategies. In the conceptual model of CCI in Figure 3.2, the institutional climate is introduced as an external environmental influence and companies as organisational environments, with the institutional climate seen as affecting companies before they take action in relation to CCI. However, carrying out CCI activities can be subject to inertia brought on by departmental politics, embedded routines and path dependency (Bowen, 2007). In order to avoid this, there is a need to recognise that companies operate in an environment consisting of other institutions and hence they need to understand their rules as well as being able to respond effectively to any changes in order to survive (DiMaggio, 1988; DiMaggio and Powell, 1991). Moreover, companies, in addition to their efforts to become more profitable, more valuable and more widespread in the world, have to deal with social and environmental problems as well as having to harmonise their philanthropic perspective with the society's values and norms.

DiMaggio (1988) argued that institutionalisation leads to managers having to relinquish their autonomy to the external organisations on which they depend for resources. In other words, the process of institutionalisation results in actors being unable to behave only according to their self-interest, for they need to weigh up how the external environment affects them if they are to perform effectively. However, the external environment is not only the environment in which all the other organisations exist, but also includes the norms and the values of the country concerned, the values of citizens of this country and the norms of the government. Additionally, Campbell (2007) suggested that public and private regulation, the presence of non-governmental and/other independent organisations that monitor corporate behaviour, institutionalised norms regarding appropriate behaviour, associative behaviour among corporations themselves and organised dialogues among corporations and their stakeholders create institutional pressures that act upon companies' social actions.

Based on the above discussion the following proposition is put forward.

Proposition 3: The institutional climate has a direct effect on managerial CCI decision making.

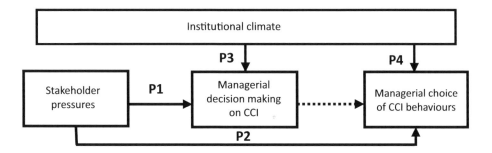

Figure 3.2   The role of institutional climate in influencing CCI

In the existing literature on CCI, several scholars investigated the institutional climate in terms of how this can affect the companies' CCI behaviours (Bennett, 1998; Brammer and Pavelin, 2005; Gan, 2006). For example, Bennett (1998) demonstrated in his study how governmental pressures can cause firms to contribute for the sake of the community and these pressures can differ from country to country. Later, Brammer and Pavelin (2005) identified national, cultural and institutional factors as external factors that may affect the companies giving behaviours and they also provided evidence of there being differences regarding these factors between countries. Further, Gan (2006) elicited that the level of public charitable need can be an indicator for companies' involvement in communities. Similarly, Marquis et al. (2007) showed how institutional pressures at the community level shape corporate social action, where cultural cognitive, social normative and regulative forces in communities generate patterns in the nature and level of corporate social action. All these examples show that institutional pressures shape managerial decisions about CCI behaviours and lead to the following proposition regarding the institutional climate:

> *Proposition 4: The institutional climate influences the managerial decision regarding which CCI behaviour the company should undertake.*

3.2.3 AVAILABILITY OF SLACK RESOURCES

Within the confines of the behavioural theory of the firm, the availability of slack resources was proposed by Cyert and March (1963) as a mechanism for maintaining harmony between the various members of coalitions, both within and outside an organisation. According to the theory, managers search for availability of slack resources in order to make a specific decision, such as to participate in CCI. Moreover, for the purposes of this research, the nature of the slack resources has a significant impact on the decision regarding CCI in terms of what is given and to whom. Additionally, in the literature, some studies have actually investigated the association of slack resources with corporate giving (Buchholtz et al., 1999; Seifert et al., 2003; 2004). Similarly, some academics have suggested that slack resources can be used in a discretionary manner (Dimmick and Murray, 1978) or for voluntary issues (Buchholtz et al., 1999).

Under the behavioural theory of the firm lens, slack resources have been defined as the disparity between the resources available to the organisation and the payments required to maintain the coalitions (Cyert and March, 1963). Moreover, the availability of slack resources enables the organisation to absorb failures and to explore new ideas in advance of actual need (Rosner, 1968). According to another definition, slack resources are defined as the pool of resources in an organisation that is in excess of the minimum necessary to produce a given level of organisational output (Nohria and Gulati, 1996). That is, in these authors' definition of slack resources, the emphasis is placed on the resources, in other words, on the inputs (ibid). Later, Bush (2002), placing the emphasis on output, proposed that firms can obtain slack resources by cutting down the amount of output that will be offered to the customers. In addition, this scholar pointed out that there are some characteristics that differentiate slack resources from buffers. That is, as well as the physical entities such as cash, people and machine capacity that constitute slack resources, a firm can use buffers to protect themselves from environmental fluctuations (ibid). These are somewhat abstract strategies, such as preventative maintenance, future contracts and sales smoothing. In other words, slack resources protect the firm from internal fluctuations, whereas buffers form barriers to those outside. Another difference between these two concepts is that firms employ slack resources and buffers under different conditions. For example, they use buffers when there is high resource dependency and slack resources in situations where there are conflicting internal and external demands (Sharfman et al., 1988).

According to Bourgeois (1981), slack resources serve four primary functions: as an inducement for organisational actors to remain within the system; as a resource for conflict resolution; as a buffering mechanism in the workflow process; and as a facilitator of certain types of strategic or creative behaviour within the organisation (Bourgeois, 1981). Taking all of the above into account, it is expected that stakeholders can be affected directly in an environment that has high slack resources in that if they are aware of their existence then they are likely to increase pressure for their distribution and vice versa. Figure 3.3 includes the assumed relation between slack resources and stakeholder pressure, which leads to the following proposition:

> *Proposition 5: The availability of slack resources has a direct effect on stakeholder pressures.*

Sharfman et al. (1988) stated that the need for slack resources in an organisation is determined at the industrial level in terms of the political behaviours of the organisation, slack resources in the market, environmental change and the magnitude of those changes, and at the organisational level by the size, and performance of the organisation. Seifert et al. (2004) gave examples of the forms of slack resources, which include extra inventory, labour, machines and space, and added that these resources can all be deployed for charitable purposes. In addition, Bowen (2007) identified slack resources as financial capital, managerial time, sheer size and scope of the firm, and technological capabilities. In the literature some studies have associated the contribution ratio with the specific forms of slack resources, such as: size (Buchholtz et al., 1999; Bartkus et al., 2002; Seifert et al., 2003; Brown, et al., 2006; Gan 2006); financial resources (Griffin and Mahon, 1997); availability of cash resources (Buchholtz et al., 1999; Seifert et al., 2003; 2004; Gan, 2006); and corporate profitability (Navarro, 1988; Adams and Hardwick, 1998).

In the conceptual model of CCI, as shown in Figure 3.3, the availability of slack resources is proposed as another influence on managerial decision making on CCI in that it would appear reasonable to assume that CCI will rise and fall according to the availability of slack resources. Further, slack resources for CCI are taken as covering cash, profitability, size, labour and machinery. This rationale yields the following proposition:

> *Proposition 6: The availability of slack resources has a direct effect on managerial decision making on CCI.*

Once managers have made the decision to contribute to society, their second step is to determine which type of CCI behaviours they will choose and it is expected that the availability of slack resources as well as their nature will affect this choice. According to the definition of CCI, as discussed in Chapter 2, corporate donations can be non-monetary as well as monetary (Seifert et al., 2004). Monetary giving can be cash giving through sponsorship, cause-related marketing (CRM) or philanthropic donation, and non-monetary giving can be the use of company services, finished-goods inventory, facilities, managerial expertise, services and the use of employee time for volunteer work. The CCI model caters for the expectation that the availability of slack resources, both monetary and non-monetary, affects the choice of CCI behaviours and this leads to the following proposition:

> *Proposition 7: The availability of slack resources influences the managerial decision on the choice between CCI activities.*

Figure 3.3 shows the conceptual model that includes the three main factors that have an influence on whether a manager elects to engage with CCI and what forms they choose to undertake, namely stakeholder pressures, the institutional climate and the availability of slack resources. The propositions drawn up after considering each of the influential factors will in turn be used to generate testable hypotheses in Chapter 7, as suitable variables can be identified for regression analysis to this end.

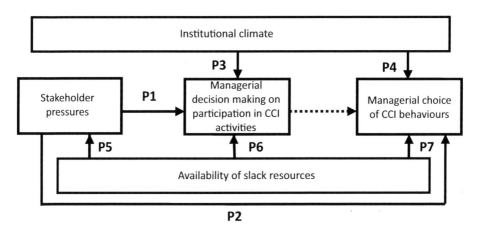

Figure 3.3   The role of availability of slack resources in influencing CCI

By way of explanation as to why there is no link in Figure 3.3 regarding the effect of institutional climate on stakeholder pressures, but there being one for slack resources and the latter, the following is put forward: the literature pertaining to the behavioural theory of the firm does not cover the influence of the institutional climate on stakeholder opinions and as the conceptual model draws heavily on this theory, it would be inappropriate to include this link, whereas the relation between slack resources and the institutional environment has been included in this literature and thus, is included. In any case whether this link exists or not is beyond the scope of this book, because its aim is to investigate managerial behaviour regarding CCI and not that of stakeholders.

More specifically, this model is to be operationalised to probe what the drivers are, in terms of company characteristics, that influence decision making on CCI by managers. In the four empirical chapters (Chapters 5, 6, 7 and 8), this model is used as the basis for examining these behaviours and the proposed determinants are tested statistically in Chapter 7 so as to establish their level of influence in this process.

4

Methodology

In the literature review chapter, Chapter 2, it was posited that there is a need to explore the forms of corporate community involvement (CCI) together, examine other institutional environments than the developed countries and to identify the motivations behind CCI decisions and the choice of CCI. More specifically, the aims and objectives of the empirical research for this book are as follows:

4.1 Aims and Objectives of the Research

- Using the behavioural theory of the firm perspective to elicit the influential determinants in relation to whether to engage in CCI and the nature of the CCI behaviours undertaken;

- to establish the amount of CCI activity that the sample companies carry out in total and on average;

- to separate the CCI actions into types so as to identify the patterns according to different industry and firm characteristics;

- to investigate whether and if so in what way the departmental structure of companies has an impact on CCI preference;

- by drawing on the extant literature, investigate which of the determinants in the conceptual model have the greatest impact on CCI decision making;

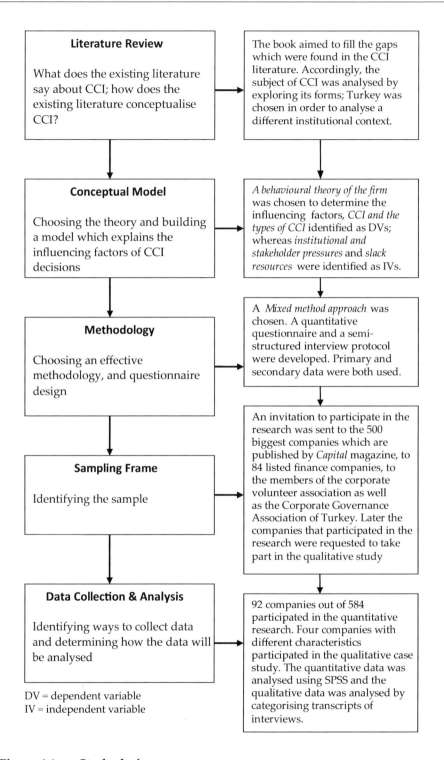

Figure 4.1   Study design

- to investigate the preferences of the aforementioned components in relation to the CCI type undertaken;

- to gain general understanding of the processes for taking CCI decisions, with regards to both engagement and form.

These objectives can only be achieved if a valid methodology is employed, whereby appropriate data is collected and robust analysis is applied and the development and justification for the chosen strategy to this end forms the purpose of the remainder of this chapter.

4.2 Study Design

The procedure employed in this book is summarised in Figure 4.1. The initial literature review has allowed for identification of the knowledge gaps, as presented in the previous section and, hence, the elicitation of areas for fruitful research. Next, the conceptual model, developed in Chapter 3, contains the presumed causal factors that have an impact on CCI decisions, which forms the foundation for evaluating the four empirical studies. Accordingly, this research in the book is complemented by four empirical studies.

4.3 Choosing the Methodology

Flick (2006) argued that the suitability of a method rests in its capacity to address the issues under empirical investigation and also contended that most phenomena cannot be explained in isolation, as there is often a high level of complexity. Regarding this, the research questions have been formulated to capture the complex nature of CCI, as discussed in Chapter 2. In general, two kinds of research paradigm, positive and normative, are put forward in the literature (Boland, 1991) on research methodologies, which are often presented as dichotomies, such as, objective/subjective, descriptive/prescriptive and rational/irrational, to represent these two forms respectively. However, this researcher has chosen to adopt a research method that lies somewhere between these two on what could be termed the positivist/normative continuum, but tending much more towards the former. More specifically, although a positivist approach predominates in this research, sometimes normative assumptions have been made in order address the related research questions with greater robustness than it would be otherwise. That is, interrogating employees about their perceptions of CCI provides explanatory information for the findings of the quantitative research. In general, the epistemological basis of this research is a positivist approach using mixed methods, whereby interview data is used to probe into the motivations behind CCI decisions.

Creswell and Clark (2007) defined the mixed methods approach as:

> *A research design with philosophical assumptions as well as methods of inquiry. As a methodology, it involves philosophical assumptions that guide the direction of the collection and analysis of data and the mixture of qualitative and quantitative approaches in many phases in the research process. As a method, it focuses on collecting, analysing, and mixing both quantitative and qualitative data in a single study or series of studies. Its central premise is that the use of quantitative and qualitative approaches in combination provides a better understanding of research problems than either approach alone (p.303).*

Further, Creswell and Clark (2007) stated that mixed method research is practical in the sense that the researcher is free to use all methods possible to address a research problem. In this book, the aim is to classify the characteristics of CCI activities, determine the influencing factors of CCI decisions and construct statistical models in order to explain what is observed from the data collected from the quantitative surveys. However, there is also the goal of eliciting a comprehensive understanding of the chosen companies' CCI decision-making processes and this cannot be achieved through surveys alone as it requires dialogue with the actors.

In sum, this researcher accepts the advantages of the mixed methods perspective as fitting with the overall aims of this book and, hence, it is adopted here. More specifically, in this researcher's opinion, using supplementary qualitative data on CCI taken from the practitioners enhances understanding of the motivation for their decision to participate as well as their preferences on what areas to donate to.

Having decided upon the methodological stance, the use of both primary and secondary data was also deemed appropriate. For the primary analysis, quantitative and qualitative surveys were designed, whereas for the secondary data, databases, websites and reports related to the firms were accessed in order to provide background and contextual data which would support and corroborate the primary data.

4.3.1 QUANTITATIVE FRAMEWORK

Bryman (2004) wrote that 'quantitative methods involve the collection of numerical data, as exhibiting a view of the relationship between theory and research as deductive, a predilection for a natural science approach (and of positivism), and an objectivist conception of social reality'. Additionally, Locke et al. (1999) stated that quantitative research deals with things that can be counted and it often uses statistical manipulations of numbers to process data and summarise results. In the literature review chapter, from the analysis of the existing studies it was observed that quantitative techniques dominate research in the CCI field, which is probably because they allow for the simple testing of hypotheses, the findings of which can be generalised while minimising the levels of subjectivity involved (Locke et al., 1999) Moreover, quantitative researchers claim that such treatments can reveal clear causal relationships between phenomena (Creswell and Clark, 2007).

4.3.1.1 The questionnaire as a research tool

Five hundred companies form the population for the questionnaire survey, the results of which are presented in Chapters 5, 6 and 7. The lack of secondary data for Turkey strengthened the case for collecting this data through a questionnaire. That is, it is posited that using a survey, despite its limited coverage when compared with other databases on CCI matters, is the most effective way of providing an overall picture of these phenomena in the focal country, Turkey. In addition, as well as the construction of the questionnaire being strongly guided by the literature, as reviewed in Chapter 2, this researcher was able to introduce elements pertaining to Turkey's specific cultural norms, values and so on, to the themes she wished to probe, which enhanced the relevance of the enquiry. In sum, the flexibility contained within a survey questionnaire on CCI has allowed for institutional elements distinct from non-Western settings to be the focal points of the analysis.

Two different questionnaires were sent out to the participant companies, the first being a CCI questionnaire and the second in relation to measuring slack resources. The reason for enquiring about slack resources through a questionnaire was because such data could not be obtained from secondary sources. In general, the key areas investigated though these questionnaires are:

- the pattern of CCI in Turkey (Chapter 5);

- patterns of CCI departmentalisation within companies (Chapter 6);

- determinants of CCI decision making and CCI behaviours (Chapter 7).

As these two questionnaires were discrete and the participants were only requested to fill them in once, the study is cross-sectional, except for those who were involved in the follow-up case study interviews. More specifically, the process of delivering the CCI questionnaire lasted from January 2008 to October 2009 and is explained in detail below. Later, during the November and December of 2008, the slack resources questionnaire involved interviews with those participants who had responded positively to the original questionnaire. Moreover, for consistency, the participants were asked to provide data pertaining to the year 2007 in both questionnaires.

The first step of the questionnaire design was to use the extant literature to identify issues that needed to be probed. Subsequently, a set of questions was devised which were split into five categories as shown in Table 4.1 below. In addition, a sixth category was added for collecting personal information about the respondents. Next, in order to limit the time demand on the respondents, certain questions which were considered to have a low relevance to the Turkish context were dropped. The references pertaining to each section of the questionnaire are shown in the right-hand column of Table 4.1.

Prior to conducting the CCI questionnaire, it was pretested to identify problems for both the interviewer and the respondents with regard to question content, order of the questions, context effects, missing instructions and formatting. With respect to this, it was decided to have four companies test the questionnaire which were chosen with the help of the Company Volunteer Association who have close relations with firms and, hence, were able to identify managers who were likely to respond positively. Further, the questionnaire was designed in English and when this was translated into Turkish this researcher became aware from the responses of some confusion in meaning and, hence, certain questions/instructions were modified. Subsequently the checked and modified questionnaire was sent to the companies in the sample, identification of which is to follow.

Table 4.1   References for the CCI questionnaire

	Corporate Community Involvement Questionnaire	**References**
Section 1	*About your company and its structure*	Business Community Involvement Survey, Australian Government Statistical Clearing House (2005);Yurtoğlu (2003); Kapopoulos and Lazaretou (2007); *Capital* magazine top 500 biggest companies index industry classification (2007).
	Questions (1–13) ownership status, nationality, size, industry type	
Section 2	*About your company's CCI activities*	Business Community Involvement Survey, Australian Government Statistical Clearing House (2005); Institute for Philanthropy, Voice of Philanthropy Survey, June 2005; Meijer et al. (2006).
	Questions (14–28) CCI, types of CCI, areas of CCI, amount of money or other resources	
Section 3	*About your company's business environment and its strategies*	Henriques and Sadorsky (1996).
	Questions (29–31) assesment of industry conditions, business nature, competitors	
Section 4	*About your company's relationship with its stakeholders*	Agle et al. (1999); Teo et al. (2003).
	Questions (32–38) government/legislator, employees,customers, shareholders/ investors, suppliers, community groups stakeholders, institutional pressures	
Section 5	*About corporate social responsibility*	Maignan (2001).
	Question 39 Company's CSR performance	
Section 6	*About you*	Taylor et al. (2007) Mori Survey.

Table 4.2   References for slack resources questionnaire

	Slack Resources Questionnaire	**References**
1st measurement of slack	Availability of slack resources was assesed according to two-item scale	Nohria and Gulati (1996, 1997); Moreno et al. (2009).
2nd measurement of slack	Relative to business profitability measure was adopted to measure slack resources	Chang and Chen (1998).
3rd measurement of slack	Availability of slack resource was assesed according to five-point scale	Luca and Atuahene-Gima (2007).
4th measurement of slack	The amount of revenue for 2006 and 2007 were requested from each company	

In order to devise the slack resources questionnaire, there was an examination of extant studies that have used a questionnaire to gather such data and all of the questions in these were adopted. Further, the questions used were taken from existing studies which are given in Table 4.2. With respect to these, the fourth measurement of revenue was available in the public domain from listed companies but had to be collected through the questionnaire for unlisted companies.

4.3.1.2 Using secondary data for quantitative analysis

Secondary data analysis has been defined as 'any further analysis of an existing dataset which presents interpretations, conclusions or knowledge additional to, or different from, those presented in the first report on the inquiry as a whole and its main results' (Hakim, 1982). Moreover, using existing databases like censuses, archives or organisational sources, such as company reports, are common ways to collect such data (Dale et al., 1988). However, Arber (2005) pointed out that one of the challenges of secondary data analysis is to address the researcher's own questions using somebody else's data, which may have been originally collected for very different purposes. Nevertheless, in spite of this, in Chapter 5, having first collected quantitative primary information, additional secondary data was collected from comprehensive archival and web-based analysis of company documents relating to their community programmes to supplement this.

4.3.2 QUALITATIVE FRAMEWORK

Qualitative research is defined as 'a situated activity that locates the observer in the world and it consists of a set of interpretive, material practices that make the world visible' (Denzin and Lincoln, 2003: p.2) and such research is conducted where it is necessary to explore a complex problem or issue, which requires deep probing (Denzin and Lincoln, 1994; Creswell, 2007). Flick (2006) explained why the interest in qualitative research has grown so much in recent decades as follows: 'Qualitative research is of specific relevance to the study of social studies, owing to the fact of the pluralisation of life in the world' (p.12). There are some examples of qualitative studies that have been conducted by researchers into CCI: in order to find out the opinions of CEOs regarding CCI activities (Burke et al., 1986), in the form of a case study of a particular CCI programme (Brønn, 2006), and in relation to the pattern of small and medium enterprises' (SME) community involvement (Madden et al., 2006). In general, the purpose of engaging in a qualitative study in the CCI field has been to obtain an in-depth understanding of the opinions of managers who are usually part of the decision process, or to provide case analysis of the CCI decision making of companies. However, as elicited in Chapter 2, in CCI research quantitative studies have predominated. Therefore, in order to capture the complexity of CCI and to find deeper explanations for the observed behaviours identified in the two surveys, in Chapter 8 there is a qualitative investigation in the form of case studies, as discussed below. Moreover, by so doing it is possible to triangulate the results of the surveys to some extent.

In sum, a qualitative approach was chosen to supplement the structured questionnaire to be used for quantitative analysis because this would provide insights into the participants' attitudes and behaviours that would be unavailable from surveys alone.

4.3.2.1 Applying case study as a research tool

Of the qualitative approaches, which Creswell (2007) listed in turn as narrative research, phenomenology, grounded theory and ethnography, in this researcher's opinion, the case study is the approach that can best achieve the goals of this book. Regarding this, Stake (2006) stated that a case study is carried out in order to understand the particularity and complexity of a single case within important circumstances. In addition, Creswell (2007) defined case study research as a 'qualitative approach in which the investor explores a bounded system (a case) or multiple bounded systems (cases) over time, through detailed, in-depth data collection involving multiple sources of information (e.g., observations, interviews, audiovisual material, and documents and reports), and reports case description and case-based themes' (p.18).

In Chapter 8, the detailed findings for four case study companies regarding the various managerial perceptions towards CCI decisions are presented. Data were collected through multiple sources of information, such as interviews, companies' reports and websites. However, secondary sources were referred to only for information about the companies. For example, to construct a table of company characteristics (see Table 8.1), it was necessary to know such information as which sectors the companies are working in or the number of employees that work in each company, which could be obtained from these sources.

Consequently, in order to achieve in-depth knowledge about the motivations for CCI activities in Turkey, a case study approach involving the carrying out of interviews was deemed the most appropriate treatment for collecting data.

In particular, probing managers in person about their CCI behaviours was considered to be the most effective way of building a clear understanding of how different firm characteristics impact upon these. In addition, a personalised approach of this nature permits the interviewer to build a rapport with the interviewee as well as providing him/her with cues as to what areas are sensitive and thus need to be handled carefully. Moreover, using the interview technique allowed this researcher to assess whether the conceptual model devised for this book reflects day-to-day reality. Further, a semi-structured format for the questions was adopted so as to provide the researcher with the opportunity to explore issues of interest more thoroughly and to seek to identify not only what participants know and think about CCI but also why they participate in it and how they formed their views. In addition, depending on the flow of the interview sometimes it was appropriate to ask questions in a different order to the proposed schedule and occasionally they needed to be repeated so as to get effective responses, but there were no omissions. The questions were formulated so as to be able to test the underpinning tenets of the behavioural theory of the firm and the aims and what kind evidence was being sought by asking these questions is summarised in Table 4.3 below.

Table 4.3   Evidence from case study question

Section 1	General issues – warm up questions	The aim is to understand if their company's stakeholders or institutional environment are important for them. Are the managers optimising the goals or paying sequential attention to goals, what level of pressure do companies receive from their external environment and how does it affect the decision making?
Section 2	Policy and structure	The aim is to learn if there is a policy. What are the influential factors which help to set this policy?
Section 3	Budget	The aim is to learn if there are slack resources. If yes, what kind of slack resources are there? How does the manager(s) allocate these resources?
Section 4	Particular cases	The aim is to dig deeper into the issue. These questions were asked to understand whether they confirmed the previous answers or in order to obtain more information about the company policies, what kind of pressure, for example stakeholder, institutional pressures are they under and so on. Also the aim is to understand how they have used their slack resources. Are there any slack resources or not, or how do previous CCI activities affect their recent behaviours and so on?
Section 5	How to deal with the regression period of time	This is another approach to learn what kind of resources companies use to perform CCI activities, the strategy and criteria of company when engaging in CCI activities and information about slack resources

In terms of the scope of the interviews carried out, in line with the literature review, it was decided to choose people working in different departments (for example corporate communication, human resources (HR) and finance) so as to gain a holistic understanding of the company perspective regarding the CCI decision-making process as well as identifying any contrasting views across a firm in relation to CCI. That is, probing different level managers who perhaps have had differing involvement in their firm's CCI was considered to be a beneficial modus operandi. The interviews were structured so as to progress from simple discussion on participants' experience of companies' CCI activities to probing their reasons and motivations for taking part in these. At the commencement of the interview, what comprises CCI activities was clearly explained to the participants so as to avoid any misunderstanding or miscommunication. Opportunity was also provided for eliciting what barriers the companies had come up against when engaging in CCI activities, their views on how to overcome such difficulties and their own opinions about their company's previous and current CCI activities.

4.4 Sampling Strategy

A sampling strategy was required which would allow for valid evaluation of the research questions. In line with previous studies, the aim was to have a large sample that would allow for effective cause–effect analysis of the model presented in Chapter 3. Moreover, a large sample size was more likely to provide a sufficient number of respondents to ensure that all sectors of industry were well represented. The sampling strategy used for the study is summarised in Figure 4.2. In order to investigate the Turkish CCI pattern, only large companies were chosen, partially because CCI research has not been carried out before in Turkey, hence it was opined that data for these would be easier to come by and partially owing to most of the existing literature having elicited that such companies are more likely to be involved in this form of activity (for example, Levy and Shatto, 1978; Adams and Hardwick, 1998; Brown et al., 2006). However, other than size, no distinction in the chosen sample was made regarding a firm's characteristics or function. In fact, the participation of companies from different industries and with different ownership status was deemed essential for a variety of patterns of CCI to emerge. Another reason for conducting the research only in large companies is because of the availability of relevant indices, which for small firms are intermittent. In terms of where to collect the sample from, Turkey's Top 500 Industrial Enterprises which is published by the Istanbul Chamber of Industry, the index of the 500 Biggest Private Companies in Turkey as well as the list of companies on the Istanbul Stock Market, were all considered.

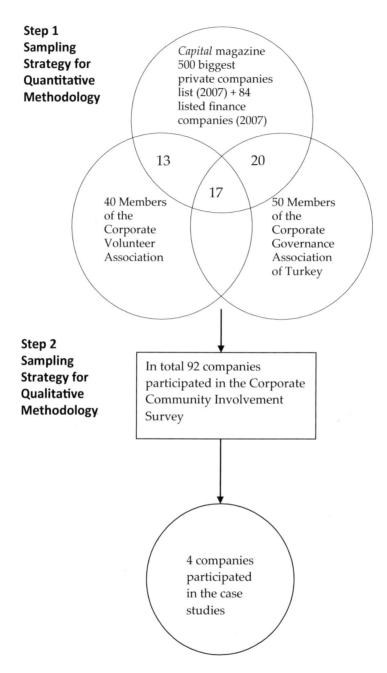

Step 1 Sampling Strategy for Quantitative Methodology

Capital magazine 500 biggest private companies list (2007) + 84 listed finance companies (2007)

13

20

17

40 Members of the Corporate Volunteer Association

50 Members of the Corporate Governance Association of Turkey

Step 2 Sampling Strategy for Qualitative Methodology

In total 92 companies participated in the Corporate Community Involvement Survey

4 companies participated in the case studies

Figure 4.2   Sampling strategy

Given the decision to use only large firms in the survey, *Capital* magazine's 500 Biggest Private Companies index was deemed appropriate as the initial sampling frame, According to a report published by *Capital* Magazine (2008), the companies in their list constitute 65 per cent of the Turkish economy, with the last company on the list having $65.9 million revenue. However, it was observed that finance companies are not included in this list, despite being some of the largest companies in Turkey. That is, according to a report published by Deloitte (2009), in 2007 the finance sector had the highest earnings of 768.6 billion TL (approximately $504 billion) and the highest profitability level, standing at $12 billion. In the same year, the finance sector growth represented 116 per cent of the increase in gross national product over the previous year.

Table 4.4 describes the industrial distribution of survey respondents and the industrial distribution of the companies in the capital list. Additionally, the finance sector portion of the list of companies in the Istanbul Stock Exchange is given in order to show how the sample reflects overall industrial distribution. It can be seen that the sample is distributed across all sectors of Turkish industry, although consumer goods has a higher representation than other industries and construction and other manufacturing a lower one. Compared to the distribution of economic activity in Turkey, where manufacturing accounts for approximately 30 per cent of gross domestic product (GDP), service industries contribute about 60 per cent and agriculture around 9 per cent, the sectoral distribution of the sample is skewed towards manufacturing because of the implicit role of firm size. That is, firms in the other two sectors tend not to be so large on average. There are a large number of small service sector firms that collectively contribute significantly to overall employment, but, because of their size, are excluded from the sample.

Besides the availability of various indices, there are also some associations in Turkey whose work concerns CCI activities and, hence, it was decided to approach two of them – the Corporate Volunteer Association and the Corporate Governance Association of Turkey – to send the questionnaire to their members, which they subsequently agreed to do. It was assumed that these companies' managers would be more forthcoming than their counterparts in providing information for the database and, thus, should be added in spite of some not matching the initial criteria, so as to enhance the quality of the data collection. As it happens, as can be observed in Figure 4.2, most of the members of these two associations are already in *Capital* magazine's 500 biggest private companies list and, thus, adding them to the sample did not distort the data collection process.

Table 4.4   Comparison of industrial distribution of survey respondents to sample frame

Industries	*Capital* Magazine 500 Biggest Private Companies List + 84 Listed Finance Companies	Industries	Total 92 Companies
IT	33	*Information & Technology*	10
Telecom	10		
Electric/Electronic	21		
Total	64		10
Ratio	**11%**		**11%**
Petrol/Gas	24	*Chemical & Pharmacy*	15
Pharmacy	14		
Chemistry	16		
Plastic	10		
Total	64		15
Ratio	**11%**		**16%**
Steel	17	*Engineering*	17
Machinery	20		
Automotive	43		
Metal	16		
Total	96		17
Ratio	**17%**		**18%**
Glass	8	*Consumer Goods*	15
Food/Beverage	74		
Jewelry	4		
Textile	61		
Tobacco	4		
Total	151		15
Ratio	**25%**		**16%**
Cement	23	*Construction*	6
Construction	11		
Total	34		6
Ratio	**5%**		**7%**
Packaging	11	*Consumer Services*	10
Media	2		
Foreign Trade	9		
Service	3		
Logistic	10		
Retail	22		
Tourism	2		
Transportation	6		
Total	65		10
Ratio	**11%**		**12%**
Tyre	3	*Other manufacturers*	4
Mine	7		
Wood	12		

Compost	4		
Total	26		4
Ratio	**5%**		**4%**
Finance	From Istanbul Stock Exchange List	*Finance*	
Total	84		15
Ratio	**15%**		**16%**
Total	**100%**		**100%**

Turning to the case study research, Stake (2006) pointed out that this does not involve sampling, but the identification of examples that can provide rich data in the field of enquiry, That is, the first criterion for choosing the case study companies for the qualitative study should be to maximize what is learnt. The potential companies for the case study research were identified from the respondents to the quantitative study through their being asked to indicate whether they would like to participate in this next research stage. Four companies were chosen from the 92 participating to be subjects for case study part of the research, the process of which is explained in detail in Chapter 8. Given the time involved and the financial limitations of this research, this number was considered sufficient for robust data collection and in any case reflected the dimensions of prior research at this level.

In sum, the sampling strategy allowed for sufficient quantitative and qualitative data to be gathered within a period of one year for testing the model presented in Chapter 3 and for addressing the research questions. The above has shown how the sample was chosen so as to be sufficiently large for effective usage in the quantitative studies (see Chapters 5, 6 and 7) as well as illustrating how the case study firms were identified for investigating, in a qualitative manner, the process of CCI (see Chapter 8).

4.5 Data Collection in the Field

This section outlines the data collection methods used and the ways in which the challenges presented (see Table 4.1) were tackled. Regarding the latter, the two key ones were ensuring an adequate number of participants was found for effective quantitative analysis and choosing the four companies that could provide the most informative detail for addressing the research aims through a case study.

The CCI questionnaire was prepared and a list of *Capital* magazine's 500 biggest companies was put on to an Excel sheet giving contact information (who to contact, the phone number, company e-mail and address) collected from their websites. In addition, the details of the 84 finance companies and those companies recommended by the Corporate Volunteer Association and the Corporate Governance Association were also put on to the spreadsheet. Next, a letter was prepared to provide those to be approached with information about the university where the researcher was studying, an explanation of the topic to be investigated, an invitation to participate in the quantitative questionnaire and the contact details of the researcher. Information regarding the support of the two aforementioned associations was also included. This letter was sent by e-mail to all the sample companies on the list and the two associations also sent it to their member companies as well giving this researcher the contact number of managers to whom they had sent it. Unfortunately, the only means of acquiring e-mail addresses in nearly all the cases was through the general information account on the company websites, which meant that they were not specifically targeted at the relevant people and also were in danger of being ignored as SPAM. As a result, only a handful of responses were received.

Consequently, another strategy was used, with the non-responding firms being phoned by this researcher, who asked for those managers who were interested in or involved with any aspect of CCI, for example those responsible for corporate social responsibility (CSR) at the company, those responsible for sponsorship activities and so on. When this strategy proved successful, the manager was asked for their direct e-mail address and detailed information about the research was subsequently provided for them. Further, in order to increase the number of survey returns, special emphasis was placed in the e-mail on the fact that the research would be anonymous, the first on CCI in Turkey and that the findings would be shared amongst the participant companies. However, even this strategy was not enough to obtain a sufficiently high level of returns and so the managers were called again and asked if they had received the e-mail and whether they had read the information letter. At this stage, those who said they did not want to participate in this research were dropped from the sample. Despite the research officers of the associations giving the required explanations and encouraging their member to complete the CCI survey, the return rate through these was quite low and, thus, the researcher decided to call the firms herself and explain the reason for doing the research.

Time was the main restricting factor for managers wishing to join in because it was decided that the questionnaire had to be filled out using a face-to-face interview prearranged by phone or e-mail. The rationale behind this was that the pretesting had revealed that the questions often needed to be explained by the interviewer if meaningful answers were to be forthcoming. Moreover, it had emerged that when people undertook the survey on their own they tended to avoid answering questions, especially those relating to the amount of donation, unless the researcher was there to explain the importance of their response as well as reasserting that none of the information would reach the public domain. As a result, it was concluded that a higher level of participation would be achieved if the researcher were present. However, because many of the managers were very busy they could not give an appointment date, so those in the sample were offered telephone interviews which greatly increased the number of participants.

Moreover, although filling in the survey was expected to take no longer than an hour this was still too long for some. Some requested information such as the amount of the total donation and the level of importance of the different stakeholders was considered too sensitive, which resulted in their refusal to engage with the survey.

The follow-up slack resources questionnaire was sent only to the participating companies, who were called again by phone to ask if they would answer questions which would take up only 10 minutes of their time; only six companies failed to do so. It turned out that in some cases the relevant manager had resigned or had failed to see the new request. These short interviews were carried out over the phone.

For the qualitative study, as explained above, four companies were chosen for case study research, with a total of 14 managers being interviewed face to face. As the companies were already respondent companies, these managers already knew what this research was about so no information letter was sent for this stage. The process of approaching these companies and deciding which ones were appropriate for inclusion, data collection methods, data transcription and data analysis are explained in detail in Chapter 8.

5

Corporate Community Involvement in Turkey: An Overview of 92 Companies in Turkey

This chapter contains the first of four empirical studies and begins with a discussion on the Turkish economic, social and cultural environment, which aims to identify key distinctions between these aspects when compared to developed countries. Next, there is presentation and analysis of the results regarding corporate community involvement (CCI) activities in Turkey, taken from the surveys, according to company size, industry sector and ownership status. Throughout this discussion, comparisons between the Turkish CCI situation and that of other countries are made. Explanation is then provided as to why certain features of CCI in Turkey are different to those in Western settings.

5.1 Culture, Economy and Society in Turkey

5.1.1 CULTURE AND RELIGION IN TURKEY

Turkish culture has several distinctive characteristics relative to the other domains about which much of the research on CCI has been carried out. First, in contrast to Anglo-Saxon countries and much of Europe, it is a secular country with 99 per cent of its population being Muslim (Turan, 1991). Regarding this, earlier research has highlighted that religion is significantly correlated with attitudes towards aspects of corporate social responsibility (CSR) (Brammer et al., 2007). In particular, these authors highlighted that 'Muslims are supportive of holding companies responsible for addressing poverty and charity, which are basic tenets of Islam but do not in general expect companies to uphold equal rights between genders' (p.240). Despite the fact that the vast majority of the population is Muslim, other religious and ethnic groups, particularly in Istanbul, have an influence on society and business that outweighs their percentage representation (Tapper, 1991; Timmerman, 1995; Turan 1991), thus providing a rich diversity of culture.

Regarding Turkey's broad cultural orientation, Hofstede's (1983) research provides a useful way for comparing it with that of other countries. Hofstede grouped countries by employing four value-oriented dimensions: (1) the level of inequality as measured by the power distance index; (2) the degree to which ties between individuals are loose (individualism); (3) the distribution of roles between genders (masculinity versus femininity); and (4) the level of tolerance for uncertainty and ambiguity (uncertainty avoidance index). Table 5.1 presents the scores for these cultural dimensions for several Western countries and Turkey and some distinct features can be seen with regards to the latter. For instance, compared with the other countries it has the lowest rate of individualism, the second highest power distance index score, the second lowest level of masculinity and also registers a high uncertainty index mark. That is, in general, its cultural mix under these classifications is quite distinct from the other countries shown in the Table 5.1, that is, a sample of Western nations.

5.1.2 THE TURKISH ECONOMY AND FINANCIAL MARKETS

Recent Turkish history has been characterised by a period of considerable growth and industrialisation following the liberalisation of the money markets (Bugra, 1994). Moreover, respective governments have made great efforts to build links with other countries, with it being a member of the Organisation for Economic Co-operation and Development (OECD) and the G20 industrial countries as well as having signed a trade agreement with the European Union (EU), which, along with other measures taken, has led to it becoming a significant destination for foreign direct investment. However, regarding Turkey's comparative economic development in general, Table 5.2 reports a range of economic and financial variables for a set of countries and it can be seen that it still clearly lags behind the developed countries, having a level of gross domestic product (GDP) per capita between three and a half and five times lower than them. Nevertheless, Turkey's economy is growing very much more rapidly than those of the West with a current annual growth rate of over 7 per cent and an average growth rate between 2002 and 2007 of 7.2 per cent (Fletcher, 2007).

Table 5.1 Hofstede's cultural dimensions for selected countries

	Power Distance Index	Individualism	Masculinity	Uncertainty Avoidance Index
France	68	71	43	86
Germany	35	67	66	65
United Kingdom	35	89	66	35
United States	40	91	62	46
Turkey	66	37	45	85

Not only is the total level of economic production in Turkey lower than in the developed countries, but it also has a very different composition. In particular, Table 5.1 demonstrates that in the other countries the percentage of employment involved in agricultural production is less than 5 per cent, whereas in Turkey this proportion is almost 30 per cent. By contrast, the levels of manufacturing employment are similar across the countries in the sample and, consequently, the more developed economies have substantially higher rates of service sector employment. Within manufacturing, Turkey has a particular presence within the textiles industry, where it has a strong competitive advantage with low labour costs and abundant raw materials. This industry was also one of the forerunner industries, developed proactively during the 1980s by the export-oriented economic strategies of the era and it has made a consistently high contribution to the national income to this day. For instance, according to the Istanbul Textile and Apparel Exporters' Association the textile and clothing industry accounted for 7.8 per cent of GDP and 19.9 per cent of industrial production in 2004.

Concerning the development of financial markets in Turkey, the Istanbul Stock Exchange was established relatively recently in 1986. Table 5.2 shows that the stock exchange is relatively small in absolute terms in comparison with more developed countries but that, perhaps surprisingly, the ratio of the size of its stock market to its GDP is comparable to Germany, though lower than other developed countries. This suggests that, of the developing countries, Turkey has a relatively well-established financial system. Furthermore, in parallel with the growth of the Turkish economy generally, the capitalisation of the Istanbul Stock Exchange National Index increased from 33.8 billion dollars to 163 billion dollars between 2002 and 2005 (Turkish-US Business Council of DEİK, 2006) and this success, in recent years, has led to very substantial fortunes being made by leading industrialists. Regarding this, a study conducted by *Forbes* magazine (2008) showed that Istanbul ranked fourth behind Moscow, New York and London in terms of the number of resident billionaires, with it having 36, whilst the others had 74, 71 and 36, respectively.

Table 5.2 Key economic indicators for selected countries

	Australia	France	Germany	Japan	Turkey	United Kingdom	United States
Economic overview							
GDP (current US$)	737,944,207,360	2,136,451,973,120	2,786,966,896,640	4,549,106,991,104	36,336,962,648	2,231,891,394,560	12,397,900,201,984
GDP growth (annual %)	2.8	1.7	0.9	1.9	7.4	1.9	3.2
GDP per capita, PPP	34,106	30,591	30,445	30,290	7,786	31,371	41,813
Unemployment, total (% of total labour force)	5.1	9.8	11.1	4.4	10.3	4.6	5.1
Composition of economic activity							
Employment in agriculture (% of total employment)	3.6	3.8	2.4	4.4	29.5	1.4	1.6
Employment in industry (% of total employment)	21.1	24.3	29.7	27.9	24.7	22.0	20.6
Employment in services (% of total employment)	75.0	71.5	67.8	66.4	45.8	76.3	77.8
Financial market development							
Market capitalisation of listed companies (current US$)	804,073,802,362	1,758,720,655,89	1,221,250,098,842	4,736,512,818,77	161,537,430,000	3,058,182,414,470	16,970,864,548,060
Market capitalisation of listed companies (% of GDP)	109.0	82.3	43.8	104.1	44.5	137.0	136.9

5.1.3 THE SOCIAL WELFARE AND LEGISLATION SYSTEM IN TURKEY

Table 5.3 provides statistics relating to Turkey's demography as well those for the same developed countries shown in Table 5.1 and it is immediately apparent that the former nation faces a range of challenges that the more developed countries do not have to. For example, life expectancy is lower in Turkey, at 71.3 years, than in any of the other countries listed. This can be largely explained by the lower overall levels of expenditure on health than in the other countries, with per capita spending equating to around $400 as compared with as much as 15 times this for the rest. Further, in education, particularly the tertiary sector, Turkey also lags substantially behind other countries, with only 15 per cent of its workforce having been educated to this level. In general, it can be seen that there are substantial deficits, in a comparative sense, with developed nations in the areas of social welfare which CCI contributions in Turkey could help to address.

Turning to legislative matters, one of the key reasons companies engage in CCI activities (Navarro, 1998) is the availability of tax deduction from profits and this also pertains to the Turkish setting. That is, a law passed in 2006 meant that cash giving and sponsorship by companies could count as an expense and, hence, be tax deductible. Additionally, by means of Turkish Law No. 5228, donations made to foundations and associations can also be deducted from tax at the discretion of the Council of Ministers. For example, if a cash money donation made by any company is not included in the approved list, as determined by the Council of Ministers, it may not be declared as an expense. However, the Council of Ministers can put some special rules into force in exceptional circumstances. Another rule which is stated in the income tax statutes is that donations made in the educational field can be deducted from tax. Regarding this, one of the biggest mobile phone operators in Turkey, namely Turkcell, put the Kardelenler Project (a project which is aimed at giving girls more modern opportunities) into force together with Çağdaş Yaşamı Koruma Derneği (the Association for the Protection of Modern Life) by taking advantage of this incentive.

Although various forms of CCI activities are undertaken by companies, because they can write them off as expenses, this cannot be the only driver, for the law was only changed recently and, yet, there is significant evidence that CCI has been engaged with for a long period of time. Therefore, it can be accepted that other factors embedded in the cultural and social norms of Turkey are influential, which these empirical chapters aim to uncover.

Table 5.3   Key social indicators for selected countries

	Australia	France	Germany	Japan	Turkey	United Kingdom	United States
Democratic Overview							
Population, total	20,399.836	60,873,000	82,468,400	127,773,000	72,065,000	60,226,500	296,507,000
Population in urban agglomeration > 1 million	12,323,665	13,633,665	6,390,835	61,390,835	61,048,252	18,430,909	128,327,946
Population in urban . agglomeration > 1 million (% of total population)	60.4	22.4	7.7	47.8	25.6	26.1	43.3
Welfare provision							
Health expenditure per capita (current US$)	3.181	3.807	3.628	2.936	383	3.064	6.657
Health expenditure, private (% of GDP)	2.9	2.2	2.5	1.5	2.2	1.1	8.3
Health expenditure, total (% of GDP)	5.9	8.9	8.2	6.7	5.4	7.1	7.2
Health expenditure, total (% of GDP)	8.8	11.1	10.7	8.2	7.6	8.2	15.9
Labour force with tertiary education (% of total)	37.7	29.8		38.8	15.0	31.2	62.9
Life expectancy at birth, total (years)	80.8	80.2	78.9	82.1	71.3	78.9	77.7

5.2 Research Methodology

The descriptive data on CCI in Turkey comprises both primary and secondary sources. The primary data are drawn from the CCI questionnaire that was developed for this book. This data provides information on the amount of donations the sample companies give to the Turkish community according to the different forms of CCI identified in Chapter 2. The data is also grouped for the sample companies according to their: size, industry and ownership status. The secondary data that was obtained from companies, their websites and from the researcher's field notes have been subject to content analysis. This involved using a largely inductive approach that allowed for the prevailing pattern, themes and categories to emerge from the collected data rather than it being controlled by predetermined factors. The constant comparative method was used for conducting the analysis (Ragin, 1989), which involved a continuous process of coding the firm data according to the areas that they focused their giving on.

5.3 Findings on Corporate Community Involvement Behaviours

The findings reveal that, on average, the companies who responded to the survey were contributing approximately YTL two million per year (around £800,000) and that the aggregate contributions were around YTL 200 million. In the UK, the Charities Aid Foundation's (CAF) top 500 corporate donors gave over £1.1 billion in 2005/2006, the equivalent number being $12.7 billion for the USA. Moreover, in Turkey's case, considerable variation in the level and composition of giving across companies is found. Next, the situation regarding Turkey's CCI is considered in terms of the types of companies that are the main givers, the sectors that are the highest donors and the form(s) of giving that are preferred.

Table 5.4   The concentration of giving among the largest companies

	Charitable Giving	Sponsorship	Cause-Related Marketing	Gifts-in-Kind	Total Giving
First Quartile (Largest givers)	91.9%	94.1%	97.3%	91.4%	93.4%
Second Quartile	4.5%	2.2%	0.1%	4.9%	3.0%
Third Quartile	2.7%	2.8%	2.5%	3.2%	2.8%
Fourth Quartile (Smallest givers)	0.9%	0.9%	0.1%	0.6%	0.7%

Table 5.4 shows the proportion of the overall level of giving attributable to four quartiles of the sample, arranged in order of firm size, that is the first quartile contains the top quarter of the respondents. It is clearly apparent that by far the greatest givers are these larger companies. More specifically, 94 per cent of overall community involvement contributions are made by the largest 20 or so donors in the sample. This finding is consistent with other studies that found that larger companies are significantly more likely to participate in CCI and that their levels of expenditures are substantially higher (Navarro, 1988; Arupalam and Stoneman, 1995; Adams and Hardwick, 1998; Bartkus et al., 2002; Seifert et al., 2004; Brammer and Millington 2004a; Gan, 2006; Brown et al., 2006). Similarly, an analysis of the Guardian Giving List for 2006 shows that the ten highest givers contributed nearly 60 per cent of the CCI carried out by the largest 100 British companies. Likewise, Brammer and Pavelin (2005) showed that around half of the total community contributions made by the largest donors in the US were made by the leading ten companies. Although these outcomes for the other nations are similar, it would appear that the concentration of giving by the large firms is more pronounced in Turkey. In terms of the actual numbers, the first quartile of firms gives YTL 189 million out of a total of YTL 200 million.

The secondary data reveals that the CCI activities of companies in Turkey are heavily influenced by a small group of leading businessmen who seek to contribute to the betterment of society through their companies. This finding is consistent with those for the UK and the US (Sharfman, 1994) and is another determinant of why it is mostly large companies that donate. Moreover, the data for Turkey reveals that these businessmen play an active role in areas such as health, education, culture and arts, which are probably more vital than similar activities in the developed countries, owing to the less advanced welfare state. Amongst these businessmen, Vehbi Koç, Kadir Has, Hacı Ömer Sabancı and Asım Kocabıyık are particularly prominent.

In the literature some studies have also found that industry sector is strongly associated with the level and composition of CCI activities (Bennett, 1998; Arupalam and Stoneman, 1995; Adams and Hardwick, 1998; Brammer and Millington, 2004a) and Turkey is no exception. Table 5.5 shows the percentages of the sample companies participating in various aspects of CCI broken down into eight industrial categories: finance, information and technology, chemical and pharmacy, engineering, consumer goods, construction, consumer services and other manufacturers. The table not only shows the types of CCI activities, as discussed in the literature review, but also separates gifts-in-kind into several categories; it can be seen that there is a preference for giving company products and donations of old equipment.

Table 5.5 Rates of participation in aspects of CCI across eight industry sectors

	Finance No=15	Information & Technology No=10	Chemical & Parmacy No=15	Engineering No=17	Consumer Goods No=15	Construction No=6	Consumer Services No=10	Other Manufacturers No=4	All Sectors No=92
Any CCI	100.0%	100.0%	100.0%	100.0%	100.0%	100.0%	100.0%	100.0%	100.0%
Corporate Foundation	13.3%	10.0%	26.7%	35.3%	35.7%	66.7%	0.0%	25.0%	25.0%
Sponsorship	93.3%	70.0%	66.7%	100.0%	78.6%	83.3%	100.0%	75.0%	84.8%
Cause-Related Marketing	26.7%	20.0%	13.3%	17.6%	7.1%	0.0%	54.5%	0.0%	19.6%
Charitable Giving	93.3%	90.0%	100.0%	82.4%	78.6%	100.0%	81.8%	100.0%	89.1%
Employee Volunteering	73.3%	80.0%	80.0%	58.8%	57.1%	66.7%	72.7%	50.0%	68.5%
Gifts-in-Kind	73.3%	90.0%	93.3%	94.1%	78.6%	83.3%	90.9%	75.0%	85.9%
Giving of Company Products	46.7%	80.0%	66.7%	64.7%	71.4%	66.7%	90.9%	50.0%	67.4%
Donations of Old Equipment	66.7%	80.0%	60.0%	82.4%	57.1%	83.3%	54.5%	50.0%	67.4%
Donations of Input/ Raw Materials	6.7%	30.0%	13.3%	11.8%	24.0%	16.7%	9.1%	50.0%	16.3%
Other Donations	33.3%	10.0%	20.0%	17.6%	14.3%	0.0%	0.0%	25.0%	16.3%

Table 5.6   Levels of contributions in elements of CCI for eight industry sectors

	Finance No=13	Information & Technology No=10	Chemical & Parmacy No=13	Engineering No=15	Consumer Goods No=13	Construction No=6	Consumer Services No=10	Other Manufacturers No=4	All Sectors No=84
Charitable Giving (YTL)	530.462	1.538.100	203.192	1.132.667	141.077	993.750	59.350	1.006.250	646.708
Percentage	37.45%	46.63%	25.43%	62.41%	2.9%	56.63%	17.95%	65.09%	31.4%
Sponsorship (YTL)	510.769	1.567.000	300.654	329.400	4.700.423	351.667	147.250	426.250	1.161.339
Percentage	36.06%	47.51%	37.63%	18.15%	96.8%	20.04%	44.54%	27.57%	57.0%
Cause-Related Marketing (YTL)	15.769	7.850	115.385	4.000	0	0	24.600	0	24.875
Percentage	1.11%	0.24%	14.44%	9.87%	0.0%	0.0%	7.44%	0.0%	1.0%
Gifts-in-Kind (YTL)	359.423	185.250	179.731	348.900	15.654	409.417	99.400	113.375	216.696
Percentage	25.38%	5.62%	22.5%	19.22%	0.3%	23.33%	30.07%	7.33%	10.6%
Total Giving (YTL)	1.312.577	3.298.200	798.962	1.814.967	4.857.154	1.754.833	330.600	1.545.875	2.033.548
	100.0%	100.0%	100.0%	100.0%	100.0%	100.0%	100.0%	100.0%	100.0%

The findings show that all the sample companies participate in some form of CCI activities, but that the particular forms engaged with vary substantially across industries. Almost 90 per cent of companies make charitable donations, more than 80 per cent engage in sponsorship of community activities and about two-thirds have an employee volunteering scheme. In contrast, only 20 per cent undertake cause-related marketing (CRM). Specifically, 54 per cent of the consumer services industry engages in CRM, which is the highest ratio of all the sectors. Moreover, a quarter of companies manage some or all of their CCI activities through a corporate foundation, which is a lower proportion than for some countries, for example the US and Germany (Seifert et al., 2004; Bennett, 1988) but higher than in the UK (Arupalam and Stoneman, 1995). This finding was somewhat unexpected, given the legacy of the Ottoman Empire foundations, as explained in Chapter 1. In addition, it emerges that the largest firms are the ones more likely to have a corporate foundation and it is the construction sector that has the highest proportion, with two-thirds of its firms in the sample having this status.

Table 5.6 extends the analysis of the variation in the pattern of CCI activities, across sectors, by focusing on the degree of involvement in the different forms of CCI, in terms of the amounts of expenditure. However, it should be noted that nine of the sample companies were unwilling to divulge information at this level of detail and, hence, the outcomes were slightly less robust than for the whole sample, but nevertheless they still provided some useful insights. For instance, it emerges that companies in consumer goods spend approximately two and half times as much as the average firm in the sample on total CCI and the Information & Technology sector gives twice as much as this average. In contrast, finance, chemical and pharmacy and consumer service companies make substantially lower investments in CCI than the average. Moreover, when comparing these outcomes with the existing evidence available for other countries, some differences are found in the Turkish setting. For example, finance sector companies register the third lowest total amount in spite of their constituting one of the largest portions of the overall sample. This would appear to contrast with Rigaud's (1991) findings for France, where overall corporate giving was heavily concentrated in the banking and insurance sectors, contributing 22.8 per cent and 7.2 per cent of all business donations, respectively. Brammer and Millington (2003) also highlighted the heavy concentration of giving in the context of the UK for the finance sectors. Further, in the US the finance sector is a big contributor to CCI at 17.4 per cent and so too is the pharmaceutical/medical sector at 29.9 per cent of total contributions (Brown et al., 2006). In addition, within the Turkish context not only does the consumer goods production sector donate by far the greatest average amount, but much of this difference can be accounted for by the levels of sponsorship it provides, which constitutes not only the vast majority of its total giving (96.8 per cent), but in actual money terms stands at over YTL four million on average for each of these firms and this represents a substantial proportion of overall giving. That is, without these donations the average total across the sectors would be much lower. Finally, in spite of the sponsorship total for the consumer goods sector appearing to be by far the largest, this form emerges as being the most important across nearly all of the sectors.

Next, linking firm ownership status with engagement in CCI activities, earlier studies have highlighted the role of individual philanthropists giving through their family companies as a possibly significant driver for the emerging patterns of corporate responsibility (Smith, 2003; Jones, 2010). Moreover, other research has questioned the contributions made by multinational companies to the communities in the countries where they have operations (Husted and Allen, 2006; Miller and Guthrie, 2007). To investigate whether these assertions hold true, Table 5.7 presents the rates of participation in the different types of CCI for the 92 companies in terms of their ownership status. It needs to be borne in mind that the categories are not mutually exclusive (that is, a company can be both a listed company and a family-owned one) and hence any observations need to be treated with some caution. However, some modest variations across the ownership types can be seen. For instance, family-managed and foreign-owned and controlled companies generally exhibit lower rates of participation in CCI than the other groups of companies. Moreover, donating through a corporate foundation for stock market-listed companies is quite common (36.7 per cent), but this is not the case for foreign-owned and controlled firms (11.1 per cent). On a different note, family-managed firms have the highest ratio of CRM donations (27.6 per cent) amongst these categories.

Table 5.8 extends this analysis by examining the levels of contributions made by these groups of companies to the various categories of CCI. The figures show that listed companies contribute the most, with average donations of over YTL 3.3 million, followed by companies with foreign operations, who donate over YTL 2.5 million on average. This finding is also consistent with a UK example investigated by Brammer and Millington (2003), which showed that, in 1999, the largest 25 givers in the UK, donating over 80 per cent of the charitable giving, were listed in that country. In addition, sponsorship is found to be the most preferred type of CCI activity in Turkey for stock market-listed companies. Moreover, the lowest levels of contributions are made by companies that are foreign-owned and controlled, giving around YTL 570,000 on average, and family-managed companies, each donating around YTL 1.3 million. These starkly differing amounts between foreign firms in Turkey and host ones, in general, raise important questions about the level of concern of outsiders for host community development. Regarding this difference, a study by the Committee Encouraging Corporate Philanthropy (CECP, 2008) in the US investigated Fortune 100 companies and found that 90 per cent of the home-grown firms companies make their donations locally, with only 8.8 per cent giving overseas.

Table 5.7   Rates of participation in aspects of CCI for firms with different ownership status

	Stock-Market Listed N=49	Foreign Operations N=66	Family Owned N=56	Family Managed N=29	Foreign Owned and Controlled N=18
Any CCI	100.0%	100.0%	100.0%	100.0%	100.0%
Corporate Foundation	36.7%	28.8%	28.6%	27.6%	11.11%
Sponsorship	83.7%	89.4%	83.9%	82.8%	77.8%
Cause-Related Marketing	20.4%	18.2%	19.6%	27.6%	16.7%
Charitable Giving	87.8%	89.4%	87.5%	89.7%	77.8%
Employee Volunteering	67.3%	77.3%	60.7%	51.7%	72.2%
Gifts-in-Kind	81.6%	86.4%	89.3%	89.7%	77.8%
Giving of Company Products	65.3%	69.7%	75.0%	68.0%	66.7%
Donations of Old Equipment	63.3%	68.2%	67.9%	62.1%	50.0%
Donations of Input/Raw Materials	10.2%	21.2%	14.3%	27.6%	16.7%
Other Donations	10.2%	19.7%	16.1%	20.7%	16.7%

Table 5.8   **Levels of contributions to aspects of CCI for firms with different ownership status**

	Stock-Market Listed N=45	Foreign Operations N=59	Family Owned N=52	Family Managed N=27	Foreign Owned and Controlled N=17
Charitable Giving (YTL)	1.017.667	881.653	304.183	951.389	122.794
Percentage	30.0%	32.0%	17.0%	71.0%	21.6%
Sponsorship (YTL)	2.017.944	1.598.644	1.324.163	294.426	334.265
Percentage	60.0%	58.0%	74.0%	22.0%	58.7%
Cause-Related Marketing (YTL)	5.967	33.703	37.010	10.907	22.353
Percentage	0.1%	1.0%	2.0%	1.0%	3.9%
Gifts-in-Kind (YTL)	317.089	232.593	123.692	83.389	90.412
Percentage	9.9%	9.0%	7.0%	6.0%	15.8%
Total Giving (YTL)	3.328.667	2.723.712	1.789.048	1.340.111	569.824
Percentage	100.0%	100.0%	100.0%	100.0%	100.0%

Regarding the Turkish companies who donate the most, probing websites revealed that they have had a significant influence on the Turkish institutional climate, in particular, in the areas of education, health, and culture and the arts where investment is necessary. In relation to education, the Aygaz Company, which is a subsidiary of Koç Holding operating in the energy sector and is the biggest Turkish LPG supplier in the domestic market, has been focusing most of its efforts on projects in this field. These projects are LPG Education Programme, the Attentive Child Campaign and the Firefly Mobile Learning Units Project and, in addition, the company has built two elementary schools in Gebze and Van. Moreover, Turkcell, the GSM-based Turkish mobile communication company, has been conducting the Kardelenler (Snowdrops) project, within the scope of its community involvement efforts and in association with the Foundation for Contemporary Life, which is one of the biggest social responsibility projects in education. Under these, many school-age girls whose families cannot afford to send them to school are granted a scholarship. By the end of 2009, 18,400 students had been granted scholarships, 7,380 Snowdrops had graduated from high school, 1,400 of them had passed the university exam and 170 of them had graduated successfully from university.

In the area of health, Tüpraş, Turkey's largest industrial enterprise, built a rehabilitation centre in the intensive care unit of Derince State Hospital in 2002 and made a donation for the completion of an additional building in 2005. The company also purchased monitors and operating tables for Körfez State Hospital as well as equipment for the Nuclear Medicine Department of Kocaeli State Hospital. Sabancı Holding, which is undertaking its CCI activities through its Sabancı Foundation, made large donations towards the establishment of health centres and to hospitals across Turkey, including: Kangal Sabancı State Hospital in Sivas, Sakarya Toyotasa Emergency Aid Hospital in Sakarya, Pembe Sabancı Health Centre in Kayseri, Sabancı First Aid Health Centre in Bursa, Özdemir Sabancı Hydrotherapy Pool in Isparta, Erol Sabacı Training and Treatment Centre for Spastic Children in İstanbul, Metin Sabancı Baltalimanı Bone Diseases Education and Research Hospital in İstanbul, Sabancı Gynecological Oncology Department in the Cerrahpaşa Medical Faculty in İstanbul and Sabancı Red Crescent Dispensary in İstanbul. Further, the Doğuş Group, one of Turkey's largest holding companies, set up the Ayhan Şahenk Foundation, the majority of its activities being concentrated on health. For instance, one project offers free healthcare services through mobile units and the number of financially disadvantaged citizens benefiting from these services had exceeded 285,000 by the end of 2006.

Turkey's extensive history and cultural richness provides many attractive opportunities for companies to donate their resources to culture and art. In relation to this, the Eczacıbaşı Group, which has its core business in building, pharmaceuticals and consumer products, is the founder of Turkey's first privately-funded museum of modern art, for which it provided the initial investment and project management finance as well as the core collection of paintings. In fact, this company has long been committed to raising public awareness and appreciation of Turkish modern art and, to this end, it has developed one of the largest permanent collections of abstract and figurative work by Turkish painters, which it has sought to exhibit in a variety of forums. Finally, the group is also a staunch supporter of the Istanbul International Festivals.

5.4 Discussion of the Findings

In this chapter, the first comprehensive insight into CCI activities of companies in Turkey has been provided. Drawing upon an extensive database compiled from corporate websites and archive documents in addition to a primary survey of 92 of Turkey's largest companies, the general pattern of CCI in Turkey has emerged. The outcomes when compared to prior studies in Western contexts have revealed a number of similarities, but there have been a number of notable differences. Regarding the former, one unexpected finding is that there is no substantial difference in the proportion of Turkish firms that work through foundations. That is, as explained in Chapter 1, it was assumed that there would be a higher proportion in Turkey, because of the Ottoman legacy. Another finding common with the extant literature is that giving appears to be concentrated in the hands of a few large givers from the biggest firms. Moreover, it has emerged that foreign CCI is substantially lower than that of domestic firms, which is also consistent with other studies. Finally, no substantial difference emerged in relation to the proportions of the types of giving in the two different contexts.

Turning to the differences that have been revealed in Turkey, in previous studies in the West the financial services sector has been a major giver, but in Turkey these do not appear to have had nearly so great an impact. This can partially be explained by the fact that most of its major banks are international brands, such as HBSC and Fortis, which being foreign owned would be unlikely to invest in CCI, given the evidence in the previous paragraph. In fact, the biggest givers in Turkey came from the consumer services sector and most of their giving, almost 97 per cent, is in the form of sponsorship. As explained in the literature review, this type of giving is largely associated with firm visibility, which suggests that it is used as a core part of these firms' business strategy. Another dissimilarity relates to the purpose of the giving, in that much of the project work described in the previous section is geared towards providing welfare services in such areas as health and education. For instance, hospital building projects and reading projects have been cited which would normally be the responsibility of the state in Western countries. The reason for this can be found in the early discussion in this chapter on how Turkey is still lagging well behind the latter in terms of welfare provision. In essence, it would appear that much of the giving is similar to the efforts of philanthropists like Rowntree and Cadbury in the pre-welfare state UK. That is, because the Turkish Government cannot raise sufficient tax revenues to provide services to all of its 80 million people, these companies, many of which are family owned, have taken on a paternalistic role. Obviously, this is only a tentative finding, but the remaining empirical chapters may well provide other evidence to support this view.

This chapter has provided an overview of the Turkish context, in relation to socioeconomic factors and the nature of its CCI activities. Moreover, a comparative analysis to flesh out the similarities and differences of CCI scholarship in Western settings has been made. In the next chapter, the survey results from the 92 companies are further analysed to elicit the organisational structure in relation to CCI as well as firm preferences for areas to make donations.

6

Corporate Community Involvement, Organisational Forms and the Preferred Areas for Investment in Turkey

Prior research has tended to focus on the influences regarding on organisational contribution to charitable or community cases, paying relatively little attention to the recipients of these donations or how firms develop preferences in respect of them. In this chapter the aim is to address this by concentrating on two main aspects of corporate community involvement (CCI) within the sample of companies in Turkey. This chapter contributes to the existing literature in two ways. First, it explores how different institutional environments can shape the departmentalisation of CCI. Second, this is one of the first studies aimed at establishing whether and how a different institutional context, to those previously researched, namely that of Turkey, might influence the preference and exclusion areas of CCI activities. This chapter is structured as follows. The next section (section 6.1) discusses the literature on the determinants that can have an influence on the departmentalisation of CCI within the firm. Subsequently, section 6.2 contains a discussion on why companies might want to invest in a specific area and in particular, sets out three main areas that need investment in Turkey. The methodology used in this chapter is discussed in section 6.3. Section 6.4 is a presentation of the findings and section 6.5 discusses the implications of the research outcomes.

6.1 Organisational Structure and Corporate Community Involvement

The first objective of this chapter is to investigate whether there is any systematic pattern between a firm's departmental structure and CCI activities. This is approached by considering the organisational structure in terms of whether a firm embeds CCI into the tasks of specific functional departments, or whether it assigns managers with sole responsibility for CCI matters. Understanding how CCI decision making is configured within a company may also explain why some companies give more than the others. For instance, it could be that those companies that have established a corporate social responsibility (CSR) department focusing specifically on CCI activities tend to give more than those who undertake them in addition to their main duties. In this section two main issues are explored, first, the theories that can account for the determinants that influence organisational structure are reviewed. Second, several studies that have been undertaken about departmentalisation and managerial attitudes regarding CCI activities in other national contexts are discussed.

The determinants of corporate organisational structure have been studied under the institutional theory lens. For example, Scott (2001) defined the institutions that can have an impact as governments, activists, trade associations, local communities, investors and customers by shaping the rules within an organisation and, hence, its structure. That is, institutional theorists argue that a society's rules, laws, certification, accreditation, social norms and values drive companies to act with consideration of this external environment so as to optimise their performance (Jepperson, 1991; Scott, 1992). Further, in Hoffman's (2001) study it was argued that organisations' functional structure and culture are determined by these institutional forces. Moreover, within this perspective it has been contended that organisations imitate high performing ones by abandoning obsolete practices. In particular, if they see their competitors making new arrangements regarding their organisational structure, such as setting up new departments owing to pressures from the above described external environment, they will imitate this behaviour to gain or maintain their legitimacy (Hoffman, 2001). In sum, taking the organisational and institutional theory optics together, how firms choose to structure their organisation is influenced by the need for efficiency in carrying out tasks, consideration of the forces of the external environment and pressures to copy arrangements in benchmarking competitors. It would appear reasonable to suggest that these motivations are the same for the arrangements of CCI within companies.

Husted (2003) provided examples of CCI activities – such as outsourcing through charitable contributions, developing an in-house programme or creating a more collaborative model which benefits both the company and the partner non-profit organisation – as activities that have to be undertaken through companies' CSR programmes. In a similar vein, Campbell (2007) stated that companies support community activities, treat their workers and customers decently, abide by the law and generally maintain standards of honesty and integrity as part of the integration of CSR into company culture. Therefore, there is considerable evidence to suggest that most CCI activities are undertaken as a part of CSR strategies and, according to organisational theory, there are two ways to integrate CSR programmes into the firm's structure. The first is by establishing a unique CSR department and the second is by distributing the tasks of CSR over various departments, such as public relations (PR), marketing or human resources (HR).

Whether firms separate the management aspects of CSR from other business functions has been the subject of a few studies. Regarding this, Husted and Allen (2006) following DiMaggio and Powell's (1983) institutional approach, put forward the following reasons why some companies do not have separate CSR departments. First, some firms consider that CSR activities can be undertaken adequately by managers who work in different units within the firm. Second, the uncertainty associated with the relationship between CSR and financial performance can prevent companies from setting up a separate department. Thirdly, the ambiguity of goals in the CSR area motivates some firms to integrate their programmes with other tasks. Where a firm decides not to establish a separate CSR department, they often view their programmes as part of PR and, hence, put it within that department (Etang, 1994). The prominence of this arrangement can be seen in research conducted in European and Asian countries, where the researchers emphasised the importance of sending the CSR relevant questions to PR departments (Welford, 2004). That is, the assumption was that CSR is used to respond to external pressures rather than other motivations (Etang, 1994). Similarly, Jamali and Mirsak (2007), looking at the Lebanese context, found that none of the sample companies had a separate CSR department or a manager who was responsible just for the CSR programme. In fact, nearly all of the managers they interviewed had major responsibilities other than CSR, working mostly in marketing and PR departments. Further, these scholars found that the departments responsible for CSR had to follow guidelines set by top management on how to handle social issues. In another more recent study on Greece, it emerged that out of 67 companies, 17 had established separate departments for their CSR practices (Panayiotou et al., 2009).

A number of academics have emphasised the importance of establishing a separate CSR department (Smith, 2003; Butler, 1991), seeing this as the most efficient way to address the values of stakeholders and improve communication with society at large, whilst making profit (Zwetsloot, 2003). That is, companies that locate their CSR activities in a specialised unit can be seen to consider these as one of their core strategies, for they recognise the importance of building a relationship between the external environment and their stakeholders so as to protect their business operations. Moreover, it has been noted in the extant literature that the departmentalisation of CSR is more common in international companies (Smith, 2003). Regarding this, The World Business Council for Sustainable Development (WBCSD), a coalition of 120 international companies, referred to the increasing calls for business to assume wider responsibilities in the social arena and pointed out that CSR 'is firmly on the global policy agenda' (Smith, 2003). Thus, it would appear that CSR activities are increasingly being seen as an important way of managing stakeholders and so need to be incorporated into firms' core objectives. This view is supported by Black (2006) who contended that companies need to develop social responsiveness capabilities which span the cultural and structural levels of the firm.

A recent study has shown that in the UK increasing numbers of companies prefer to separate their CSR activities from other business functions by establishing CSR departments (Smyth, 2007). Moreover, in the US, since the 1970s, CSR officer has become a new position on the organisation chart in many companies (Eilbirt and Parket, 1973). Further, according to the CSR Globe Report based on the Institute for Corporate Culture Affairs (ICCA) survey initiated in 2008, the majority of the participating companies indicated the presence of a managing body responsible for their CSR activities, with 31 per cent actually stating that they had a separate department or office responsible for the coordination and implementation of CSR policies and strategies. In addition, 19 per cent had a corporate communications department which was undertaking CSR activities and a further 16 per cent named the sustainability department as the body responsible for this. Corporate citizenship, corporate external affairs or environmental affairs were also among the frequently cited terms for CSR-managing bodies of companies covered by the survey.

The effect of top-level management on CSR adaptation has been identified, with some suggesting that corporate strategy is significantly influenced by the personal values of top managers (Guth and Tagiuri, 1965; Lincoln et al., 1982). A study by Juholin (2004) discovered that in many cases in Finland the management of CSR is located at a very high level in the company hierarchy, thus underlining the importance in strategic positioning. A similar top management effect on CSR decisions was found in Hungary, where according to Fülöp et al. (1999), top management is motivated to exert their discretionary influence in developing the ethical practices of a company. Another study conducted in Italy probed the reasons for companies adopting socially responsible behaviour, and established that the influence of top-level management in the CSR decision-making process is paramount (Tencati et al., 2004). Moreover, these scholars reported that the most frequently cited advantages of CSR were benefits to company image, providing opportunities to improve relations with the local community and motivating top management to act in an ethical manner.

6.2 The Motives for Prioritising and Excluding Different Types of Corporate Community Involvement Activities

By undertaking CCI activities companies can show their community that they care about the problems around them, but they can also benefit in a number of other ways. For example, if a company is having difficulty finding trained employees, it can work closely with high schools and universities so as to rectify this. More widely, the ways in which companies engage in CCI and the activities they prefer are shaped by the local institutional environment. That is, as several scholars have contended (Matten and Moon, 2004; Campbell, 2007; Marquis et al., 2007) the institutional environment is a key determinant for the actions of decision makers in companies. In relation to the focal nation of this research, namely Turkey, the local conditions are explored in order to elicit what leads to companies having preferences in CCI involvement. This is addressed, first, by examining the general literature concerned with why multinational companies participate in CSR in emerging or developing market contexts. Subsequently, there is analysis of Turkish education, healthcare and environmental matters, the salience of which in this particular context being provided by the presentation of some comparative figures with the other countries.

In general, the literature suggests that multinational enterprises (MNEs) are uniquely situated for helping to solve local problems, such as human rights (De George, 1993), environmental protection (Gnyawali, 1996) and worker's rights protection (Klein, 1999; Miller and Guthrie, 2007). Further, Frynas (2001) stated that multinational firms, beyond their purely economic role, could be expected to play a constructive part in the macro-level development and governance of a country. For example in this regard, De Jongh (2004) pointed out that MNEs in South Africa have been fighting against unemployment, poverty and HIV–AIDS in order to manage social risks. Miller and Guthrie (2007) highlighted that CSR of this type represents actively adopted strategies in response to the pressures corporations face in the local institutional environments in which they are embedded. Likewise, Husted and Allen (2006) in their study pointed to institutional pressures guiding decision making with respect to CSR, after eliciting that MNEs operating in Mexico placed similar emphasis on global CSR issues, such as environmental conservation. In another study that investigated Spanish multinationals it was found that institutional forces determine the companies' CSR projects. For example, they show that CSR projects have been shaped according to the ethical index criteria rather than by carrying out strategic analysis of stakeholder demands (Madariaga and Valor, 2004). Knox et al. (2005) argued that companies usually prefer to invest in the area(s) where there is a direct impact on their core business. For instance, a car manufacturer might be expected to invest in vehicle safety or the environment, rather than dealing with low-income housing or adult illiteracy (ibid). This is based on the premise that they invest in areas where there is a chance of using the participation to build the infrastructure for their business. Alternatively, Frynas (2001) found that oil companies often engage in community projects in order to maintain a stable working environment and to appear to be socially responsible. In sum, the evidence points to local conditions exerting a substantial impact on CCI decision making.

In Turkey, education, healthcare and the natural environment are key areas that need local investment. According to the Economist Intelligence Unit report (2008), although Turkish primary school enrolment is compulsory and its duration has been raised from five to eight years, now covering ages six to 14, in some undeveloped or conservative provinces in the east and south-east up to 40 per cent of girls may not be enrolled. This has resulted in great inequalities of educational achievement between social classes, regions of the country and between boys and girls. Additionally, there is poor general educational provision in rural areas, where shortages of books, buildings and personnel are serious problems (Williamson, 1987). According to an Organisation for Economic Co-operation and Development (OECD) economic survey (2008), the three key reasons for investment in education are as follows: first, the number of schools is still insufficient to keep up with the growth rate of the school-age population; second, educational enrolment in Turkey lags behind comparable middle-income emerging countries, notably with regard to post-primary school education for girls; and third, in 2005 only 36 per cent of the population aged between 25 and 34 had at least an upper secondary education, much lower than the EU19 and OECD averages of 70 per cent and 77 per cent, respectively.

Aktaş (2005) pointed out that in the period from 1923 to 2006 the number of universities increased from one to 77, student enrolment went from 2,914 to 2.1 million and the annual number of graduates increased from 321,000 to 324,000. Much of this increase can be attributed to Government initiation of the establishment of 25 new universities across the country in 1992. In addition to these newly established small city universities, several foundation universities were also set up and, according to a Ministry of Education report in 2005, there were 53 state and 24 foundation universities in Turkey. Most of the foundation universities were established by Turkish holding companies in 2001 and since this time there has been a substantial increase in the enrolment of students. However, these improvements have proved insufficient to cater for the demand for higher education places. In 2003, 1,451,811 high school graduates and senior high school graduates took the nationwide competitive entrance examination to the universities, but only 311,498 applicants were successful (21 per cent) (Tansel and Bircan, 2006). Moreover, these authors point out that in developing countries deficiencies in the educational system, such as an inadequate number of universities, large class sizes and low public educational expenditure, are often cited as the reasons for the high demand for private tutoring in relation to which Turkey is no exception (ibid). Finally, in the ranking for education in the latest version of the global competitiveness report, Turkey got 77 points for its quantity of education and 70 points for its quality, which means that the system does not produce sufficient technically trained people.

Turning to the data relating to healthcare, the number of doctors/nurses per person, consumption of medicine, the quality of health services and the eligibility to those services are indicators of a country's level of provision and overall development. In relation to which, in 2006, Turkey had 1.5 physicians per 1,000 population, which is less than half of the OECD average of 3.1. Despite increasing numbers of doctors in recent years, it continues to have the lowest number of physicians per capita among all the OECD countries (Data Monitor, 2009). Similarly, there were only 2.0 nurses per 1,000 population in 2008, a much lower figure than the average of 9.6 in OECD countries. The number of acute care hospital beds in 2008 was 2.8 per 1,000 population, which is less than the OECD average of 3.8. In general, it has emerged in an OECD report that Turkey has the lowest health spending per capita among OECD countries (OECD Health Data, 2009).

Turkey has a complex healthcare system that includes both state and private sectors, which are both coordinated by the Ministry of Health. In recent years, the healthcare services provided by hospitals have been improved by importing large quantities of modern machinery and equipment (Data Monitor, 2009). In 2006, the Ministry of Health initiated a project, whereby several medical centres would be built in three major cities to provide health facilities in 13 regions throughout the country. Moreover, the Turkish Government is encouraging foreign companies to invest in the healthcare industry. The private hospitals, which have also improved their medical equipment in recent years and charge less than rivals in other European countries, have witnessed an increasing number of patients from there as well as the Middle East. In fact, this sector provides 25 per cent of the total heath expenditure for the nation, with many people paying their insurance premiums to these private companies in addition to their regular contribution to state insurance systems, in order to receive a better quality of healthcare when they are ill. In sum, there is still much room for greater provision of medical supplies, equipment, hospitals and personnel that could be realised by collaborations between private companies and non-governmental organizations (NGOs).

The natural environment is seen as another important area for investment in relation to air quality, water quality, land use and ecosystem health along with social and cultural matters. In an OECD Environmental Outlook (2008) the major current environmental issues are specified as climate change, pollution and resource depletion. Complementary to the Environmental Law and its regulations, other laws and international conventions governing the protection of the environment have come into force in Turkey in the years since 1983. The following is an account according to a report published by the Regional Environmental Centre (Okumuş, 2002) on Turkey's natural environment, with regards to its air, water, waste, soil and protection of nature conditions

Regarding air, it emerges that Turkey has been producing fewer harmful emissions since the 1990s, because in urban areas domestic coal with high sulphur content is prohibited for heating, being replaced by imported coal with lower sulphur content. However, the illegal use of domestic coal for heating is still a significant contributor to urban air pollution. Natural gas is being supplied to the big cities and at the time of the report made up about 10 per cent of Turkey's total energy supply. Industrial emissions, coupled with those attributable to industrial power use, was responsible for almost 40 per cent of the total SO_2 (oxygen saturation) pollution in Turkey and motor vehicles are still a significant source of carbon monoxide, hydrocarbons and nitrogen oxides. Further, as a result of rapid economic development, uncontrolled urbanisation and rapid high growth, rates in air pollution remain a current environmental problem in the Turkey of today.

The report also stated that annual consumption of drinking water was almost 74 cubic metres per capita, when the EU average was about 100 cubic metres over a year. In relation to this and other water issues, the financing of investments for water supply, sanitation, sewage treatment and solid waste disposal is still a heavy burden for the central government, with significant pressure to increase the proportion of the population connected to the sewage treatment system, which currently stands at only 12 per cent. In addition, strategies for the management of water resources in water basins are required and the relevant legislation needs to be better enforced. In terms of municipal waste, volumes have increased in line with the increase in the country's population and the changes in lifestyle, from 15 million tonnes in 1991 to 22.8 million tonnes in 1996 and although composting plants have been installed in some cities, in other centres disposal practices vary from land fill to dumping in quarries, streams and even the sea. Therefore, strategies on the management of municipal waste need to be developed and technical support provided.

The main problem with soil in Turkey is erosion, with losses being estimated at one billion tonnes, most of it washed out to sea. In fact, this affects 81 per cent of the total land surface. This situation is exacerbated by the fact that agricultural land as with urban land can be built upon easily, for there are no laws about land use and there are no stable policies which support ecological cultivation. Furthermore, information relating to the natural environment in Turkey shows the need to increase public awareness through education programmes on nature conservation (OECD Environmental Outlook, 2008). Companies in Turkey may choose to act more responsibly towards environmental issues and integrate eco-friendly systems into their daily operations and also donate to and initiate projects with those NGOs that have environmental concerns.

6.3 Research Methodology

The data analysed in the remainder of this chapter are obtained from the same questionnaire as that used in Chapter 5. Binary variables were constructed for each priority and exclusion that took a value of 1 if the area was prioritised or excluded and zero otherwise. Additionally, secondary research analysis was undertaken using the Global Insight and MarketLine databases to collect facts related to the Turkish environment, health, and socio-political situation that help shed light on the Turkish institutional context, as presented in Section 6.2.

Although the sample of firms comprises 92 companies, drawn from the 2007 *Capital* magazine listing of Turkey's 500 largest companies, not all engaged in charitable giving and as a result the findings relate to 84 companies. Additionally, the classification related to departmentalisation was achieved by asking interviewees their job title and their responsibilities and from this the location of the management of CCI within the firm was deduced. Regarding this, job titles were subjected to an open coding process that led initially to the identification of 15 classifications, but further analysis of the characteristics of these 15 classifications supported a reduction to five final locations, these being CSR, human resources management (HRM), external relations, central administration and other internal functions and the details of this process can be seen in Table 6.1.

6.4 Findings

The analysis in this section focuses on three objectives. Firstly, identifying the sample's departmental distribution in terms of where CCI decisions are taken. Secondly, to investigate the allocation of responsibility for the management of CCI within the firm and thirdly, to elicit whether there is a relation between preferences and the location of responsibility for the management of CCI. In order to meet the first objective, as explained above, the job titles of the managers who described their job or part of their job as making the decisions on CCI activities were categorised under five main departmental categories. To achieve the second objective, the association between the location of internal control and composition of firm CCI expenditure is enlisted. To attain the third objective, the areas of community involvement that are identified by firms as particular priorities and as those they exclude are probed.

In Table 6.1 the Turkish sample is shown and the importance of corporate communications and HR departments in CCI decision making is evident. That is, 24 corporate communications managers stated that CCI activities were part of the description of their main job and 22 HR managers responded likewise. Once these job roles are reduced to the five aforementioned categories, it emerges that those departments responsible for HR, external relations and central administration have the greatest engagement in the management of CCI activities, standing at 22, 32 and 25 firms each in the sample respectively, and thus, accounting for over 85 per cent of the total. It is notable that only two of the firms sampled reported that they had a CSR manager and presumably a department.

Table 6.1   Departmental categories

Groups	Categories	Number	Final Categories	Total Number
Group 1	CSR manager	2	CSR	
				2
Group 2	HR manager	22	HRM	
				22
Group 3	Corporate communications manager	24	External relations	
	PR manager	6	External relations	
	Marketing	2	External relations	
				32
Group 4	Finance	7	Central administration	
	Top level	3	Central administration	
	General manager	3	Central administration	
	Assistant of general manager	4	Central administration	
	Deputy general manager	4	Central administration	
	Senior-level manager	4	Central administration	
				25
Group 5	Operations manager	3	Other internal	
	Quality control manager	2	Other internal	
	Strategy manager	3	Other internal	
	Production manager	3	Other internal	
				11
			Total	92

Turning to the relationship between firm characteristics and the location of CCI responsibility within a firm, Table 6.2 gives the average number of employees and the company age for each of the five departmental categories. From this data, it can be seen that the group of the youngest companies of medium size prefer to carry out their CCI activities through the external relations function and small companies tend to arrange their CCI activities under other internal functions. Additionally, the data show that the largest and older companies prefer to undertake their CCI activities under the CSR department. This finding is also consistent with the existing literature, which states that larger companies tend to separate their CSR department (Smith, 2003). Moreover, ownership characteristics and the sector that the companies are in vary across organisational form. The distribution does not show a clear difference in this variation, but it can be observed that 72.7 per cent of family-owned companies and 90.9 per cent of listed companies prefer to undertake their CCI activities as other internal functions. Further, 40 per cent of engineering companies prefer to use their central administration and 45.5 per cent of these companies choose other internal functions in order to engage in CCI activities.

Table 6.2   **The characteristics of the firms and the choice of organisational form**

	CSR Department	HR Department	External Relations	Central Administration	Other Internal Functions
N	2	22	32	25	11
Number of employees	150,000	18,989	54,352	12,917	4,148
Company age	42.0	33.7	30.8	35.5	42.5
Ownership characteristics					
Listed on the stock market	100.0%	40.9%	46.9%	52.0%	90.9%
Significant government ownership	50.0%	9.1%	3.1%	0.0%	9.1%
Joint venture	50.0%	50.0%	37.5%	24.0%	9.1%
Family owned	0.0%	68.2%	56.3%	60.0%	72.7%
Family managed	50.0%	27.3%	21.9%	40.0%	45.5%
Significant foreign ownership	50.0%	40.9%	43.8%	20.0%	0.0%
Sectoral breakdown					
Finance	0.0%	13.6%	21.9%	20.0%	0.0%
High technology	0.0%	9.1%	12.5%	8.0%	18.2%
Chemicals and pharmaceuticals	0.0%	31.8%	15.6%	4.0%	18.2%
Engineering	50.0%	9.1%	12.5%	40.0%	0.0%
Comsumer goods	0.0%	18.2%	9.4%	8.0%	45.5%
Construction	0.0%	4.5%	6.3%	4.0%	18.2%
Consumer services	50.0%	9.1%	15.6%	12.0%	0.0%
Other sectors	0.0%	4.5%	6.3%	4.0%	0.0%

Table 6.3 describes the distribution of the location of control over CCI and it can be seen that the aggregated composition of CCI activity varies for the different departments that are responsible for giving. It emerges that the vast amount of it is carried out within an external relations function. 32 companies (35 per cent) out of the 92 prefer to carry out their CCI activities in this way. Only two firms (2 per cent) have a separate CSR department, whilst 22 firms (24 per cent) have it as an HRM function; 25 firms (27 per cent) have placed it with central administration and 11 (12 per cent) as another form of internal function. The high proportion of firms that manage their CCI through the external relations function is consistent with the findings in the study on the UK by Brammer and Millington (2003), which showed that the highest proportion of giving came from the marketing and PR departments. In the study presented here, the marketing and PR departments are considered in the subgroup of the external relations function in addition to the corporate communications department. However, in Brammer and Millington's 2003 study, 35 per cent of the sample arranged CCI activities using the CSR department, which is very different from the Turkish case, with only 2 per cent of the sample doing so.

Table 6.3   Patterns in the size of CCI expenditure and the choice of organisational form

	CSR Department	HR Department	External Relations	Central Administration	Other Internal Functions
N	2	20	32	23	7
AVG CCI (YTL)	9,730,000	503,262	4,158,413	666,652	690,277
MAX CCI (YTL)	19,250,000	4,675,000	60,780,000	4,050,000	3,750,000
MIN CCI (YTL)	210,000	5,000	30,000	30,000	1,500
AVG CASH GIVING (YTL)	7,537,500	153,929	968,827	257,717	221,388
(PERCENTAGE OF TOTAL)	77.5%	30.6%	23.3%	38.7%	32.1%
AVG SPONSORSHIP (YTL)	1,765,000	138,690	2,948,724	163,347	204,444
(PERCENTAGE OF TOTAL)	18.1%	27.6%	70.9%	24.5%	29.6%
AVG CRM (YTL)	15,000	81,547	1,155	13,478	389
(PERCENTAGE OF TOTAL)	0.2%	16.2%	0.0%	2.0%	0.1%
AVG GIFTS IN KIND (YTL)	412,500	129,095	239,706	232,108	264,055
(PERCENTAGE OF TOTAL)	4.2%	25.7%	5.8%	34.8%	38.3%

Table 6.4   Patterns of CCI priorities across alternative organisational forms

	CSR Department	HR Department	External Relations	Central Administration	Other Internal Functions
N	2	22	32	25	11
Education	100.0%	90.9%	100.0%	92.0%	90.9%
Heathcare	0.0%	54.5%	50.0%	32.0%	36.4%
Arts culture	50.0%	54.5%	71.9%	56.0%	45.5%
Sports	50.0%	50.0%	53.1%	40.0%	54.5%
Environment	100.0%	59.1%	68.8%	56.0%	36.4%
Religion	0.0%	9.1%	6.3%	12.0%	9.1%
Youth	50.0%	50.0%	43.8%	40.0%	27.3%
Elderly	0.0%	18.2%	18,8%	20.0%	45.5%
Inter aid	50.0%	9.1%	9.3%	8.0%	9.1%
Political	0.0%	0.0%	0.0%	0.0%	0.0%
Animal rights	0.0%	4.5%	3.1%	0.0%	0.0%

(All figures are % of firms in the category that expressed a positive preference).

As pointed out in Table 6.3, a high proportion of the firms in the sample prefer to arrange their CCI activities as an external relations function and these companies also contribute a large part of the overall giving. Moreover, although companies that carry out their CCI activities through a CSR department represent the lowest number in the sample, these have a bigger budget for their CCI activities than those where corporate giving comes under the other three business functions. In the sample, on average, the level of CCI expenditure by firms that manage their CCI as an external relations function is more than three times as high as the level of expenditure made by companies that manage it in their CSR department, 12 times as high as the level of expenditure made by firms who manage it through HRM and central administration and 17 times as high as the firms who manage it through other internal functions.

Table 6.4 explores the relationship between organisational structure and CCI prioritisation. Formal t-tests of differences in priorities for CCI between groups of firms classified according to their choice of location of responsibility for CCI revealed that there were no statistically significant differences, largely because of the size of some of the subsamples. Therefore, the differences identified must be seen as indicative rather than definitive. Nonetheless, a few differences are worth highlighting. First, the proportion of arts and culture and environment projects are higher in the firms that manage their CCI through the external relations function. Second, the proportion of firms that prioritise projects associated with sports is higher in the firms that run CCI projects under the external relations function and other internal functions. The areas of preferences show a few differences across the different types. First, the extent to which firms prioritise arts and culture is significantly higher in firms that manage their CCI through an external relations department rather than through any of the alternatives. Second, investment in the environment is lowest when the giving is the responsibility of other internal functions. Third, investment in animal rights is seen only in those firms running their giving under their HR or external relations departments. In the literature review, it was noted that having a separate CSR department for engaging in CCI activities was considered preferable by many companies in Western contexts, but only two of the firms in the Turkish sample donated in this way. These two firms expressed a strong preference for donating to education and the environment. However, no strong systematic relationship between the types of CCI and departmental location is found. This is inconsistent with existing studies that were discussed in section 6.1 (Smith, 2003; Butler, 1991; Panayiotou et al., 2009). For example, Brammer and Millington (2003) found that a number of significant differences exist in the proportion of firms that prioritise particular aspects of CCI across the alternative locations of responsibility for its management. As explained previously, these authors concluded that different sectors tended to arrange their CCI similarly because of pressure from stakeholders. Therefore, this finding suggests that the form of stakeholder pressure in Turkey has not resulted in similar standardised CCI arrangements. Further evidence to support this is presented in Chapter 7, where it emerges that customers have a negative influence on CCI decision making, which is not the case in Western contexts. In sum, these outcomes indicate that most Turkish firms do not shape their organisational structure so that their giving is part of their business strategy, but rather their CCI activity is an add on to other roles and more geared towards being benevolent than is the case for their Western counterparts. This matter is returned to in the case studies in Chapter 8.

Overall, education is the most preferred community involvement activity with around 95 per cent of firms expressing a preference for involvement with it. Regarding this, there are many ongoing projects currently being carried out by companies in Turkey (for example, the Snowdrop Project – a joint educational project developed by Turkcell GSM operator with the Association in Support of Contemporary Living which provided a scholarship to 5,000 female students in the year 2000), which they engage in to fill the gaps in the public system. However, rather than putting forward an altruistic motive, evidence in some of the relevant literature points to strategic reasons for giving to education. More specifically, some authors have argued that the changes in business environment, arising from global competition and global market conditions (for example, the speed of technological innovations) require a skilled labour force and this puts pressure on companies to improve the quality of their workers (Stout and Schweikart, 1989; Lin and Hunter, 1992), which will substantially depend on the performance of the educational institutions, academic programmes and so on (Celik and Ecer, 2009). This would suggest that the multinational companies in the Turkish sample have strategic motives for donating to education but, given the last finding, organisational altruism appears to be a strong driver for domestic firms. The environment is found to be the second most important area of preference with 64 per cent of companies contributing to this area. This finding is consistent with the discussion in section 6.2 of this chapter, where it emerged that companies, in the interests of their business, like to engage in donating through infrastructure building so they can operate more effectively in the market.

Around 55 per cent of firms stated that they prioritise involvement in community projects involving the arts and culture. Turkey's cultural richness embraces a diverse and heterogeneous set of elements that are derived from Ottoman, European and Middle Eastern traditions. In particular, Istanbul has been home to countless societies and cultures and historically has a very rich cultural heritage. In 2010 Istanbul was the European City of Culture, which meant that more projects related to culture and arts were generated and viewed internationally during that year. The rich cultural heritage of Istanbul is seen in many other cities of Turkey. According to the data of the Turkish Ministry of Culture and Tourism, there are 99 museums directorates attached to the Ministry and, there are 92 private museums and 1,204 private collectors. However, this number is low if it is compared the heritage of Turkey and also with other countries. For example, in the UK there are about 1,860 museums accredited by the Museums, Libraries and Archives Council as meeting their minimum standards (Museum Association, 2009). Therefore, Turkey needs more protection in terms of its cultural heritage and because the Government has more pressing demands on its resources then firms often engage in this area, especially through their foundations.

As expected, approximately 45 per cent of firms expressed a preference for involvement in healthcare, which was discussed in some detail in section 6.2. The fourth most popular area for giving is sport and, although companies help with this, the area is underdeveloped because the Government cannot afford to invest in it. Keskin (2009) noted that in developed countries sports tourism constitutes 32 per cent of total tourism activities, but this ratio is very low in Turkey. Moreover, Keskin (2009) also pointed out that, with the exception of the areas of soccer, basketball and volleyball, there is no investment aimed at increasing the numbers of professional sportsmen and sportswomen and, as a result, Turkey has a very low participation rate in local and international sports activities. Because of this, the Turkish Government, in order to draw the attention of the private sector to sports and increase sponsorship, set up a programme – the 'Turkish sports meet their sponsor' campaign. The main aim of this programme is to increase the number of licensed sports people in various sports activities, to promote local sports activities and to increase sports tourism.

Investment in youth also constitutes 45 per cent of the CCI preference of Turkish companies. About one-third of the population is under 18 and need good education and training if they are to achieve their potential, but serious challenges still remain in relation to this. Williamson (1987) highlighted this issue by providing the following examples: the overproduction of university graduates who cannot be properly employed and also a heavy reliance on formal examinations as a way of assessing people, which leads to a kind of veneration of certification and highly stylised learning, which stresses memorisation of facts rather than the development of analytical skills. Further, migration from rural areas is adding to the already severe problems of demographic pressures in the cities, in relation to educational resources and also regarding HR planning for the economy. In sum, the results show that some companies are keenly aware of these problems for young people and are engaging in CCI to alleviate the situation. Very few firms stated that they prioritise CCI activities in the area of religion and, additionally, none of the firms invest in politics.

A few significant differences are revealed regarding the location of CCI within the firms and CCI priorities. First, the proportion of arts and culture and environment projects is higher for the firms that manage their CCI as an external relations function. Second, the proportion of firms that prioritise projects associated with sports is higher in those firms that run their CCI projects under an external relations function and other internal functions. However, in general, there are no striking differences between the department in which CCI activities are undertaken and areas of priorities. Prior research has also investigated the areas of priority in relation to several countries. For example, Brammer and Millington (2003) found that education is the preferred area of support for UK companies, followed by the arts, medical research and disability and sickness. In France, Rigaud (1991) elicited that one-third of all French company donations involve 'social and humanitarian causes and issues', whilst in the US 31 per cent of giving goes to health and social services, 25 per cent to education and 14 per cent to community and economic development, but only 3 per cent of community expenditures are oriented towards the natural environment (committee Encouraging Corporate Philanthropy, 2009).

Table 6.5 extends the analysis to report the relationship between the location of control over CCI and the incidence of exclusions regarding CCI activities. As is clearly seen, very few differences arise in the pattern of exclusions from involvement across the different forms of organisation. However, exclusion of international aid is seen only in two organisational structures (HR and central administration departments) and giving to the elderly only comes from firms whose CCI comes through the external relations department. Overall, no distinct pattern emerges in relation to department and exclusion type, which again, as suggested in Chapter 3, indicates that giving is determined by other factors, especially the preferences of the shareholder/owner, Moreover, this lack of a pattern gives further weight to the position put forward above that much giving is for benevolent purposes rather than strategic ones. Additionally, formal t-tests of differences in exclusions for CCI between groups of firms classified according to their choice of location of responsibility for CCI revealed that there were no statistically significant differences, largely because of the size of some of the subsamples.

Table 6.5   **Patterns of CCI exclusions across alternative organisational forms**

	CSR Department	HR Department	External Relations	Central Administration	Other Internal Functions
N	2	22	32	25	11
Education	n/p*	0.0%	0.0%	0.0%	0.0%
Healthcare	n/p*	0.0%	6.3%	4.0%	9.1%
Arts culture	n/p*	0.0%	0.0%	0.0%	0.0%
Sports	n/p*	0.0%	0.0%	0.0%	0.0%
Environment	n/p*	0.0%	0.0%	0.0%	0.0%
Religion	n/p*	45.5%	62.5%	36.0%	54.5%
Youth	n/p*	0.0%	0.0%	0.0%	0.0%
Elderly	n/p*	0.0%	3.1%	0.0%	0.0%
Inter aid	n/p*	9.1%	0.0%	4.0%	0.0%
Political	n/p*	63.6%	75.0%	56.0%	45.5%
Animal rights	n/p*	4.5%	15.6%	8.0%	9.1%

*   Not provided.

(All figures are % of firms in the category that expressed a positive preference).

Most of the companies indicated that involvement with politics is excluded (60 per cent of firms) and the reason for this is as follows. Prior to the military coup d'état in Turkey in 1980, religious divisions were exploited by both right-wing and left-wing groups for their different political ends and the situation degenerated into a virtual civil war (Williamson, 1987). Since then, because of continued polarisation and the wish of most people to modernise Turkish society away from the former militarist orientation, many sections of society including business steer well clear of getting involved in politics. Moreover, there has always been the danger that fundamentalist Islam and pan-Arabism could intervene in the system, which would lead to the undermining of 'Kemalist principles' championed by wide sections of the population that are in danger because of the religious fundamentalists. Nowadays, these issues are more pressing because of the government of the AKP (Justice and Development Party), whose aim is social and economic reform that replaces the secular state system with one founded on Islamic law (White, 2002). In sum, modernisation is the goal of Turkish businesses but through increased prosperity rather than political patronage.

Giving to the area of religion is excluded by 49 per cent of firms. As pointed out in Chapter 5, although Turkey is 99 per cent Muslim, it is a secular state and ever since the 1920's rule of Kemal Attaturk, most of establishment have avoided mixing religion with the affairs of state and business. This holds true for many firms for, as pointed out above, they do not get involved in politics. Moreover, there is no history of strong fundamentalism in the country and the leaders of industry were largely educated in non-Muslim settings. However, as also pointed out above, in recent years there has been a shift towards desecularisation by the ruling AKP, which might explain why a substantial number of firms do not rule out donating to religious causes. Further, the Islamist movement in Turkey encompasses a variety of people with contradictory motivations and goals and sometimes radically differing interpretations of fundamental religious principles (White, 2002) and not knowing what people stand for may also put businesses off religious donations.

Exclusion of the areas of politics and religion is also consistent with the UK data as shown in Brammer and Millington's (2003) study. They reported that 63 per cent of firms in their sample excluded political causes and 74 per cent excluded religious causes from their CCI activities. A similar finding is seen in analysis by Seigfried et al., (1983), which suggests that in the US most of the companies studied declared religion and politics as the most common exclusions. In addition, the third most cited area of exclusion, although with a much lower percentage than religion or politics, is animal rights. In Turkey, activist groups such as Turkey Animal Protection Association (THKD), Homeless Animals and Nature Protection Association (EHDHK) and Helping Street Animals in Turkey (DOHAYKO), try to solve the stray animal problem. Although a law to protect animals was passed in 2004, there is no supporting incentive or campaign established by governmental agencies or by the private sector. Moreover, although the number of firms who said they exclude animal rights from their giving was small, only a small percentage actually gave to them, as can be seen in Table 6.4, which suggests that they are largely disinterested and so this is left to a few activist groups.

International aid is found to be another area of exclusion for a small number of companies, because investment needed in Turkey is seen as the highest priority. However, international aid is being given in two ways: first, by participating in the international campaigns of big international non-profit institutions like United Nations Educational Scientific and Cultural Organisations (UNESCO) and Unite for Children (UNISEF); or second, donations can be made for only a specific period of time when it is needed. Natural disasters, such as earthquakes, floods or diseases like swine flu are examples of donation for a specific period of time. However, although the rest of the world also needs charitable donations, the amount donated by companies located in Turkey is nowhere near as much as for companies located in developed countries. Thus, this finding was also expected.

Finally, it should be noted that the two companies that had CSR departments were unwilling to provide any information on exclusions. This lack of willingness could be due to their already using CCI in a strategic manner as in the West and therefore they consider this be restricted information that they do not want their competitors to get hold of.

6.5 Discussion of the Findings

This chapter has discussed the allocation of responsibility for the management of CCI within the firm and the areas of preferences according to the location of responsibility for the management of CCI. Firstly, whether any systematic patterns in company choices of organisational structures in terms of how their community involvement is managed has been probed. The results suggest that, in contrast to the other research which has been done in the UK and the US, there is no clear pattern in Turkey. One possible reason for this is that no strong stakeholder affect has yet emerged and much of the CCI activity is still at the benevolent stage influenced strongly by investors/owners. Moreover, it has emerged that the vast majority of CCI activities are carried out as an external relations function and engaging in CCI under a CSR department is rarely the case. However, the budget for CCI where there was a CSR department was strikingly high. In sum, this suggests that companies in Turkey are still not ready or willing to establish separate CSR departments and for them CCI activities are viewed as extra responsibilities in their job roles.

Secondly, the areas of preference that the companies wish to engage with in their CCI activities, or choose to avoid, has been investigated. It emerged that, as with the UK, education had the highest priority for giving. However, in Turkey's case much of this form of donation is to address gaps in the public education system as opposed to strategic positioning in the UK's case. Moreover, the ranking of the three most popular exclusions, politics, religion and animal rights, are consistent with studies that have examined the situation in the UK and the US. In addition, the preferred and excluded areas which have been found in this chapter are consistent with the argument advanced in section 6.2 which is that the country's particular economic, social, cultural context may influence companies when engaging in CCI activities. Finally, the lack of a pattern in the organisational structures in relation to priorities and exclusions also suggests CCI in Turkey has different motivations to Western nations, because of its different history and institutional configuration, a matter investigated in detail in Chapter 8.

7

Decisions Regarding the Scale and the Composition of Corporate Community Involvement Activities

As noted in Chapter 2, a considerable amount of extant research has examined the different determinants affecting the amount of corporate community involvement (CCI) that UK and US firms have engaged in. However, researchers have yet to explore the drivers for investing in the different types of CCI, nor have they yet investigated the nature of trade-offs of these types in firm CCI strategies In order to address this, in this chapter there are four key objectives. First, having provided a broad examination of the relationship between companies and their community, previous studies are built upon by exploring this in relation to different types of CCI. Second, the aim is to test the factors that impact upon CCI decision making by applying three determinants taken from the behavioural theory of the firm – namely stakeholder pressures, the institutional climate and the availability of slack resources – as the independent variables, as well as employing a set of control variables taken from previous research. Third, given the lack of availability of secondary data, as explained previously, a measure is devised for assessing the impact of the presence or absence of slack resources on CCI behaviour. Fourth, drawing on institutional literature, a set of institutional variables are constructed and subsequently included in the model for investigating CCI decision making.

7.1 Empirical Model and Hypotheses Development

In this chapter, the determinants of CCI behaviour for firms in Turkey are investigated within a model derived from the behavioural theory of the firm (Cyert and March, 1963). In particular, the focus here involves probing the impact of stakeholder pressures, the institutional climate, availability of slack resources and a set of firm and industry characteristics on firm choices regarding CCI. The basic model for this investigation is shown in the following equation and, when addressing this, the four previously identified types of CCI are considered as well as their aggregate amount.

> *Corporate community involvement = f(stakeholder pressures, institutional climate, availability of slack resources, size, industry, company ownership).*

7.1.1 STAKEHOLDER PRESSURES

Mitchell et al. (1997) stressed the need to explore how and under what circumstances managers can and should respond to the various stakeholder types. That is, managers should be aware of the validity of diverse stakeholder groups and should attempt to respond to them within a mutually supportive framework (Donaldson and Preston, 1995), because this is important for the achievement of the organisation's objectives (Frooman, 1999). Additionally, Brammer and Millington (2004a) argued that companies practising stakeholder management can achieve sustainability and maximise their profits. However, stakeholder management is not only applied to achieve sustainability and profitability, as it is also important for companies regarding their legitimacy (Donaldson and Preston, 1995). Regarding the lattermost, according to Craig (2002), sometimes companies have to strive to attain legitimacy in unknown environments, where how they should act is not straightforward and stakeholder management can help in this quest.

Moreover, Kaler (2006) has suggested that stakeholder management is an important driver for implementing corporate social responsibility (CSR) strategies within companies. That is, he argued that the stakeholder environment is an important consideration for managers if they are to achieve organisational goals. To see whether this assumption is valid in the field of CCI, this researcher, in the conceptual framework in Chapter 3, put forward that the pressure from stakeholders has a marked impact on the managerial decision to engage in CCI. Previous studies have provided some evidence for this contention (Besser, 1999; Adam and Hardwick, 1998 Brammer and Millington, 2003; Meijer et al., 2006) and in particular, Brammer and Millington (2004b) found that the management of corporate giving is significantly influenced by powerful stakeholders. However, given the shortage of scholarship on this matter, especially in relation to a non-Western country context, in this case Turkey, it is important to examine this further. That is, it may well be that a significant difference emerges when probing such a virgin context with regards to such investigation. Therefore, consistent with this enquiry of establishing whether this stakeholder link exists it is hypothesised that:

> *Hypothesis 1: Other things being equal, the total amount of corporate community involvement CCI increases if managers receive pressure from their stakeholder(s).*

Agency theory proponents have argued that investor/owner stakeholders are those that put most pressure on managers to seek profit maximisation (Werber and Carter, 2002). Therefore, in the context of this book, it would appear reasonable to assume that these people will prefer that managers donate in cash, because it is tax deductible and has less impact on profits than non-cash giving (Navarro, 1988). At the same time, sponsorship is expected to be promoted by the investor/owner, because engaging in such activities makes the company's name more visible in the eyes of their customers and society, which can also positively affect the bottom line, something mentioned in some of the related literature (Harvey, 2001; Menon and Kahn, 2003). In the context of Turkey most of the big companies have the owner's family name in their title (for example, Koç Holding, Borusan Holding, Sabancı Holding) and when they sponsor events this helps to improve their reputation in the eyes of society, which provides yet another incentive for such giving. Moreover, the Turkish Government is another important stakeholder that is likely to have had a positive influence on cash giving owing to its passing of the Turkish tax deductible law 5228 in 2004, which applies to cash donations. Lastly, sponsorship and cause-related marketing (CRM) types of CCI are more visible to customers (McDonald, 1991) and, hence, it is they that are expected to put pressure on companies to engage more in sponsorship and CRM than other types of CCI. These three key assumptions lead to the generation of the following hypotheses.

> *Hypothesis 2: With regard to the pressures on managers in relation to different types of CCI, shareholders/investors direct their CCI towards cash giving and sponsorship.*

> *Hypothesis 3: Government/legislators' actions have mostly influenced cash giving for CCI activities.*

Hypothesis 4: With regard to the pressures on managers in relation to different types of CCI, customers have a preference for sponsorship and CRM.

7.1.2 INSTITUTIONAL CLIMATE

As discussed in Chapter 3, according to the behavioural theory of the firm, companies need to consider environmental conditions and economic actors in order to gain a unique survival advantage (Cyert and March, 1992). The theory also suggests that economic actors set rules, norms and practices which are not necessarily determined by the demands of the community in which they exist. In the case of CCI, these economic actors, such as the institutions and associations that companies are members of, can require them to engage in certain types of CCI activities that are not necessarily expected by the community itself. For example, in the case of Turkey, if a company is a member of the Corporate Volunteerism Association, its membership is expected to develop projects in which their employees are involved (for example, employees go to the local schools and help students with their homework or other duties).

Meyer and Rowan (1977) argued that as states and large organisations extend their dominance over more arenas of social life, organisational structures increasingly come to reflect the institutionalised rules of the society in question. As a result, organisations become increasingly homogeneous within given domains and increasingly organised around rituals of conformity to wider institutions (DiMaggio and Powell, 1983). These wider institutions may also create pressure for companies to engage in CCI activities as they could well see these as helping to protect their legitimacy and, hence, their survival. Regarding this, a number of studies have suggested that the institutional climate shapes companies' socially responsible behaviours (Bennett, 1988; Brammer and Pavelin, 2005; Gan, 2006). In an early study, Bennett (1998) demonstrated that there are significant differences in national approaches to the management of companies regarding philanthropic giving. Later, as discussed in Chapter 3, Brammer and Pavelin (2005), analysing the data of the top 100 UK and US corporate community contributors, found that national, cultural and institutional factors explain why companies' giving behaviours are different in these two countries. Additionally, Gan (2006) indicated that when the economy is weak and charitable donations need to increase, companies which are acting altruistically are the ones who step in. He also noted that companies give more when everyone else is also donating more (ibid), thus suggesting that competitors' behaviours also affect companies' CCI behaviours. All these examples provide evidence that the institutional climate shapes managerial decisions on the amount of CCI. This leads to the fifth hypothesis.

> *Hypothesis 5: Other things being equal, the total amount of corporate community involvement increases if managers are subject to pressure from the institutional climate.*

It has been contended that normative, mimetic and coercive pressures constitute the components of institutional pressures (Teo et al., 2003). Regarding the foremost type, Werber and Carter (2002) argued that membership of organisations increases the degree of such pressure on firms. In relation to the focus in this research, in recent years Göcenoğlu and Onan (2008) in Turkey suggested that the adjustment of Turkish Association Law, so as to be compatible with that of the European Union (EU), has accelerated growth in non-governmental organizations (NGOs) and has created a better environment for civil participation. In particular, the Corporate Governance Association of Turkey (TKYD), the Employee Volunteerism Association of Turkey (OSGD) and the CSR Association of Turkey are organisations supporting CCI that have substantially increased their profiles in recent years. In addition to this, companies situated in Turkey are also members of The United Nations Global Compact, Business in the Community, Global Reporting Initiatives (GRI) Organisational Stakeholder Encouragement Programmes and the United Nation's Development Programme (UNDP). Within the perspective of Teo et al. (2003) mentioned above, it can be assumed membership of organisations intensifies the normative pressure on companies to engage in more CCI. Moreover, when this researcher probed the websites of these non-profit organisations, their mission statements referred to their supporting philanthropic and sustainable projects through cash giving, gifts-in-kind and CRM types of CCI. For example, companies implementing UNDP projects are required to take action on such matters as poverty reduction and environmental sustainability. Therefore, it is expected that companies that belong to such organisations prioritise these forms of CCI in their donations, rather than sponsorship, owing to the normative institutional pressures they experience.

Turning to mimetic pressure, a study conducted by McWilliams et al. (1999) pointed out that competing firms may be forced to imitate other companies' social strategies in order to gain competitive parity, especially in a highly competitive market place with substantial uncertainty. In relation to CCI, in the extant literature it has been concluded that under such institutional pressure firms opt to engage with or increase their level of sponsorship activities (DiMaggio and Powell, 1983; Shaw and Amis, 2001). Finally, with respect to coercive pressure, institutional theorists have argued that firms that share the same organisational field feel obliged to take actions that fit with those of powerful ones in order to gain or protect their legitimacy (Jennings and Zandbergen, 1995). With regards to CCI, there is no reason to expect any preference for a particular type when coercive pressure is exerted to any degree. Therefore, in line with this discussion the following hypotheses are developed.

> Hypothesis 6: Managers who are influenced by normative institutional pressures are more eager to engage in cash giving, CRM and gifts-in-kind types of CCI than sponsorship.

> Hypothesis 7: Managers who are influenced by mimetic institutional pressures prefer to engage in the sponsorship type of CCI.

> Hypothesis 8: The presence of coercive institutional pressure is not responded to by managers with any preference regarding CCI type.

7.1.3 AVAILABILITY OF SLACK RESOURCES

The behavioural theory proposes that the availability of slack resources plays a crucial role in resolving the goal conflict of coalitions and preventing organisations from breaking apart (Cyert and March, 1992). Slack refers to profits and excess inputs, such as redundant employees, unused capacity and unutilised capital expenditure (Nohria and Gulati, 1996). In the wider context, Bourgeois (1981) stated that slack is 'the cushion of actual or potential resources which allows an organisation to adapt successfully to internal pressures for adjustment or to external pressures for change'. Extending the availability of slack resources to the CCI decisions issue, scholars have argued that the availability of slack is an important catalyst for engaging in such activities. In terms of their origins, McElroy and Siegfried (1985) argued that profitability creates slack resources that can be used to support charitable giving. However, although most studies used profitability to measure slack and found a strong relationship between charitable giving and financial performance (McGuire et al., 1988; Waddock and Graves, 1997), some studies have failed to elicit this link (for example, Seifert et al., 2003). This inconsistency in findings could be down to the narrow measure used to define slack, for it excludes the other aspects highlighted above (Adams and Lamont, 2003). Clearly, new measurements of slack are necessary to establish more conclusively whether a relationship between the availability of slack and charitable giving can be found and two are employed in this book, as explained in subsection 7.2.2.3. below.

Moreover, under the behavioural theory of the firm lens it is argued that slack plays an important role in maintaining the harmony between the stakeholder groups (Cyert and March, 1963). In addition, within this perspective, the availability of slack makes it easier to respond to the pressures that come from the institutional climate. Regarding CCI, it is expected that when slack is abundant there will be a high level of donating, whereas the converse will occur when it is scarce. This leads to the final two hypotheses.

Hypothesis 9: The availability of slack resources encourages managers to engage in corporate community involvement activities.

Hypothesis 10: Meeting pressures from stakeholder groups and the institutional climate is easier when slack is abundant.

7.1.4 CONTROL VARIABLES

7.1.4.1 Size

Size has often been investigated in prior CCI studies (Levy and Shatto, 1978; Burke et al., 1986; Useem, 1988; Navarro, 1988; Arupalam and Stoneman, 1995; Adams and Hardwick, 1998; Dennis et al., 2007). For example, Brammer and Millington (2004a) reported that company size is an important correlate of visibility, reasoning that large firms make a high level of charitable donations because they exhibit this feature and as a result society may put pressure on them to give more. Their later research confirmed that more pressure from their stakeholders than from smaller firms increases the amount of firms' corporate charitable contributions significantly (Brammer and Millington 2004b). Seifert et al. (2004) similarly contended that large firms have greater visibility, which attracts greater public scrutiny and hence, a higher standard of corporate citizenship. As a result of the observations of the existing studies it is predicted here that CCI activity is strongly positively correlated with size.

7.1.4.2 Industry

The empirical literature on CCI has found that industry differences are an important determinant of corporate giving (Useem, 1988; Arupalam and Stoneman, 1995; Adam and Hardwick, 1988). That is, firms in the same industry face the same environmental conditions and this tends to streamline their involvement in corporate giving (Seifert et al., 2003). Moreover, Brammer and Millington (2004a), after considering companies which operate in consumer goods are high-wage and are stiffly regulated, argued that industry type and structure may have a significant impact on the delegation of the management of corporate donations. Additionally, Amato and Amato (2007) found that industry type explains 20–22 per cent of the total variation in giving.

7.1.4.3 Company ownership

The influence of corporate ownership on corporate contributions is another topic of interest in the debates pertaining to the field of CCI (Bartkus et al., 2002; Zhang et al., 2009). More specifically, most of the studies have analysed the relationship between giving to charitable causes and the availability of stock held by insiders (Atkinson and Galaskiewicz, 1988; Wang and Coffey, 1992; Bartkus et al., 2002). Additionally, whether a firm is state owned or not (Zhang et al., 2009) or whether it is local or a subsidiary of a foreign multinational firm (Committee Encouraging Corporate Philantropy 2009), has been found to determine the amount that companies choose to donate.

7.2 Methods

In order to test the hypotheses put forward in the previous section, estimates are made for the equation put forward in section 7.2 for CCI as a whole as well as for the four different types. As explained previously, 92 responses were received, however some companies refused to disclose the total amount they spent on CCI and there is also missing data from the part of the questionnaire enquiring about slack resources, as explained below. As a result of the former situation, the total number of observations was reduced to 76 companies for this study.

7.2.1 DEPENDENT VARIABLES

As explained in the literature review of Chapter 2, prior studies have tended to address corporate philanthropic giving and CCI separately. Regarding this, corporate philanthropy has been measured by defining the total amount of money given in donations (Arupalam and Stoneman, 1995; Adams and Hardwick, 1998; Brammer and Millington, 2004a; Gan, 2006; Brown et al., 2006), whereas CCI has been taken as being the amount of pre-tax profit that companies give for community investment (Atkinson and Galaskiewicz, 1988;

Brammer and Millington, 2003) or the total amount of cash contribution, which includes both philanthropic giving and giving for strategic purposes (Brown et al., 2006). As pointed out earlier, the lack of availability of companies' financial reports or other databases containing these types of information for companies in Turkey has meant that the primary data taken from the survey are to be used in this particular study. The companies concerned were probed about their donation amounts for four measures of CCI, namely cash giving, sponsorship, CRM, gifts-in-kind (for example, companies were asked, 'Approximately how much cash has your company donated to charitable/philanthropic giving in the last year?' and so on) and these were subsequently aggregated. Sixteen different intervals of money amounts were specified for the respondents and the mid value of the interval selected was taken as the value for the analysis.

When it came to assigning scores to the different CCI types, it soon became apparent that the donations were heavily biased towards cash giving and after some preliminary analysis it emerged that for consistent investigation across all four types of giving there would have to be a very low cut off point if meaningful results were to be achieved. That is, because many firms do not engage in these other aspects or only to a limited extent, skewness was found to be a problem that needed to be overcome. Therefore, initially, a relatively low 20 per cent was chosen for each type to represent the boundary in terms of the binary variables for each CCI form, that is a 1 allocated for this score and above and 0 otherwise. However, even this failed to produce any meaningful outcomes and it had to be reduced further to 10 per cent, before this was the case. Moreover, in similar studies it has been common practice to take the log of total giving as the dependent variable rather than actual values as this linearises the data to achieve greater accuracy (Buchholtz et al., 1999; Campbell et al., 1999). To summarise, the dependent variables are defined as follows:

Total CCI giving: Log of the total amount of CCI

For the binary variables a score of 1 is allocated when:

1) Cash giving is 10 per cent or more of the total

2) Sponsorship is 10 per cent or more of the total

3) CRM 10 per cent or more of the total

4) Gifts-in-kind is 10 per cent or more of the total

7.2.2 INDEPENDENT VARIABLES

7.2.2.1 Stakeholders

In the questionnaire, stakeholders were classified into six categories: government/ legislators, employees, customers, shareholders/investors, suppliers and community groups. Following Brammer and Millington's (2004a) study, the respondents were asked to evaluate stakeholder pressures using a seven-point Likert scale (1 = strongly disagree, to 7 = strongly agree) regarding the relevance of a set of statements to their experience. For example, in order to measure pressure from government/legislators: 'we have received a significant amount of pressure from government/legislators concerning our social responsibilities' was the question. However, although a set of statements were drawn up for each stakeholder type, subsequent analysis of the responses led to only those related to salience providing meaningful data. In sum, salience of the six aforementioned stakeholder types for each firm were employed as the independent variables.

7.2.2.2 Institutional climate

In order to measure institutional pressure, the procedure developed by Teo et al. (2003) was adopted, which measured normative, mimetic and coercive types. That is, these authors assigned a set of statements to each of these forms of pressure and these were slightly modified for the survey questionnaire as shown in Table 7.1.

As can be seen in the table, Teo et al. employed two types of normative pressures. However, analysis of the responses to the survey questionnaire revealed that those responses pertaining to the second type were substantially more comprehensive and complete than those for the first and, hence, only these were included, that is, normative b. Participants were asked to rate each item on a seven-point Likert scale (1 = strongly disagree, to 7 = strongly agree). Next, the software programme SPSS was used for confirmatory factor analysis to assess whether statement responses clustered around the appropriate institutional pressure type and the results of this can be seen in Table 7.2. In the social sciences the lowest scores for variance of a ratio should be between 0.30 and 0.40 (Neale and Liebert, 1980; Cathell and Baggaley, 1960). As seen in Table 7.2, ratios of variance are high and this suggests that the factor structure of the scale is strong (Gorsuch, 1974). Subsequently, these ten items were taken to be the independent institutional variables, which were inputted into SPSS to obtain measurements for the three institution pressure types: normative, mimetic and coercive.

Table 7.1   Questionnaire items for measuring normative, mimetic and coercive pressures

My firm operates in an environment where there are institutionalised norms that encourage CCI, as in business publications, business school curriculum and other educational venues in which corporate managers participate	normative (a)
My firm belongs to a trade or employer association that advocates or promotes socially responsible behaviour	normative (a)
My firm is regularly involved in institutionalised dialogue with unions, employees, community groups, investors and other stakeholders	normative (a)
My firm operates in an environment where the discourse of social responsibility is prominent in the socio-cultural system	normative (a)
When assessing our CCI activities, we also consider our rivals' CCI programmes	mimetic
In designing our CCI programme, we model our activities on those of other organisations perceived as successful	mimetic
Competitors with well-developed CCI programmes are perceived favourably by others in our industry	coersive
Undertaking CCI activities is normal in our industry	coersive
We have a high degree of awareness concerning the CCI activities of our rivals	mimetic
Our competitors have used CCI to their advantage	mimetic
Our firm's success depends significantly upon our participation in CCI	coersive
CCI is something we feel we must do	coersive
We actively participate in industry, trade or professional associations that promote CCI	normative (b)
Significant pressure to engage in CCI is placed upon us from industry and professional sources that support CCI	normative (b)

Set of statements to evaluate types of institutional pressures adapted from Teo et al. (2003).

Table 7.2   Factor loadings for institutional variables

Item	Institutional normative Factor #1	Institutional mimetic Factor #2	Institutional coersive Factor #3
We actively participate in industry, trade or professional associations that promote CCI	0.784		
Significant pressure to engage in CCI is placed upon us from industry and professional sources that support CCI	0.784		
When assessing our CCI activities, we also consider our rival's CCI programmes		0.783	
In designing our CCI programme, we model our activities on those of other organisations perceived as successful		0.727	
We have a high degree of awareness concerning the CCI activities of our rivals		0.867	
Our competitors have used CCI to their advantage		0.546	
Competitors with well-developed CCI programmes are perceived favourably by others in our industry			0.736
Undertaking CCI activities is normal in our industry			0.795
Our firm's success depends significantly upon our participation in CCI			0.688
CCI is something we feel we must do			0.701

7.2.2.3 Slack resources

As explained in Chapter 3, the slack questionnaire involved integrating suggestions for its indirect measurement from three sources because firms were reluctant to provide actual figures regarding this. However, perhaps because of this heterogeneity, it transpired through confirmatory factor analysis that these did not load effectively. Consequently, the two questions drawn from Nohria and Gulati's (1996, 1997) studies, were the ones used pertaining to a decrease in employee engagement and a drop in operating budget. More specifically, these two questions asked what would be the consequences of a 10 per cent fall in the availability of these two operating factors. The loading values for these two items, which were employed as the slack resources variables, can be seen Table 7.3 and subsequent analysis through SPSS provided a single measure.

Table 7.3   Factor loadings for slack resources variables

Item	Slack Resources Variable Factor #1
Assume that due to some sudden development, 10 per cent of the time of all people working in your firm has to be spent on work totally unconnected with the tasks and responsibilities of your department. How seriously will your output be affected over the next year?	0,930
Assume that due to a similar development, your firm's annual operating budget is reduced by 10 per cent. How significantly will your work be affected over the next year?	0,930

7.2.3 CONTROL VARIABLES

7.2.3.1 Firm size

Firm size was used as a control variable, because extant studies have revealed that this can affect the amount of total giving. In order to measure each firm's size, respondents were asked how many employees, in total, were working in the company throughout the world including in Turkey. That is, for companies with international operations the global number of employees was taken as a more appropriate measure than their domestic total. Measuring size using the number of employees can be found in previous studies (Arupalam and Stoneman, 1995; Johnson and Greening, 1999; Brown et al., 2006).

7.2.3.2 Industry variables

The companies in the sample were assigned to a particular industry depending on their major activities, as discussed in the methodology chapter (Chapter 4). That is, using *Capital* magazine's industry classification, each firm was allocated to one of seven sectors: information technologies, chemistry and pharmacy, engineering, consumer goods, construction, finance and consumer services, for which seven sets of dummy variables were created. Previous literature has used a similar procedure to establish which types of industry participate most in CCI activities (Brammer and Millington, 2004a; Arupalam and Stoneman, 1995). In particular, Arupalam and Stoneman (1995) found that companies in industries which have more direct contact with customers, for example the financial, food, alcohol, tobacco and leisure industries, give relatively more to charities ceteris paribus, because of the potential usefulness of giving in that it creates a favourable public image.

7.2.3.3 Ownership status

The companies were asked several questions regarding ownership status. Questions of the survey on ownership status were designed to explore the ownership characteristics of each company that participated in this survey, the responses to which have been discussed in Chapter 5, where it emerged that all of the firms engaged in some sort of CCI, with family-managed, foreign-owned and controlled companies generally exhibiting lower rates of participation than other types of companies. In fact, it was revealed that the lowest contributions were made by companies that are foreign-owned and controlled and for this reason only foreign ownership was chosen as a controlled variable to measure ownership status, for which a negative sign is expected.

7.2.4 EMPIRICAL APPROACH

Multiple regression was used to see which of these independent variables influence the total amount of CCI and decisions regarding the compositions of such activities. This form of analysis has been defined as 'the statistical technique that allows the researcher to identify a set of predictor variables which together provide a useful estimate of a participant's likely score on a criterion variable' (Chang 2007). That is, multiple regression analysis involves measuring the naturally occurring scores on a number of predictor variables in order to establish the best fit equation (Field, 2005). In this particular research a total of 19 independent variables were identified, as discussed above, to find the best prediction for each of the five dependent variables pertaining to CCI. However, the existing literature stresses that statistically multiple regression analysis requires a large number of observations (Chang, 2007). This means that the number of cases in the research must substantially exceed the number of predictor variables that has been used (Kelley and Maxwell, 2003). Regarding this, Howell (2002) put forward that there should be ten observations per independent variable, whereas others have argued that this should be as high as 40, but Chang (2007) suggested that this need only be a minimum of five. For this analysis the number of observations is 76 and the number of independent variables 19, which would lead to the ratio being too small. However, because only eight of these variables registered as significant in the regression analysis, as will be shown, this meant that this ratio was just under ten, which consequently is acceptable

Because the sample size is small, the usual straightforward approach of ordinary least squares (OLS) is not appropriate and instead a stepwise approach is adopted for the regression (Howell, 2002). The binary logistic is used to estimate CCI types. This method allows for identification of the most parsimonious model(s) with the greatest statistical power and involves stepwise calculation 'by entering each variable in sequence and its value assessed. If adding the variable contributes to the model then it is retained, but all other variables in the model are then re-tested to see if they are still contributing to the success of the model. If they no longer contribute significantly they are removed' (Brace et al., 2009). That is, this technique allows for elimination of most of the models under consideration leaving one or a small number of acceptable ones that correspond to the best fit equation(s) with the lowest number of variables (Shtatland et al., 2001).

7.3 Findings

This section presents the results of the OLS stepwise method to elicit an econometric model of CCI incorporating the independent variables described in the previous section. According to the statistical analysis that provides means, standard deviations and Pearson correlations between the dependent and independent variables, the magnitude of the correlation coefficients shows initial evidence that multicollinearity is relatively low. That is, variance inflation factors (VIFs) are not reported, that is the scores are less than ten, indicating that there probably is no cause for concern (Myers, 1990).

Table 7.4 presents the results of the stepwise regression analysis, with Model 1 referring to the variables that influence the total amount of CCI, whereas the moderation effect of slack resources on the stakeholder and institutional variables are presented in Models 2 and 3. Subsequently, Table 7.5 presents the stepwise binary regression analysis for four specifications that differ according to which of the dependent variables is scoring. That is, each of the types of CCI is employed as a binary variable (cash giving, sponsorship, CRM and gifts-in-kind), registering 1 where present and 0 otherwise. With the exception of Models 2 and 3, the set of independent variables is the same in all the others. However, the models only contain those variables that registered as significant through the stepwise regression analysis. Next, each model is considered in turn to assess whether they support or refute the hypotheses put forward in section 7.1 In Model 1, it can be seen that the perceived level of pressure from two stakeholders has a significant positive effect on CCI, these being the shareholder/investor (p=0.001) and community groups (p=0.042). However, in this model customers (p=0.016) and government/legislative (p=0.015) stakeholders have a significant, but negative effect, on total CCI. Therefore, the evidence supports acceptance of Hypothesis 1 purporting that stakeholders do influence CCI donation, because four of the six identified stakeholder groups are found to have an impact, either positive or negative, on the total amount of CCI in Turkey, This finding is also consistent with earlier studies, such as that of Brammer and Millington (2004a), who found that the management of corporate giving is significantly influenced by the extent and type of managerially perceived stakeholder pressures. They also noted that a firm's choice of departmental responsibility for charitable giving may arise from a desire to cope efficiently with prevailing stakeholder pressures from investors, consumers, legislators and community groups. This is also consistent with earlier suggestions that acting responsibly results in a trusting relationship between the firm and its stakeholders that enhances competitiveness and financial performance (Jones, 1995) and differentiates the firm from others in the eyes of consumer and investor groups (McWilliams and Siegel, 2000).

From the websites of these companies, as is discussed in detail in Chapter 5, it emerged that in many cases CSR policy is integrated with the philosophy of the founders who are actively involved in efforts to alleviate social problems. In particular, family-owned companies participate to this end often through a 'waqf' (foundation) has pointed out has its origins in the Ottoman Empire. This could shed light on why there is a positive association between shareholder/investor group, for over half the sample firms are family owned and many of their proprietors serve this role. That is, this supports the evidence in Chapter 5 that owners are closely linked to CCI giving in many Turkish companies, and they consider engaging with this as their philanthropic duty.

Moreover, in Turkey, given the strength of the activism exhibited by community groups, such as civil organisations and NGOs, the positive link between CCI and pressure from these stakeholders is understandable. In addition, regarding this, the existence of the Turkey Third Sector Foundation (TUSEV) creates a knowledge base and momentum for civil society strengthening initiatives. Further, CSR in Turkey is supported by external drivers, such as international organisations and NGOs (Göcenoğlu and Onan, 2009) and Turkish businessmen have established civil organisations, such as The Turkish Foundation for Combating Soil Erosion, for Reforestation and the Protection of Natural Habitats (TEMA), The Educational Volunteers Foundation of Turkey (TEGV) and Community Volunteers Foundation (TOG). One further reason for this positive association is the fact that many businessmen are on the board of directors of various non-profit organisations and community groups, hence they are brought closer to recognising what is needed and acting upon it through their firms' CCI budgets.

However, the results do not show that if companies receive pressure from government/legislator stakeholder groups they tend to engage in more CCI activities, but actually imply that the opposite is the case. With respect to this, earlier studies, when investigating the role of the legislative bodies as corporate stakeholders, have claimed that governments can have a positive impact on corporate strategy and performance (Freeman, 1984; Watts and Zimmerman, 1978). These authors, amongst others, concluded that this is because they may engage in CSR so as to reduce the risk of governmental intrusions (Watts and Zimmerman, 1978; Clarkson, 1995). The negative relationship found here could be down to the high demands placed on firms by the government, in relation to corporate taxation and other forms of regulation that can squeeze their CCI budgets. Moreover, there is much bureaucracy involved in complying with these regulations, which could be tying up employee time, hence reducing the possibility of them supplying their labour for CCI. Further, whereas in many Western countries there are clear laws about delivering and recording CCI, in Turkey, as stated in Göcenoğlu and Onan (2009), no such legislation exists, which again can explain why no positive relationship is found. Finally, in relation to this result, the tax exemption law is highly restricted to certain areas of giving, with many projects falling outside those that can receive reductions. Hence, when a company is introduced to a project it is unlikely to donate without tax breaks and given that most CSR/CCI, as revealed in previous chapters, would appear not to be strategically planned, it will not necessarily then decide to give elsewhere.

In relation to the significant negative consumer influence on CCI finding, in Turkey there are no organisations like the ethical consumer or fair-trade groups seen in the UK and other developed countries, which result in this type of pressure being important in decision making. However, this situation would only suggest a neutral relationship and not a negative one, whereby lack of this form of pressure would appear to lead to more CCI activity. One tentative explanation for this could lie in the philanthropic sense of responsibility put forward in Chapter 5 amongst a substantial number of big entrepreneurs. That is, the weakness or lack of consumer organisations to exert power may have resulted in these companies' managers/owners seeing it as their duty to help address these failings of civil society in the form of giving assistance to those in need. If this were the case, then there is a marked contrast to the underlying motives for donating in Turkey's case than have emerged in most Western studies. This matter is returned to in the motivations section for CCI engagement in the reporting for the case study investigation in Chapter 8.

In Models 4, 5 and 6, the only significant positive effect found is that of suppliers (p=0.024) on cash giving. In other words, there is no support for any of the hypotheses that predicted that types of CCI can be associated more strongly with certain stakeholders than others, namely H2, H3 and H4. This implies that, although shareholders/investors and community groups apply pressure on firms to engage in CCI, they do not specify which type. The only positive influence found is that of suppliers influencing cash giving, which was not proposed in any of these three hypotheses and, hence, no explanation for this is offered.

In relation to institutional pressures, the only significance of the three forms is normative pressure (p=0.014) which thus provides weak evidence in support of Hypothesis 5. That is, managers in Turkey would appear to model their CCI so as to fit with the normative behaviours expected within the country. According to DiMaggio and Powel (1983), such a situation leads to increased isomorphic behaviour, which implies that many of these firms are embedded in Turkish society as members of business, professional or other organisations, such as political organisations and civic groups. However, the other two types of pressure do not register significance, that is, there is no evidence of mimetic or coercive behaviour. With regards to H6, H7 and H8, Models 4 to 7 give no evidence of types of pressure being associated with a specific preference for a particular form of CCI and, hence, these are rejected.

Model 1 provides no significance for there being a positive relationship between having slack resources and total CCI and so H9 is rejected. Models 2 and 3, in Table 7.4, show the results of the moderation effect of slack resources for both institutional/normative and investor/shareholders on total CCI. As can be seen, this is only significant for investor/shareholder pressure and therefore H10, which purports that slack resources will moderate when companies try to satisfy both the requests of stakeholder groups and the pressures that come from the institutional environment, is only partially accepted.

Table 7.4   Stepwise regression results for total giving

Variables	Model 1	Model 2	Model 3
Constant	8,471	6,235	12,658
	(0.913)***	(1.621)***	(2.270)***
Control Variables			
Size	2,146	2,224	2,304
	(0.421)***	(0.435)***	(0.407)***
Foreign owned and controlled	-1.579	-1.551	-1.359
	(0.469)***	(0.499)***	(0.465)***
Stakeholders			
Government/legislators	-0.370	-0.401	-0.382
	(0.148)***	(0.174)**	(0.163)**
Customers	-0.265	-0.284	-0.208
	(0.107)***	(0.117)	(0.109)*
Shareholders/investors	0.648	0.595	-3.398
	(0.181)***	(0.189)***	(1.225)***
Community groups	0.242	0.250	0.228
	(0.117)**	(0.123)**	(0.114)**
Institutional Factors			
Institutional normative	0.478	-1.351	0.407
	(0.189)***	(0.305)	(1.90)**
Moderation Effects			
Slack		0.486	-1.043
		(0.305)	(0.503)**
Slack x institutional normative		0.411	
		(0.288)	
Slack x shareholders/investors			0.880
			(0.266)***

The dependent variable is a log of the total amount of Corporate Community Involvement.

Figure in parantheses are standard errors. *, ** and *** denote significance at the 90%, 95% and 99% level of confidence respectively.

No. of Observations = 76

Model 1: $r^2 = 0.488$

Model 2: $r^2 = 0.528$

Model 3: $r^2 = 0.587$

Table 7.5   Stepwise regression results for forms of giving

Variables	Model 4	Model 5	Model 6	Model 7
Constant	-0,817	0.026	-2.148	0.078
	(0.484)*	(0.228)	(3.99)***	(0.228)
Control Variables				
Size				
Finance				
Information technologies				
Chemical pharmaceutical				
Engineering				
Consumer goods				
Construction				
Consumer service			2.148	
			(0.748)***	
Foreign owned and controlled	-1.786			
	(0.750)***			
Stakeholders				
Government/legislators				
Employees				
Customers				
Shareholders/investors				
Suppliers	0.415			
	(0.184)***			
Community groups				
Institional Factors				
Institutional normative				
Institutional mimetic				
Institutional coersive				
Slack Resources				
Slack				
No of Observations = 76				

Model 5   The dependent variable is 10% or more of the total sponsorship.

Model 6   The dependent variable is 10% or more of the total cause related marketing.

Model 7   The dependent variable is 10% or more of the total gifts-in-kind.

Figures in parentheses are standard errors. *, ** and *** denote significance at the 90%, 95% and 99% level of confidence respectively.

Model 4   The dependent variable is 10% or more of the total cash giving.

With regards to the control variables, as expected a strong positive significance is found between size and CCI amounts in Model 1. This is consistent with existing literature (Buchholtz et al., 1999; Galaskiewicz, 1997), which has established that larger firms give more than smaller ones. However, Table 7.5 indicates there is no significant relation between firm size and managerial preference for CCI. This result was expected because, as stated in some existing studies (Griffin and Mahon, 1997; Buchholtz et al., 1999), size itself only tells part of the story, for large firms are not necessarily profitable ones. Therefore, assumptions like, for instance, they would prefer to give in cash, may not hold because they have little or no spare cash and choose to give support in other forms. However, the results for Model 1 demonstrate no evidence of a relationship between industry type and CCI amount. That is, there is no evidence that certain firm sectors are more generous than others in their giving. On the other hand, some systematic variation across sectors for the types of CCI is found. For instance, it emerges that the consumer service industry has a preference for engaging in CRM activities (p=0.004), which suggests that Turkish firms use this form of CCI to promote their public profile. Finally, it can be seen that foreign ownership/control is significantly negatively associated with total CCI at the 1 per cent level. In other words, there is strong evidence supporting the descriptive findings and reports from the literature (Brammer and Millington, 2003) presented in Chapter 5 that foreign firms give substantially less. In terms of choice of CCI for these firms, a strongly positive and significant result is delivered for cash giving (p=0.029), which would indicate further that these companies have a lower tendency than domestic ones to engage in those activities that involve higher levels of continuous commitment.

7.4 Discussion of the Findings

The purpose of this chapter has been to examine variables drawn from the behavioural theory of the firm in relation to their impact on companies' scale of CCI and preferences regarding type of CCI. Very few empirical studies on CCI have addressed the different forms, both individually and as whole. In fact, most of the extant literature, as it emerged in Chapter 2, has been focused on analysing philanthropic donations. Moreover, this work has made a contribution by engaging in using primary research data for the Turkish context given the lack of secondary data and, consequently, has involved devising a novel set of procedures for investigating CCI. In relation to this overall goal, this researcher posits that previous studies have had a tendency to limit the CCI locus for investigation because they have relied on variables obtained from published indices relating to corporate discretionary donations as a dependent variable and because they have mainly concentrated on measuring cash philanthropic donations.

Given the decision to employ primary data for the statistical analysis, the survey questionnaire had to probe the different amounts each firm estimated that they gave to the four different measures of CCI identified in Chapter 2: cash giving, sponsorship, CRM and gifts-in-kind. These were subsequently aggregated so that tests could be carried on five dependent variables, a procedure not previously employed in the field. In relation to overall giving, for Model 1 (see Table 7.4) a value of $r^2=0.488$ was obtained on SPSS, which meant that the outcomes from its application were valid. That is, according to this ratio, this confirms that the collective effects of all the independent variables have provided a significant explanation for CCI activity as 48 per cent of them can be explained by this. This ratio is high if it is compared with previous studies (Arupalam and Stoneman, 1995; Campbell et al., 1999).

Novel measurement techniques have also been used to measure the independent variables in that the data collected in relation to these was of a primary form. That is, the managers of the survey companies were asked to indicate their perception regarding a variety of stakeholder and institutional pressures on their CCI giving behaviour. Another contribution to research in the field has been with regard to the availability of slack resources where, rather than using financial data, Nohria and Gulati's (1996, 1997) double item scale has been adopted and applied to the CCI context. It is suggested that this approach could be applied in future studies when reliable financial data is unavailable.

The findings in this study have potential theoretical and practical implications for scholars, corporate executives and NGOs, as discussed next.

7.4.1 THEORETICAL IMPLICATIONS

The results have provided strong support for the position put forward in previous studies (Brammer and Millington, 2003 and 2004a; Moir and Taffler, 2004; Wei-Skillern, 2004; Meijer el al., 2006) that stakeholders have an influence on the total amount of CCI. However, one anomaly has emerged in the results and that is the negative and significant impact of the government and customer stakeholders in this process. Tentative explanations have been provided for this, but in general they appear to give evidence that the Turkish context in relation to CCI is markedly different to that of the West, where these other studies have been focused. That is, future researchers on this subject matter may need to expect these types of negative stakeholder pressures when investigating non-Western countries. Additionally, the empirical evidence has provided support for there being an institutional effect on managerial CCI decisions, which under the behavioural theory of the firm is associated with the need to avoid uncertainty. However, the results were only significantly positive for normative institutional pressure, which implies that firms focus on involvement with domestic institutions/organisations rather than concerning themselves with mimetic and coercive pressures coming from within the industry itself. In other words, in Turkey it would appear that the emphasis placed by firms on belonging to society is a key driver of their CCI giving. This could be a form of strategic positioning to ensure legitimacy, but it could also involve altruistic behaviour aimed at plugging gaps in welfare provision, as suggested in Chapter 5, a matter that is returned to in the analysis of the interview data in Chapter 8. This too raises an important issue mentioned in the previous chapter, that of whether in other non-developed and lesser-developed country situations, domestic firms use corporate giving in an altruistic fashion to a greater extent than in the West.

7.4.2 PRACTICAL IMPLICATIONS

The evidence on CCI from Turkey is useful for other developing countries around the world with cultural, legal, economic and ethical backgrounds differing from developed countries. That is, from the 76 companies surveyed listed in the 500 biggest private companies for that nation, it has been learnt that the pressures from shareholder/investors and community groups positively affect their decision to engage in CCI. This is in contrast to the findings for developed countries, where these stakeholders were elicited as having a negative influence on certain types of CCI. The outcomes regarding Turkey thus imply that managers should have more concerns about meeting the two aforementioned stakeholders' demands rather than concerning themselves with, in particular, those of the consumer, for the significance for the latter was negative. Moreover, this could be the case in other non-Western contexts, in particular, because consumer groups are absent and, thus, this may need to be taken into account by managers. In relation to government pressures, the evidence has suggested that too many regulations with too much red tape can have a negative impact on the willingness to engage in CCI. Turning to the matter of institutional pressures, with there being a normative significant outcome, this would appear to indicate that in the Turkish situation, managers of Turkish firms highly value engaging with domestic organisations as an effective means for embedding themselves in society, which maybe foreign firms should consider doing as an uncertainty avoidance strategy.

8

Four Companies' Process of Managerial Corporate Community Involvement Decision Making

The previous studies relating to corporate community involvement (CCI) forms have mostly used quantitative methods with a large sample size. However, several of the authors in the extant literature have called for more qualitative studies into the topic so as to elicit more comprehensive understanding of its various aspects (Burke et al., 1986; Brønn, 2006; Madden et al., 2006) Taking up this challenge, in this chapter the findings of four case studies conducted in large companies situated in Turkey are presented, with the decision-making process separated into five categories: motivation, managerial structure, budget, slack resources and criteria for choosing which CCI activities to engage in. Additionally, the case study findings are used to assess whether different types of industry lead to different outcomes to the quantitative results presented in Chapter 7. There is also consideration as to whether the core concepts of the behavioural theory of the firm are supported in the process of CCI decision making observed in the case study companies.

8.1 Research Methodology

8.1.1 HOW WERE THE FIRMS SELECTED?

Four cases were chosen from the 92 companies that participated in the survey for the qualititative analysis. The main criteria for identfying which companies to involve was ensuring that they came from different industries, were of different sizes and had different ownership structures. This approach allowed for further investigation into the outcomes obtained from the survey in Chapter 7, with regards to whether having any of these characteristics has an impact on CCI motivations. In particular, varying the composition of the firms chosen allows for assessment as to whether different types of firms act differently in relation to the behavioural theory of the firm. Table 8.1 summarises the major contextual differences between the four cases examined and pseudonyms are used to protect their identities

Table 8.1   A summary of the key characteristics of the four cases

Case No.	Name of Company	Industry Sector	Ownership Status	Type Of CCI	Managerial Positions of Interviewee	No. Of Respondents	Workforce Size
1	ESA	Engineering and Construction, Energy, Real Estate, Trade and Manufacturing, Retail	Turkish-owned holding company	*Philanthropy*: Cash giving, gifts-in-kind, employee volunteerism *Sponsorship*: Cash giving	Foundation manager, Director of culture and art programme, Assistant director of culture and art programme, Human resources manager	4 managers	< 50,000
2	GAYA	Finance	Joint venture of two Turkish companies and one MNC	*Philanthropy*: Cash giving, employee volunteerism, gift-in-kind *Sponsorship*: Cash giving, gifts-in-kind, CRM	Head of events and sponsorship sections, Events and sponsorship associate with corporate identity and communication department, Head of corporate communication department	3 managers	< 50,000
3	INTENT	IT	Subsidiary of MNC	*Philanthropy*: Cash giving, employee volunteerism, gifts-in-kind	University relations manager, CSR manager, marketing manager	4 managers	< 1,000
4	ASTON	Petroleum and Gas	Subsidiary of Turkish holding company	*Philanthropy*: Cash giving, employee volunteerism *Sponsorship*: Cash giving	Head of corporate communications, corporate communications manager, deputy of corporate communications manager	3 managers	< 2,000

8.1.2 HOW THE PARTICIPANTS WERE SELECTED

The interviewees spanned various hierarchical levels, but were mainly from corporate communications and marketing departments. However, the titles and department names varied widely from company to company. In each case the manager was nominated by the firm as having responsibility for a firm's various CCI activities and the most experienced person in the most senior managerial position was interviewed first. Other managers or assistant managers were chosen when data could not be obtained from the first interviewee so as to ensure that there was comprehensive coverage of the data for each firm's CCI activities. Each case began with the first interviewee being asked to give an overview of their CCI activities and, subsequently, they were probed for further information on those aspects with which they were familiar. At the end of the interview they were asked to put forward the name(s) of others who should be spoken to (for example, a manager from the marketing department or human resources (HR) department) regarding CCI. In total, three or four people were interviewed from each company over a two-month period, there being a total of 14 interviews, with an average length of approximately one hour.

8.1.3 DATA COLLECTION METHOD

Data were collected from multiple cases. The reason for choosing a multiple-case method is because it is more compelling and the overall study is therefore, more robust. Multiple case allows for cross-case analyses. The data for this study are analysed across all of the cases in order to identify similarities and differences. In this way further insight into issues concerning CCI decisions can be explored. Qualitative research interviews were used to collect information from the multiple cases for, as Kvale (1996) suggested, qualitative research interviews seek to describe the meaning of central themes in the world of the subjects. According to Flick (2006) and Guion (2006) interviews are particularly useful for reaching the story behind a participant's experiences, because the interviewer can pursue in-depth information around a topic. Interviews may be useful as follow-up to certain responses to questionnaires. Data was collected from semi-structured interviews with a variety of managers in each firm and the interviews contained both unstructured and structured components in order to allow respondents to relate and reflect on their experiences of the CCI decision-making process. This also allowed for questions to be shaped according to the run of the conversation.

The interview also facilitates a more purposeful collection of information around similar themes to those explored in the conceptual development section. A vast amount of qualitative data were collected for the purposes of data analyses. Sometimes, during the interview the complexity of the CCI behaviours led to questions not being understood very well by the interviewees. That is, the interviewees asked what the researcher meant by some questions and sometimes explanation of terms from the terminology of the field of CCI needed to be defined for them For these reasons, in order to collect the right information that was needed for this study, Bryman's (2001) guidelines were followed for conducting the interviews in order to deal with this. In addition, questions related to companies' strategic decisions created a problem. For example, the managers found the question about operating in a recession time to be problematic. That is, many were unwilling during the interview to share information about how they manage their budget during such times, but after some persistence by the researcher and clear explanation as to why she needed to know, all of the firms except ASTON did eventually provide this information.

As explained in the introduction to this chapter, the case study questions schedule draws upon the underpinning conceptual arrangements contained within the behavioural theory of the firm. Consequently in accordance with this perspective the questions were grouped under five main themes:

1. What are the motivations behind CCI? (What are the reasons for engaging with it? What was the catalyst for taking up CCI activities? Is this the founder's idea or a decision made by headquarters? What are the pressures from the internal and external environments?)

2. Who is involved in making CCI decisions? (Managers, employees, company owners and/or CEOs? How do each of the relevant people participate in the process of decision making?)

3. What is the budgeting procedure? (Does the budget come from specific projects which have been undertaken in the company? Was some proportion of money allocated to the company's foundation? Under this theme, the aim is to discover how companies use their local budget, global budget and departmental budget for their CCI activities.)

4. How do slack resources affect decisions about CCI? (What difference does the availability or unavailability of slack resources make?)

5.   What are the criteria used to decide which areas of CCI to undertake? (The areas preferred/excluded, having a policy not to donate cash, to promote brands and/or to be sustainable.)

8.1.4 DATA TRANSCRIPTION

The question schedule was designed in English then translated into Turkish by a native speaker of Turkish and then translated back into English. The face-to-face interviews were recorded on audiotape, following Creswell's (2007) suggestion and were subsequently transcribed by a professional transcriber before being subjected to content analysis. The average length of these audiotape records per person was approximately 20 pages and all of the contributions were subsequently translated into English. Later, this researcher read both the English and Turkish versions of each transcription in order to identify any inconsistencies, which were subsequently addressed.

8.1.5 DATA ANALYSIS

Strauss (1987) suggested that reponses from each interview should be grouped under the categories that emerge from the literature. Moreover, when analysing content or transcripts, there should be a search for general information regarding relationships between categories of data as well as identification of the themes and issues of interest that arise (Creswell, 2007). In this particular research, unlike with grounded theory, most of these themes have already been determined and relate to the the underlying concepts in the behavioural theory of the firm. Moreover, the question schedule was constructed with these themes in mind. Subsequently, each category of responses was revisited to check whether any important information relating to the different themes had been overlooked. Finally, the data was assesed to establish the degree to which they supported the five basic tenets of the behavioural theory of the firm.

8.2 Findings: How and Why Corporate Community Involvement Decisions are Taken by Companies

8.2.1 MOTIVATIONS FOR CORPORATE COMMUNITY INVOLVEMENT

In general, it emerged from the interviews that the companies engaging in sponsorship were keeping this separate from other CCI activities for, as they explained, sponsorship is seen as an activity that serves their companies' commercial purpose and, hence, is undertaken within the marketing department as a part of advertising strategy. It was found that other CCI activities are undertaken by central administration or a corporate communications department and are viewed as being for more benevolent purposes. That is, apart from sponsorship, the companies group all CCI activities as philanthropy.

In Chapter 7, it was found that specific stakeholders, such as customers, the government, investor/owner and community groups, have had an influence on managerial CCI decisions. However, no such influence on the selection process used for choosing specific types of CCI emerged. Additionally, the quantitative analysis revealed that normative institutional pressure has influenced managerial CCI decisions. By contrast, the case study research shows that investor/owner stakeholders have the greatest influence on managerial CCI decisions. Moreover, this type of stakeholder has an effect on the type of CCI chosen. Further, regarding institutional types of motivation in the case companies, it is found that there is strong cognitive motivation in decision making in relation to philathropic activities. Campbell (2006) defined cognitive motivation as the perception that people have that they ought to be engaging in societal activities for moral reasons. In fact, this researcher saw that this form of motivation for engaging in CCI is strongly apparent in all four companies, in relation to their concerns about Turkey's environmental, economic, cultural and societal conditions.

The second column of Table 8.2 summarises the attitudes towards CCI in each of the case study companies. From these it is clear that the companies display strong cognitive institutional characteristics as defined in Campbell (2006). In fact, it is found that in all three of the Turkish companies the degree of commitment of their owners to the development of Turkish society is the key driver for CCI activities. Further, the cognitive perception of the need to act in a fair and responible manner is also found at INTENT, in spite of it being a subsidiary of a multinational company, but perhaps to not quite so great an extent as for the domestic firms. The table also provides a list of the stakeholders that influence the decision-making processes in each company and the types of institutional pressure that has led to their current CCI position. Moreover, for the three Turkish companies, which are large and international, it emerges that the founder or family members are still on the board of directors or are general managers. That is, it would appear that the owner/founder's opinion on CCI is still important in the Turkish context.

Table 8.2   Motivations for engaging in CCI activities

Company Name	Attitudes towards CCI	Which Stakeholders Affect the CCI Decisions	Which Institutional Pressures Influence which Type of CCI
ESA	The Company's mission dictates that it must be involved in, and continuously increase, its contribution to the communities where it works. Aim to elevate Turkish youth endeavours in modern education, culture and sports.	The company's founder, the company owner/ general manager, company employees, community groups.	• ESA displays *Cognitive Institutions Characteristics* for philanthropic type of CCI
GAYA	There have to be footprints in places where corporations pass by. Therefore, the company adopted the slogan 'We are a bank of culture and arts'.	The company founder, the manager of the company, non-profit foundations, the company's other establishment, the company's partners, the company's employees, community groups.	• GAYA contains *Cognitive Institutions Characteristics* for philanthropic type of CCI • High level of *Normative Institutional Pressure* for philanthropic type of CCI • Medium level of Mimetic Institutional Pressure for sponsorship type of CCI
INTENT	Giving back to the communities, behaving like a good citizen.	Employees, the headquarters' corporate citizenship and corporate affairs programmes, community groups	• INTENT contains *Cognitive Institutions Characteristics* for philanthropic type of CCI • Medium level of *Normative Institutional Pressure* for philanthropic type of CCI
ASTON	If my country exists then I exist as well.	The company founder, customers, dealers, community groups.	• ASTON contains Cognitive Institutions Characteristics for philanthropic type of CCI • Medium level of Normative Institutional Pressure for philanthropic type of CCI

In order to understand how CCI activities are undertaken by holding companies, which pertain to conglomerates working across industry sectors, ESA was chosen as an example. This holding company was established through a partnership between two businessmen and after ten years it was transformed into a joint stock company. A key motivation for the company becoming engaged in CCI activities was that one of its founders died in a plane crash and his sporting background provided a springboard. That is, the other owner of ESA decided to commemorate his name by engaging in sporting activities and later establised a sports club that belonged to the holding company. Later on the surviving owner established a foundation to coordinate all of these activities.

The economic, cultural and societal situation in Turkey compelled ESA to diversify its CCI activities and nowadays they embrace sports, education and arts. However, the managers expressed the view that the most important challenge for Turkey is in the field of education. These types of giving indicate cognitive motives are strong for ESA. Regarding how this particular company sees this challenge one foundation manager stated:

> ESA believes that education is the most important matter for Turkey. We can still observe that many years have passed since the establishment of the Turkish Republic. Turkey still has not yet resolved problems in education. In a country where the population is as young as ours, we believe that education is extremely important, and has to be superb for the future of Turkey. Because of that we established ESA High School in order to develop more creative, self-confident students. Now Turkey has taken this education system that we started in 1994 as a model for itself and started to implement it. So, I think we have made a substantial contribution to Turkey in this issue too. In addition to that, the earthquake which happened in 1999 has expanded our company policy on education. Many schools were destroyed during the earthquake. In those years there were no schools left for children to go. So we built a school in that area in 40 days for those kids.

Moreover, the quote below shows concern for the arts has influenced ESA's decision making with regards to their giving:

> If you asked why we are giving to arts, investing in the arts area, it is something which Turkey really needs. By organising concerts at certain times of the year, we aim to bring to Turkey's most talented artists, musicians or the most famous musicals of the year. We try to sell the tickets for these concerts at a very low price because we have a mission to make Turkish society more aware about what is going on in the world.

It emerged from this particular case that the main driver behind CCI activities is the owner, who is at the same time the general manager of the company. Issues such as deciding which areas to give to and deciding on the amount of money that is to be allocated are all ultimately down to him, but it is the managers who work for the foundation of the holding company who are responsible for the ongoing projects. However, lower-level managers are also able to propose CCI projects and to share their opinions about ESA's CCI activities. With regard to construction project managers in particular, if they decide to engage in CCI activities in a place where construction work is being undertaken, the structure of the holding company allows them to do so. The HR manager described this situation below:

> *For construction we consider our project managers' suggestions. Some CCI projects have been done according to their views. Because they see the necessity of CCI where these constructions have been undertaken by ESA, resources for CCI activities have been allocated.*

The second case, GAYA, is a finance company and it began to engage in CCI activities in the area of arts and culture 65 years ago when the founder of the company said that 'we are a bank of culture and the arts'. That is, the aim of this company was to fill a perceived gap in this area and it came to play a leading role in funding the first children's theatre in Turkey and a supporter of various other theatres across Turkey. To enhance their engagement in this area, GAYA, early on, established a separate publishing company, the purpose of which the corporate communication manager explained:

> *GAYA established a separate publishing company that pursues profit, but it never makes a profit. Our purpose in establishing this publication company is beyond making a profit; our aim was to fill a gap in the field of culture and the arts, in our book list you cannot see big selling publications like bestsellers released by commercial publishers. We aim to fill a certain gap; publishing books that are translated into Turkish for the first time or the books of Turkish writers from ancient times that have been forgotten.*

It became apparent from the interviews that the arts have always been GAYA's first preference for CCI and it has carried out its philanthropic activities through membership of various foundations. Being a member of these various foundations is company policy, because they view giving back to society as an important role for them. At the same time, one of their mangers is a member of the board of these foundations – this means that the company is pressurised into acting according to the rules set by the board and therefore both cognitive and normative institutional motivations can be seen in GAYA's case. Some of the board memberships of managers in this organisation are as follows: the corporate communications manager is on the board of trustees of the Istanbul Foundation for Culture and Arts (IKSV) and the general manager of the company is on the board of directors of the Educational Volunteers Foundation of Turkey (TEGV) as well as being the Chairman of the Board of Directors of the Private Sector Volunteer Association (OSGD). Some examples of philantropic activities which have been undertaken because managers are members of non-profit organisations were summarised by the corporate communication manager of GAYA as:

> *I am on the board of trustees of IKSV. I represent my company at IKSV. My membership of IKSV led GAYA to sponsor the events that are organised by IKSV like sponsoring the Izmir Culture and Arts Foundation to bring the Vienna Philharmonic to Turkey. We also gave money to the Ankara Music Festival. Also, we support the Istanbul Biennial that is organised once in every two years. We also organised an event with one of our credit card brands as a part of our sponsorship project. At the same time we have an archaeology sponsorship, and also, a sponsorship related to Aphrodisias, and a Çatal Höyük sponsorship. The one for Aphrodisias, which is carried out by the Geyre foundation ... or to put it more accurately, we act as a sponsor for the Geyre Foundation. All of these sponsorships are realised because of our managers' membership of various foundations.*

GAYA merged with another bank in 2006 so projects that had started in this other bank were taken up. More specifically, the holding company that this bank was a subsidiary of already had various ongoing philathropic projects that it wanted GAYA to participate in. In other words, some of GAYA's CCI has been shaped by normative institutional pressure from this change in its business operations. Examples of work that has been undertaken because of this merger were described by the deputy communications manager:

> *The company that we merged with asked us if we could support their CCI projects. We discussed what we could do and we decided to set up a reading room. Additionally, beyond setting up that room, the owner of the holding of this company was the chairman of the Clean Sea Association, and through them we got involved in a sea pollution campaign.*

Moreover, representatives from GAYA stated that it was important to engage in sponsorship activities if other companies in their sector were engaging in the same activities, thus demonstrating mimetic institutional pressure was present. This influence was explained by the marketing manager as:

> *Feedback that we receive about the other companies' sponsorship is important for us. For example, you see that a brand X becomes a sponsor for something else, and it happens to be much hotter, and to make a tremendous impact, and so you conclude that you should to be a sponsor to similar events.*

The third case, INTENT, is a subsidiary of a multinational company in the information technology (IT) sector. As a global company, it follows the same mission statement on CCI strategy in all of the countries that it operates in. The multinational company already has global strategies on CCI activities and its Turkish subsidiary has been included in the plans for future activities. However, because INTENT is part of Turkey's emergent market and its income only represents a small part of the firm's overall revenues, it has only recently been earmarked for CCI investment. Moreover, it has been grouped with other subsidiaries of the organisation in the same region as part of its business strategy. The CCI developments at the time of the interviews were described by the new corporate communications manager of the company:

> *Now, if we were to briefly look through history, despite the fact that all of these projects had been taking place in the world for many years, it is very unfortunate that this started only five to six months ago in Turkey. The reason why it started so late is that Turkey appears as a very small company within the organisation, so it follows that the budgets and revenues are also small. But now, it introduces a new organisation as of the 1 January 2009. You know, it is called the Central Eastern Europe. Turkey is within this group because it is among the growing countries; because it is an emergent market. Of the 15 countries, Turkey is the second largest. There has been substantial success for the last few years and it draws a lot attention in the sense of sales, for instance. So headquarters says, 'From now on, I want to invest in here too.'*

As shown in Table 8.2, a range of different stakeholders affect the development of CCI projects within the company. The first and oldest of this subsidiary's philanthropic projects is the university relations project, which has been conducted by a group of volunteer employees in the area of education. In addition to this, the Global Corporate Affairs and Citizenship programme was instigated by INTENT and began on a voluntary basis. Because the subsidiary became classified as a growing company by headquarters, the latter eventually provided funds for this programme. However, the rules set out by headquarters encourage INTENT to follow their lead regarding CCI activities and, thus, normative institutional pressure is observed. Nevertheless, the managers of INTENT aim to select philanthropic projects that are most beneficial to Turkish society from the pool of CCI projects recommended by the parent company. The situation was explained by a manager of the company engaged with CCI on a voluntary basis:

> I mean it's not like there we are, just sitting and agreeing to make the most of the investment in education in Turkey ... our company globally makes the most of the investments in education anyhow, but we choose to focus on education in Turkey. It overlaps, maybe more developed countries can prefer to say, 'let's give some priority to culture and arts' but here we have a very big potential in the issue of education already, there is too much necessity, and so on. The young population does not seem to know their potential yet but we know that there is potential. This therefore happens to be a naturally developing process.

Clearly from this statement it can be seen that there is a cognitive motive underlying INTENT's giving.

ASTON, the fourth case, is a subsidiary of a holding company and the inclinations of the founder of the parent company, as with all the other companies of Turkish origin in this study, was the starting point for engaging in CCI activities. That is, the mindset of this person together with the scope of the company business activities has influenced its CCI activities. A strong sense of responsibility towards Turkish society – in particular human development, environmental consciousness and economic sustainability – emerged as key concerns of this company. As can be seen from the following quote, cognitive motives are also important drivers for ASTON's role as a donor:

> Aston, like all companies of the other companies under our holding, acts in line with principle of 'if my country exists then I exist as well' which is the heritage of our deceased original owner. Within such a persepctive, volunteer activities have been carried out both individually and corporately since the first day of establishment.

The holding company has a corporate social responsibility (CSR) department which sets the rules for CCI activities throughout the organisation and ASTON is often pressured to adopt the philanthropic activities started by it. This situation is a typical example where normative institutional pressures are present and it was summarised by the corporate communication manager as:

> *The inquiry for some of the philanthiropic projects comes from the CSR department. As a matter of fact, there are some projects conducted by the Holding by itself as you stated, and some others which it conducts to flourish synergy within the group. All the employees of the Holding and group companies participate in those anyway. Of course, those companies which fit to certain criteria ...*

Therefore, although ASTON has its own separate philanthropic projects which are driven by cognitive institutional pressures, they receive a medium level of normative pressure from the parent company regarding which CCI activities to engage in. In addition to this, ASTON undertakes ongoing corporate research to measure the expectations of its stakeholders, in particular, seeking customer opinion and the views of its dealers which consequently also has an influence on the CCI programmes. The corporate communications manager explained this as follows:

> *Our company, since the year 1961, when it introduced a clean alternative fuel to Turkey, has continued a close relationship with its customers. Our company, as a brand which is currently involved in more than 100,000 households per day, is accepted as 'A Part of the Family'. Our company evaluates the requests of its stakeholders and makes contributions to the community in line with such requests as its responsibility. For example our company conducts surveys twice a year in order to measure the expectations of its stakeholders, and the perception of the company. In line with the studies of the year of 2007, our company noticed that the stakeholders expected some improvements in areas such as training, health and culture and art.*

In sum, three key observations have emerged regarding the motivation for Turkey's CCI. First, there is evidence that there is a strong influence of the founder/owner on the CCI decision-making process, which is consistent with the findings from the quantitative study in Chapter 7. Moreover, although the findings show that customer, investor and community groups can have an impact on CCI decisions, this appears to be a subsantially lesser driver than the proclivities of the founder/owner, with the exception being the foreign-owned subsidary INTENT. This owner/founder influence leads to the conclusion, drawn in previous chapters, that CCI by large companies in Turkey is still at an early stage because there is little other institutional pressure when compared with the developed countries. For example, in this regard in the USA and the UK, changes in ownership status, company profit, managers' opinions, tax regulations, public expectations and industry conditions all exert an influence on CCI (Navarro, 1988; Adams and Hardwick, 1998; Buchholtz et al., 1999). Second, these cases also show that cognitive institutional pressures are predominant in all cases over other forms, with INTENT again being the exception.

8.2.2 MANAGERIAL STRUCTURE

This subsection explores the relationship between managerial structure and CCI in terms of where decisions are taken and who is involved in making them. In general, it transpires from the case study firms that a distinction is made between project management and budgetary control as well as there being a clear understanding of the role of the senior management/investor/ owner in relation to CCI delivery. Moreover, cash donations or gifts-in-kind can come from either or both of the budgets allocated to philanthropic and/ or sponsorship activities. With respect to who is involved in CCI decisions, it is found that middle-level managers are held responsible for maintaining existing CCI projects. In all four companies, if it becomes necessary to revise existing projects, or implement new ones, middle-level managers need to inform higher-level ones about this.

Table 8.3 illustrates the organisational structure of the four case companies in relation to who is responsible for each of the different types of giving. It is notable that there is a clear separation between sponsorship and philanthropy for the three firms than engage in the former, namely ESA, GAYA and ASTON. That is, sponsorship activities are carried out in a separate department related to corporate identity, marketing and brand image or is the responsibility of the general manager as in the foremost case, thus indicating that this activity is seen as central to a firm's business strategy. Moreover, in GAYA, INTENT and ASTON philanthropic activities are the responsibility of the corporate communications department.

Table 8.3   **Managerial structure**

Company Name	CCI Types	Department Responsible for CCI Decisions	Managers Involved in CCI Decisions
ESA	Philanthropy: cash giving, gifts-in-kind	Foundation	Managers, company owner/ general manager
	Philanthropy: cash giving, gifts-in-kind, employee volunteerism	Project based	Managers who work on the project, company owner, general manager
	Sponsorship: cash giving	None	General manager
GAYA	Philanthropy: cash giving, employee volunteerism, gifts-in-kind	Corporate communications department	Middle-level managers in the department, general manager, deputy general manager
	Sponsorship: cash giving, gifts-in-kind, CRM	Image and branding department	Middle-level managers in the department, general manager, deputy general manager
INTENT	Philanthropy: cash giving, employee volunteerism, gifts-in-kind	Corporate communications department	Manager in the department, volunteer managers, senior manager at the headquarters
	Philanthropy: Cash giving, employee volunteerism, gifts-in-kind	Volunteer management board	Volunteer manager, top-level managers at headquarters
ASTON	Philanthropy: cash giving, employee volunteerism, gifts-in-kind	Corporate communications department	Middle-level managers in the department, general manager
	Sponsorship: cash giving	Marketing department	Middle-level managers in the department, general manager

In ESA, most CCI activities are undertaken by a foundation that is funded by profits and the managers who work for it are involved in the CCI decision-making process for the company. In addition, philanthropic projects are proposed by senior managers, but these are paid for in the form of internal budgets, gifts-in-kind and/or voluntarism. In GAYA, new sponsorship projects or revisions are normally discussed amongst middle managers in the brand image department. Proposals are then taken to senior management, who then decide whether to pass them to top management for approval. The procedure was described by the brand and image manager of the finance company:

> *If I offer a sponsorship with regard to one of my brands, we have to explain this to the manager of that brand in the first place. First of*

all, inquiries are brought to us, we eliminate them and if any suit us, we go up to the Brand Manager and say, 'This one suits your targets as well, what would you say to that?' The deputy general manager who manages that brand should approve of this as well as us. If he also approves, and if it is something major, then this shall most definitely be referred to the CEO for the final decision.

In the case of ESA, the final decisions related to philanthropic CCI are taken by the general manager who is the owner of the holding company. That is, the main role of those managers who work for the foundation is to conduct those projects that have been specified by the general manager and the board of directors. For example, the holding company has involved itself in sponsorship only once and this decision was taken by the general manager. The foundation manager of ESA described this issue in this way:

When it is to be done through the foundation, and if we are asked 'what shall we do?', then we give our opinion, but the decision to do it is taken by the general manager.

In fact, in all four companies there is evidence of top-level managers proposing new projects or opposing those that have been decided upon in the programme set by the middle managers. In such cases, the middle-level managers have to revise and rearrange the company's CCI activities according to what they have been told by upper-level management. For example, GAYA has a separate publication company, the administrative board of which has to make direct requests to the finance company's CEO for funds or other forms of donation for a particular project and, if he thinks that it is feasible, he assigns it to the middle-level managers to coordinate the activity:

... after all, our publication company has a separate publication board. So, they are the ones to decide which book to publish. There is a publication company that we owned and also managers of the galleries. All these have their own general managers, but of course, there are bank managers on the board of directors. The decision is taken by our upper level management ... sometimes these decisions are taken in the meetings which our general manager and our deputy manager attend. These decisions are taken by top management and we execute it.

However, the respondents from both ESA and INTENT pointed out that for them some aspects of philanthropic CCI are also 'bottom up'. For instance, in INTENT sometimes the employees of the company set up a team to maintain a CCI project separately from those that are being undertaken by the corporate communications department. A manager of INTENT explained this situation in this way:

> We set up a core team in university relations three years ago. This team, besides their main jobs, give extra time for this project in order to realise it. For example, I have been running university relations for three years, but this is not my real job, I do this voluntarily.

In a similar vein, ESA supports CCI projects proposed by its employees, if construction managers are prepared to support them. Table 8.3 illustrates these two different philanthropic types and their alternative management teams. A similar scenario is also found at INTENT, where the different forms of such giving were described by the HR manager of ESA:

> Since we are engaged in construction works, our engineers,and project managers are engaged only with their own work. In addition to that, while they are carrying out their work, they also consider making a contribution to the area where they construct these buildings. That is entirely something regional. For instance we built a power plant in Bursa, and completed the power plant as the contractor. But right next to it, we also built a technical school. The management of the construction must have somehow figured it out and the local administrators must have suggested new philanthropic projects.

In sum, Table 8.3 shows that the structure of the managerial teams that work on CCI projects are more or less the same in all four organisations, with the general manager/owner having the final say. Moreover, all four organisations have departmental mechanisms to undertake CCI activities which are completely separate when both philanthropy and sponsorship are engaged with.

8.2.3 BUDGET

This section considers how the case companies set budgets for CCI activities. There are three main reasons for including budgeting procedure as one of the themes: first to understand better the process and procedures of CCI decisions; second to specify the conditions according to which companies differentiate their CCI activities; and third to show companies' perceptions of the degree of importance of CCI activities. In general, from the interview data it emerges that the main distinction regarding the budgeting procedure relates to whether these four companies are consumer oriented or not. That is, with ASTON and GAYA, both consumer-oriented companies, sponsorship activities are considered separately from philanthropic ones, as the former are central to their commercial strategies and, consequently, these two budgets are split between two departments. By contrast, ESA and INTENT, which are not consumer-oriented companies, engage in little or no sponsorship, preferring to focus on philanthropic activities.

Table 8.4 shows the time frames for budget allocation as well as from where it is acquired for each case company. As can be seen, most monies are allocated on a yearly basis, however there are two key exceptions. First, ESA would appear to employ a greater degree of commitment than the other compnies, because any donations are allocated to a whole project rather than on this annual basis. In relation to INTENT, it is notable that the local funding from the subsidiary itself is much more tightly monitored, once every three months, implying that the parent company does not wish to grant too high a degree of autonomy. When the companies were asked, 'From where does the money come for your CCI activities?', in general, it turned out that each provided funds differently. In the case of ESA, money for philanthropic activities comes from both the foundation of the holding company as well as their construction budget aimed at projects. For INTENT there are also two sources of money: the global budget administered by headquarters and the local budget which comes out of its own coffers. With regards to GAYA and ASTON, it emerges that the budgeting procedures are similar in that a specific amount of money is allocated to each department who arrange their CCI activities according to this budget. For example, the marketing department of GAYA know at the beginning of the year how much money they can spend on marketing activities and they allocate money from this alotment to their sponsorship activities. The budgeting procedure is explained in more detail in the following paragraphs.

Table 8.4   Budgeting procedure

Company Name	CCI Types	Time Frame	Allocation Location
ESA	Philanthrophy	Yearly basis	Foundation budget
	Philanthropy	Duration of the project	Project basis budget
GAYA	Philanthropy, sponsorship	Yearly basis	Departmental budget
INTENT	Philanthropy	Yearly basis	Global budget
	Philanthropy	Quarterly determined	Local budget
ASTON	Philanthropy, sponsorship	Yearly basis	Departmental budget

ESA manages its philanthropic activities within two separate budgets, with the first budget being managed by the foundation and the second pertaining to the running of projects which have been undertaken by the construction subsidiary of the holding company. The foundation manager of ESA explained how the foundation of the holding company creates its budget in order to engage in various philanthopic projects in the following way:

> *Our foundation is a shareholder in the holding company (6 per cent) and the construction company (6 per cent). But when you say the 6 per cent part, that is a fixed asset, to make it current you must definitely sell it on the stock market and some cash must come. So that is one of our incomes. Our second income is, on the other hand, 1 per cent of the profit of the construction company, which we take every year. One per cent of the companies affiliated to the holding is appropriated to us, is given to us. Apart from that, there are incomes secured by the foundation that come from those immovable properties in kind which have been among its assets for years. Moreover, if you take it as an income, there are some small size incomes from full members that belong here, sports members and rental incomes from tennis courts or halls, and from leases for small scale sports organisations.*

The philanthropic activities which are undertaken through the projects' budget are not usually sustainable ones. The HR manager of the holding company explained this second budgeting procedure:

> *Yes, that's our company's way anyway. It has projects, its income comes from its projects, and profits left from such projects. Thus, all expenses required are met through those projects. That may be an expense like buying iron, or an expense like buying concrete too, or an expense of paying salaries, or, if the project requires such philanthropic donations, that would be given within that budget too.*

INTENT is a subsidiary of a multinational company and, as explained above, in 2009 the headquarters increased the budget allocated to CSR projects for Turkey because it identified it as one of a group of countries experiencing strong growth that it wanted to invest more in. With this new conviction, the company hired a new CSR manager and set up a new department, the budget for which is determined by negotiations with headquarters, but the latter has the final say. That is, as it now has a new organisational structure, the company also has an extra budget for its philanthropic activities, drawn from these negotiated local arrangements. The nature of the combination of the new and old budgeting procedures was explained by the company's new CSR manager:

> *For the CCI projects planned for the next year, we made our projection for the first time and sent our budget request for undertaking such projects to our headquarters. Now, I made my preparation, as I've told you, as to how much I will be asking from the local budget, and how much from the global, I took that up to my manager, and together with her, we revised them again. After that I sent it abroad. We've got four quarters per year. At the beginning of the year we have to draw up a budget. The budget that comes from abroad is project based. We can't say 'such a project came up, let me take some part of the budget that came from X project, and transfer it there'. That's 100 per cent clear. The money that will be used from the local budget is not specified at the beginning of the year. I am trying to request the money quarterly. Let's say I have spared a quantity x for the first quarter for X project, and when I get to the second quarter, I notice that an amount has been left over there. This is the money that I can transfer to the project that comes up.*

As pointed out above, the budgeting procedures for ASTON and GAYA are similar. That is, both companies have departmental budgets to engage in CCI activities, with sponsorship activities being undertaken under the marketing department's budget and philanthropic activities funded through the corporate communication department's budget. The corporate communications manager of ASTON explained how the budget for his department is allocated:

> *We form the budget in line with the scope of the project. All factors ranging from implementation of the project to its communication are considered.*

The budget for GAYA allocated from the corporate communications department is aimed at involvement in long-term sustainable philanthropic projects. Moreover, usually these two companies set up their budget on a yearly basis for their philanthropic activities. However, in both companies sponsorship budgets are less reliable. The communications manager of GAYA described the situation:

The budget is already there. We receive a target at the beginning of each year, so our budget is certain anyhow in line with that budget. It happens to be served to us somehow each year. We then break it down with respect to departments. In that breakdown are the marketing plans of the product sides determined in accordance with their marketing targets. They share such plans with us. We make a distribution among them, and they tell us their own preferences and wishes, they tell us what they have in mind to realise. So, we set up the communication department and its budget in that sense but, later, it happens to undergo changes due to transactions within the period. But you can never keep what you fix at the beginning of the year constant, or unaltered till the end of the year. It's the same in every country, but in Turkey particularly, you know, all kinds of things like influences from surroundings, social effects, economic effects.

In sum, the budgeting procedure varies across the case companies in relation to size, ownership characteristics and country of domicile of the parent company. More specifically, ESA, a large Turkish holding company, chooses to distribute much of its aid through a traditional foundation, but also, so as to ensure local practice, allocates other funds to sustainable projects. Regarding INTENT, a foreign-owned subsidiary of a large multinational enterprise (MNE), it does not have a foundation but it has been involving itself in local sustainable projects – mainly on a voluntary basis backed by a small internal expenses budget. However, in relation to the period between budget reviews for these local projects, ESA aims at preplanning for sufficient funds to ensure sustainability and project completion, whereas INTENT now has to assess its budgetry position on a quarterly basis. This suggests that the foreign subsidiary's CCI activities are more elastic to changes in market condiditons, which in turn implies that it is less tied to cognitive and normative pressures of the Turkish market than stakeholder demands, regardless of the wishes of local managers. Regarding the other two Turkish companies, their annual budget reviews of CCI would appear to be tied in with their overall business strategy, in that the activities of philanthropic giving and sponsorship are embedded in two different departments central to their economic plannning. Moreover, although there was the expressed wish from many of the interviewees for budgets to be long term and, hence, deliver sustainability and strong relations with the community, many of them recognised that their contribution was subject to changing socieconomic conditions.

Finally, Levy and Shatto (1978) advised that charitable giving should be investigated in relation to overall financial strategy and that its perceived importance should be judged in terms of the degree to which budgeting for it is sustainable and clearly allocated to core departmental or senior managers. In all four cases here, it has emerged that CCI activities, regardless of motivation, are being seen as a key element of corporate strategy, as specific budgets have been allocated for donorship in relation to both monetary and non-monetary giving.

8.2.4 SLACK RESOURCES

The effect of slack resources has also been analysed in Chapter 7 and no relationship with CCI was found, but the case study results would appear to reveal a different picture. That is, when the interviewees were asked about their CCI behaviour and the availability of slack resources during a recession, many stated that there was a direct link between the two when there was a recession in Turkey. Regarding this, Table 8.5 details the responses given by three of the companies' managers to questions about the availability or non-availability of slack resources and it can be seen that they provided similar answers. In relation to this, the ASTON representatives, as explained earlier, refused to contribute such information because it was not company policy to do so.

To summarise, all of those who responded said that during times of recession budget shortages can affect CCI decisions in two ways, depending on the severity of the situation. That is, if there is a small decrease the companies tend not to engage in new projects, but instead try to find ways to reduce such factors as expenses so as to ensure the survival of existing projects. However, if there is a dramatic budget decrease then ongoing projects have been known to be stopped. The impact of slack resources on CCI outcomes in each company is explained in greater detail next.

Table 8.5   Availability of slack resources

Availability of Slack	Budgetary Outcome	CCI Outcome
Slack resources are available	Enough budget, cash resources	Sustainability – new project – revise existing projects
Limited slack resources are available	Budget decrease, not enough cash money	Reduce the size of the project – consider CCI alternatives to cash especially for philanthropic projects such as employee or gift-in-kind resources – no new projects – try to maintain the existing projects with limited budget
Slack resources are not available	No budget, dramatic decrease	Stop the projects – freeze all CCI activities

ESA was facing restrictions on the amount of money allocated for the philanthropic budget, which had led to the company postponing their newly planned projects. That is, the holding company preferred to engage in long-term projects and, hence, it was prioritising the maintenance of its existing projects. As the foundation manager of the holding company elucidated:

> *Our foundation is a shareholder in our holding company and our construction company. At present they have dropped but we have 6 per cent of the shares. At the moment, the stock value of the holding company has dropped, that is its market value. However, this was in the proximity of 15 million dollars, when you take 6 per cent of that, we had an asset amounting to 700,000 dollars, we covered our budget by selling those stock shares. But, to be frank, we also have some difficulty at present since the values have excessively dropped. In the meantime, things run with the support of The construction company. We were about to construct a school this year, this new technical school. We have started out in a temporary building now. However, we have had to postpone it on account of this economic crisis.*

GAYA was experiencing budget cuts, however, there had as yet been no substantial drop in philanthropic activities. This was because the managers viewed sustainability and continuation of philanthropic activities as being more important than sponsorship activities and, thus, if there was need for a budget cut the company would curb the latter before cutting the former. Regarding this, the brand manager of the company said:

> *It's like this, first and foremost, communication, as I said, is something that's very continuous. I mean, at the point you fail to ensure continuity in communication with your customers, your work is all garbage. Therefore, if we happened to have held very intense campaigns last year, and if we are all silent about that subject this year; sometimes the advertisements of your rivals influence your performance positively. Whoever is the leader in the market benefits their rivals' marketing activities. This is the reason why we do not prefer to cut either our sponsorship or philanthropic activities. However, if there is a need to make cuts we will definitely start from our sponsorship activities because we put too much effort into our philanthropic activities and we do not want to ruin all these efforts in one instance.*

Although INTENT was affected by the recession, the company had not stopped any of its ongoing philanthropic projects, but instead it had imposed certain restrictions. However, if the revenue of the company had dropped dramatically, the company would have frozen all philanthropic activities as it had done before. This situation was summarised by the corporate communications manager:

> *For one thing, we will not be suspending any of our projects. All of them will be continued in the year 2009. That means that we will not stop any project regarding CCI. But of course, as I said earlier, we are cutting down our budgets in the face of financial constraints. However, no project will be abandoned. There are none, but if there are substantial drops in our budgets for instance, if there were substantial drops in our revenues, our net profit as well as our budgets would be affected. In past times, we went through a period where everything stopped because of budget limitations.*

Within INTENT, the budget was set by headquarters and the company had enough slack resources for the budget not to be affected too much that year. However, during the recession the company had focused its efforts on long-term projects so as maintain a high public profile of reliability. Nevertheless, the manager with responsibility for university relations did admit that if the recession had continued over several years they would have had to reconsider the situation. He summed up the situation as follows:

> *Now, naturally, if the economy gets worse, shortages affect our activities as well as everything else, but we have already decided on our activities, and a part of their budgets for this year has already been determined. We will be more selective with regard to projects. Our company believes that if you don't ensure continuity, what you do today will be forgotten tomorrow, therefore a philanthropic project is something that needs to be continuous. For this reason, we will again keep on with our work, even if at a minimum, so as to ensure that continuity. But, I have to admit that if we happened to be receding for three years, five years consecutively, then it might be reflected in our activity.*

Another important issue which was explored in the case studies was how recession affected the types of CCI activity. More specifically, the aim was, first, to elicit whether sponsorship and philanthropic giving were treated differently when there were limited slack resources. That is, was one form of donorship given greater protection during such times? Second, there was the question as to whether gifts-in-kind, such as employee labour, are preferred over cash giving during times of slack resources.

When it comes to the trade off between philanthropy and sponsorship during times of austerity, although two of the sample companies declared that they were undertaking sponsorship, namely ASTON and GAYA, as explained above, only the latter was prepared to share information about this. Regarding the latter, its managers highlighted the importance of the company's philanthropic activities. For them such activities were being undertaken for prestige and the sustainability of these projects was seen to be more important than maintaining sponsorship projects. This situation was expanded upon by the brand manager:

> We are expecting to cut down the sponsorship budget during the recession time. Our philanthropic projects are small projects so this means they involve such tiny expense that cutting them would be detrimental. So, what I'm trying to say is that we would cut down a major item like a sponsorship budget, instead of cutting down 15 small jobs, that would have a negative effect on our brand. That is, in those charity acts, in works which are legacies of the corporate culture, no cut downs are implemented.

All four companies highlighted that cash resources were their preferred type of CCI when engaging in both sponsorship and philanthropic projects. However, if there was a shortage of these then company characteristics and market conditions specified what kind of resources the companies could use as an alternative. For example, the corporate communications manager of GAYA stated that they had a large amount of employee resources that they could use and when there was a budget shortage, they had started to use them in the ongoing projects. In fact, this strategy had the advantage that it put their workers closer to their consumers and, consequently, they started to design new projects using their employee resources. In INTENT's case, where they did not have slack labour resources, gifts-in-kind were used as an alternative to cash resources. In addition, one manager at the company pointed out that employing labour on projects was a decision taken not because of lack of finance, but often was more appropriate. Moroever, ESA is not in a consumer-oriented industry, it is in the business to business (B2B) sector, and because they deal in large quantities of building materials they preferred to use gifts-in-kind. For example, they preferred to construct new hospitals or schools in the areas where they were constructing their buildings.

In this section the way in which slack resources affect CCI decisions has been explored by finding out from the interviewees what happens during a period in which there are not enough. In general, it has emerged that slack has enabled all of the case companies to undertake projects and they all stressed the importance of making these sustainable wherever possible as this was good for public visibility. Moreover, the respondents explained that during times of low or no slack resources they would substitute cash with non-cash resesources, such as using their employees or gifts-in-kind. In addition, they reported that under such circumstances they would not embark on new projects, preferring to protect the long-term ones so as to avoid damage to their reputation. Finally, all the respondents admitted that if a dramatic fall occurred in the company's budget, existing CCI activities would be terminated or frozen.

Table 8.6   Criteria for engaging in CCI activities

Company Name	CCI Types	Areas as a Criterion	Commercial Motive as a Criterion	Sustainability as a Criterion
ESA	Philanthropy	Education, culture and arts, sports	None	Established foundation in order to do sustainable projects for founded schools and cultural institutions and sport centre
GAYA	Philanthropy	Culture and arts, environment, education		Do at least three to five years' time-based projects for the environment and education
	Sponsorship		Build relationship with a brand, competitors actions	Sponsor the exibitions since 1964 at the chosen four different art galleries in four different cities
INTENT	Philanthropy	Headquarter's corporate citizenship and corporate affairs programmes (School reform and talent, culture % arts, communities in need)	Build awareness of usage of technology	Adapt chosen headquarter's projects to Turkey for long-term basis
ASTON	Philanthropy	Environment, culture and arts, education		Organise long-term education compaign, build schools
	Sponsorship		Strengthen coporate identity	

8.2.5 CRITERIA

In this section the criteria used by the case companies when deciding upon their CCI activities are probed. In the first instance, when asked, 'What criteria did you use in selecting this CCI activity?', representatives from all four companies began by explaining the areas that their companies are involved in, which, by and large, are clearly set out in their mission statements. As can be seen in Table 8.6, all four companies use similar categories when making decisions on what to invest in, namely preferred area, commercial motivation and the sustainability of the project. However, in INTENT's case, the multinational subsidiary, it is only allowed to enter into types of corporate affairs and citizenship programmes as stated in the parent company's rules. Regarding commercial motivation, all the companies, with the exception of ESA, put this as a criterion for CCI choice. Finally, respondents from all of the case firms stressed the importance of the duration of their CCI programmes in terms of there being a preference for long term, sustainable CCI projects.

Education, the arts and culture are areas in which all four companies expressed a preference for undertaking CCI activities and for GAYA and ASTON environmental issues were also identified. Additionally, ESA invests in sports and INTENT has been donating to health matters. As explained above, one of GAYA's managers is on the board of an environmental foundation, and for this reason the company has chosen to support a project in this area. More specifically, as the corporate communications manager explained:

> Why did we pick the TURMEPA project? It is because we were sensitive to the environment. And when caring for the environment, there is no other foundation working on sea cleanliness or another foundation working so prevalently. That is why we selected TURMEPA.

Whilst GAYA, INTENT and ASTON indicated commercial motivation in relation to CCI choice, ESA did not and, in fact, the HR managers of that company said that they did not even keep records for most of their projects that they engage in. In GAYA and ASTON's cases, undertaking sponsorship activities for expliciting commercial positioning is being used in order to promote the brand and, thus, to reach their consumer market more effectively. As the brand/image manager of GAYA put it:

> The marketing/communications department plans the next year's marketing projects. Doing this we ask questions like 'Who is our target

> *customer?' 'How we can communicate with our target customer?'*
> *and of course these answers are given as a result of various intense*
> *research. Actually, there are numerous methods of communication, and*
> *sponsorship activities are only one of them. So in order to increase our*
> *brand recognition by our target customers we use sponsorship.*

In the case of INTENT the situation is somewhat different where, although the respondents expressed a commercial interest in relation to carrying out CCI activities, they do not choose to engage in sponsorship, preferring to engage in projects that are aimed at accruing financial benefits owing to positive visibility. More specifically, given it is a computing company, the company managers are intent on targeting the young Turkish population as a future investment and, thus, ensuring good prospects for the nation's IT development. The advertising manager of INTENT summarised their stance as follows:

> *We are undertaking a university relations project because we need*
> *to come closer to the young generation. We need to be intimate with*
> *them for the future of the company and we need them to get acquainted*
> *with us. Since our company works for corporations and doesn't have a*
> *consumer leg, it is not a company expending huge sums on marketing.*
> *But the people who will constitute corporations in the future are*
> *students, therefore we want them to know us thoroughly, understand*
> *us, and know our technologies.*

Sustainability of CCI investment emerges as being a common criterion for the case companies. That is, all four use this measure to determine whether to donate or not. Expressly, the brand/image manager of GAYA stated that if a project was not continuous, then this could lead to the relevant community perceiving that the company had lost interest in their needs and, hence, this would be bad for the brand image. INTENT and ASTON representatives stated their desire to pursue continuity as they viewed this as a prerequisite for projects that could have a substantial impact on society. Similarly, the sustainability criterion at ESA was outlined by its foundation manager:

> *What we care for in the work we conduct is that 'it is continuous, it is*
> *sustained'. That is to say, one day a person may hold an activity in any*
> *sense, that may be sports or that may be arts as well. We do not consider*
> *that a one-off event has much of a meaning. What's important is that it*
> *has attained continuity, that it has been sustained.*

Table 8.7   How the core concepts help to explain the process of CCI decisions

Problemistic Search	Quasi-Resolution of Conflict	Uncertainty Avoidance	Slack Resources	Organisational Learning
Search is stimulated by a problem and is directed towards finding a solution to that problem.	The coalition represented in an organisation is a coalition of members having different goals. The theory proposes to pay sequential attention to goals in order to solve the conflict. This means that companies assess the internal logic at a point in time.	The organisation seeks to avoid uncertainty by following regular procedures so as try to influence/internalise/negotiate with the environment. The overall aim being to decrease unpredictable future impact.	If enough slack resources exist to meet all demands and those resources are distributed so as to meet these demands, the coalition is a feasible one. Slack plays both a stabilising and adaptive role.	The organisation will use standard operating procedures and rules of thumb to make and implement choices.
Search for CCI will be undertaken in response to pressures/problems which are received from the external and internal environments.	Companies will pay sequential attention to stakeholders' requests on CCI activities.	Both the use and design of CCI activities will be influenced by uncertainity avoidance.	Unavailability of slack resources will constrain and mold CCI responses.	Managers will revise and renew the CCI activities based on previous experience and over time companies set rules for CCI practices.
In the case of CCI, pressures from stakeholders to engage in it can create problems and managers can overcome these by conforming with their requests. That is they identify the first solution that will not compromise with the overall strategic goals of the firms.	Deciding what type of CCI companies choose to do involves sequential attention to the requests from stakeholders until a suitable compromise is reached that allows for equilibrium to be restored.	In order to overcome the negative effects of uncertainity, managers are forced to shape their CCI activities under mimetic and normative pressures.	Availability of different types of slack resources including cash, employee time and gifts-in-kind facilitates companies' engagement in a range of CCI activities.	Organisations' past CCI activities shape their current ones.
Comply with the theory. Companies engaged in problemistic search when a problem occurs. Two different sources of problem were found: First the investor/owner stakeholder created one by pushing managers into engaging in CCI. Second, in response to the challenge to achieve some specific goals, such as expanding into a different market place, promoting a brand or increasing employee motivation. CCI used as a simple solution.	Do not agree with the theory. CCI outcomes are determined by the determinant stakeholder, namely, the owner/founder in the case of the Turkish-owned companies and the parent company is most influential in relation to the mulinational. That is there is no sequential resolution of conflict amongst the various stakeholders.	Agree with the theory. There is substantial evidence that to cope with uncertainity the firms responded to normative and mimetic pressures by when deciding upon the nature of their CCI activities.	Partial consistency with the theory. The company representatives generally considered avaibility of excess cash resources as slack that could be used for CCI. However, excess employee time or excess gifts-in-kind were not considered in this and what is more, during times of recession they were often seen as useful substitutes for cash.	Partially complies with the theory. There was no evidence of organisational learning feedback from previous projects shaping one in terms of philanthropic giving but some existed for sponsorship. Moreover, given that criteria were now in place for CCI decision making in all cases, it is expected that this will result in future organisational learning.

8.3 Discussing Core Concepts of the Behavioural Theory of the Firm According to the Results Obtained from the Cases

In Table 8.7, a brief summary of this section is given. The first row describes the explanation of each core concept. The second summarises how CCI can be explained according to the core concepts' point of view. The third row asks what is expected to be found according to the theory. Finally, the fourth row shows how much the theory is capable of explaining the process of CCI decisions in the case companies.

In Chapter 7, three core concepts of the behavioural theory of the firm, namely, stakeholder pressure, institutional climate and slack resources, were analysed in relation to their impact on firms' CCI behaviour. In this section, a slightly different approach is adopted, whereby five elements coming from the same theory are investigated using the outcomes from the case study interviews to elicit greater understanding of CCI decision making in the Turkish context, these being: problemistic search, quasi resolution of conflict, uncertainty avoidance, slack resources and organisational learning. That is, next, each of these theoretical concepts is considered in sequence, along with assessment as to whether or not the outcomes from the qualitative investigation support the propositions put forward by proponents of the behavioural theory of the firm.

Problemistic search: This refers to the notion put forward by proponents of the behavioural theory of the firm that managers have to be faced with a problem before they are galvanised into taking action. More specifically, in this study this action pertains to making decisions about becoming involved in CCI activities. Further, under this lens it is contended that managers do not optimize the goals, they pay sequential attention to a problem and they do not try to reach the best and most effective solution. That is, as Cyert and March (1963) proposed, they react to pressure to search for a suitable answer as challenges arise, rather than strategising in a way that predicts them and how to manage them. In addition, it is contended that the first satisfactory alternative that fits with existing policy goals is adopted, with there being little searching for alternatives. In general, these problems can arise from either the internal or external environments.

Turning to CCI, under the above perspective it would be assumed that problems are instigated by pressure from stakeholder(s) or something else in the institutional environment, which the the manager needs to take action on and so the search for a solution would begin. In terms of the evidence from examining the actual process of CCI decisions for the four cases, problemistic search was observed in the Turkish-owned companies as a response to high pressure from their investor/owner stakeholders. Another important point which needs to be underlined is that problemistic search occurred in these companies when they decided to engage in their first CCI activities, in that the founder/owner triggered this and the managers were tasked with the role of designing CCI programmes in response. Further, in section 8.2 it emerged that the founder/owner of these firms expressed a preference for philanthropic cash giving over other forms of CCI, thereby limiting their managers' options during their problemistic search. Moreover, respondents from these companies pointed out that during difficult times the results of problemistic search often lay in engaging in non-cash activities, such as employee volunteerism, gifts-in-kind and cause-related marketing (CRM). By contrast, in the case of INTENT, the foreign subsidiary, the problemistic search would appear to be bounded by longer-term strategic goals aimed at increasing its share in the domestic market. In this regard, in section 8.2 there are number of contributions from respondents of this company portraying this practice. Therefore, it can be concluded that although problemistic search is apparent in all four case companies, the way in which solutions are found would appear to be determined by the degree of embeddedness of the firm in its society as well as the preferences of the owner/founder regarding CCI activities.

Quasi resolution of conflict: According to this concept of the theory, the criterion used to make a choice is that the alternative selected should allow for suffcent consensus amongst the coalition of conflicting interests in relation to an organisation so as to enable it to operate effectively. Under this perspective, external stakeholders, including for instance shareholders, bankers, governments, suppliers and customers, are members of this coalition, all of whom form alliances to achieve their goals. The devices employed to this end are local rationality (each subunit tackles problems within their area of expertise), acceptable but not necessarily optimal, decision rules and sequential attention to goals (Cyert and March 1963). Turning to CCI decision making, in Chapter 7 it emerged that the salient external stakeholders who exerted the greatest pressure on managers were, from most to least, shareholders/investors, community groups, government legislators and customers (the latter two being negative). However, when it comes to the three Turkish-owned companies in the qualitative study, the interviewees invariably reported that the owner/founder was by far the dominant stakeholder and, hence, the basic tenets in relation to the behavioural theory would appear not to hold. That is, because of this overwhelming power in the decision-making process, the type of CCI was not determined through quasi resolution of conflict. In the case of INTENT, there was some evidence of employee pressure guiding decisions on some projects, but much of the CCI decision making was controlled by the parent company. There was also some evidence of employee involvement in the process for ESA.

In terms of the situation within the firms, in all of the four cases companies, it was observed that each had either set up a department to deal with involvement in different types of CCI activities or had allocated responsibility to an existing department or departments. However, where potential conflict arose amongst the the middle managers, the final decision rested with senior managers or the owner in the case of the Turkish firms and headquarters in INTENT's. In other words, there was no evidence of sequential consideration of different internal coalition members' interests.

Uncertainty avoidance: Cyert and March (1963) stressed uncertainty as a feature of organisational decision making with which organisation must live and these they cited as the behaviour of the market, the behaviour of competitors, the future actions of governmental agencies and so on. Proponents of the theory argue that organisations seek to avoid uncertainty by following regular procedures and by following a policy of reacting to feedback, rather than forecasting the environment. Uncertainities also exist in relation to CCI decision making, for managers may not know how and in which ways to engage in CCI activities effectively. Moreover, they may often feel obliged to undertake activities that are in line their competitors in the industry and, yet, do not want to go against the value and the culture of the community with which they are involved. Therefore, in order to manage uncertainty it is assumed that they try to mimic the behaviour of other firms in their industry, whilst at the same time ensuring that their actions are consistent with the values and norms of the society at large.

In Chapter 7, the responses to the survey revealed that normative institutional pressures were an influential factor employed by firms to overcome uncertainities. Regarding the four cases, apart from ESA, as shown in Table 8.2, acceptance of normative institutional pressures from the parent companies meant that uncertainty in CCI decision making was reduced. Moreover, the evidence in this table regarding the four case studies also showed the presence of the other types of institutional pressure to limit uncertainty. For example, respondents from all four companies expressed the view that they aimed to ensure that their CCI behaviour would bring positive future reactions from the Turkish population and, therefore, engaged with them to negotiate the best ways forward. In other words, they were willing to submit to cognitive institutional pressure. More specifically, the three Turkish companies' interviewees explicitly stated that they wanted to show Turkish society that they were commited to the Turkish culture, value and norms. Moreover, they all want to be seen as benefactors and forerunner companies that were working to extend the scope of Turkish welfare provision. In the case of INTENT, being a subsidiary of a company in another country could create greater uncertainty than for domestic firms and, hence, backed by the parent company they have become involved with philanthropic projects as a strategy for its reduction, through winning support from the potentially hostile host society. In the cases of GAYA and ASTON, these companies are both in industries where sponsorship is a common form of CCI and, thus, they have chosen to mimic their competitors' behaviour as a means to reduce their uncertainty in the market place. That is, they have used sponsorship to present a postive public profile.

Slack resources: As explained previously, slack has been defined as the disparity between the resources available to the organisation and the payments required to maintain the coalition of interests (Cyert and March, 1963). When adopting this concept for the field of CCI, the coalition refers to the group of stakeholders, both internal and external, who often have different preferences in respect of CCI activities. Moreover, under the behavioural theory lens it is contended that the availability of slack resources will lead the company to consider coalition requests, that is, in the CCI situation those of its stakeholders. On the other hand, during times of shortage of slack some stakeholders will not get their needs met. Slack has already been tested in Chapter 7 in accordance with this perspective as being one of the key determinants in CCI decision making. However, no relationship was found in the regression analyses. In this chapter the findings have been reporting for when the interviewees from the case companies were asked what happens during recession periods when there are few or no slack resources. The respondents from INTENT said that when this occurs employee volunteerism and gifts-in-kind types of CCI are substituted for cash donations and a similar approach of non-cash giving in times of hardship was also expressed by those from the other reponding companies. However, spokespeople from all of the companies stressed the importance of engaging in sustainable projects that they would able to continue funding even when there were few or no slack resources. That is, they all considered it bad for the firm's image if projects were wound up earlier than planned. During time of excess, in contrast to the behavioural theory, it emerged that the three Turkish firms satisfied the founder/owner's needs rather than attempting to placate their other stakeholders. In the case of INTENT, the emphasis was placed on fitting in with the parent company's set of rules on CCI rather than other stakeholders' needs, but local projects involved employees being awarded a fair degree of autonomy. Thus it can be seen, in contrast to the outcomes in Chapter 7, that changes in the levels of slack resources do have an impact on CCI decision making, but the ways in which this was reported are not entirely consistent with the behavioural theory of the firm propositions.

Organisational learning: According to the theory of interest, organisational learning occurs when organisations use standard operating procedures and rules of thumb to make and implement choices, and in the short run these procedures dominate the decision made (Cyert and March, 1963). Moreover, under these assumptions managers would revise and renew CCI activities based on previous experience and over time set rules for future practice. That is, these authors contended that organisations exhibit adaptive behaviour over time. The important point in this study is to observe whether or not feedback from past CCI activities have involved learning, whereby for new projects modifications to improve effectiveness have been undertaken by the four companies studied. However, from the responses during the interviews there is no direct evidence of philanthropic giving involving historical learning. That is, in spite of representatives from all the case study firms stating that they use a set criteria to guide their CCI decision making, none of them proffered that these had been modified as a result of reflections on earlier CCI activities. In any case, given the dominant role of the firm owner/founder, in relation to the Turkish companies for philanthropic giving and their aim of providing sustainability, there would have appeared to be few if any opportunities for managers in these companies to engage in retrospective organisational learning, as described above. Nevertheless, the fact that they do have criteria in place for guiding their CCI decision making implies that there will be organisational learning opportunuties in the future provided they are permitted to avail thierselves of them. Regarding sponsorship, GAYA and ASTON interviewees explained that their marketing departments responsible for such arrangements had carried out market research to improve their performance and so, in a sense, this can be seen to have involved organisational learning. However, no explicit changes to any procedures were highlighted by those engaging in sponsorship and all such activities appeared to be confined to fairly narrow commercial goals, such as promoting the brand.

9

Conclusions and Future Directions

9.1 Aims and Research Questions

This book has investigated the corporate community involvement (CCI) activities of the largest corporate givers in Turkey. Initially, there was examination of the extant research for two reasons: to establish what the existing studies have found regarding CCI and to identify the gaps in the field. Subsequently, having decided upon the locus for the investigation, the underpinning tenets of the behavioural theory of the firm were drawn upon to help shape the conceptual development and, thus, be able to construct a model containing testable determinants of CCI behaviour. Chapter 5 contained a comparative overview of CCI activities in Turkey with Western contexts, using data taken from a survey of 92 large Turkish firms as well as secondary data obtained from firm websites. In Chapter 6, the CCI structure in the survey companies was probed as well as their preferences in their giving. The conceptual model for establishing the determinants of the amounts and types of giving was operationalised through identification of the dependent and independent variables for the subsequent regression analysis in Chapter 7. This analysis had the goal of testing a set of hypotheses that predicted these determinants regarding CCI behaviour. In the final empirical chapter, Chapter 8, the aim was to provide more in-depth analysis regarding firm CCI decisions through case studies. Moreover, the information obtained from these was used to test the validity of some of the underlying concepts in the behavioural theory of the firm.

The three research questions restated below are now considered in turn in light of the evidence.

1. What are the determinants of CCI decision making and how do they affect CCI decisions and the choice of CCI behaviours?

2.   How are firms carrying out CCI activities?

3.   What is the firm process of taking for CCI decisions and choosing the relevant form(s) of CCI within the firm?

9.2 The Determinants Influencing the Choice of Corporate Community Involvement Behaviours

In order to elicit the determinants that influence CCI behaviour, firstly, the relevant extant literature was reviewed. Regarding this, it emerged that earlier studies investigating philanthropic giving have focused mainly on cash giving (for example, Levy and Shatto, 1978; Adams and Hardwick, 1998; Brammer and Millington 2004a; Gan, 2006; Brown, et al., 2006; Amato and Amato, 2007). A full list of the correlates between philanthropic giving and the influencing independent variables is provided in Table 2.6 and it can be seen that few studies have investigated philanthropic giving with regards to its influencing variables across all types of CCI activities (for example, Clarke, 1997; Zhang et al., 2009). At the same time the studies on cause-related marketing (CRM) and sponsorship conducted in the field of marketing were explored and it was decided that these should also be researched under the umbrella of CCI. The decision to investigate CCI behaviour drawing these aspects into one study formed a novel approach to the subject matter.

The aforementioned partial examination of the CCI activities has also resulted in limited conceptualisation of CCI behaviour determinants. That is, prior studies have depended on the orientation of the researcher and the type of CCI under investigation. Regarding this, it was found that conceptually most research into CCI has been framed by a variety of theories, namely: stakeholder theory (Besser, 1999; Meijer et al., 2006; Adams and Hardwick, 1998; Brammer and Millington, 2003); institutional theory (Burke et al., 1986; Bennett, 1998; Campbell et al., 2002; Madden et al., 2006); resource dependence theory (Seifert et al., 2004); agency theory (Clarke, 1997; Werber and Carter, 2002); and altruistic theory (Moir and Taffler, 2004; Campbell, 2006). As a result, there is still a need for theory (ies) that can provide explanatory power for CCI behaviour as a whole. Some progress to this end has been made in this research by applying the basic tenets of the behavioural theory of the firm to the four types of CCI in aggregated form.

As mentioned in Cyert and March's (1992) study, the behavioural theory of the firm provides an explanation for the various decision-making processes within the organisation as well as the reasons for action. Thus, it was decided to probe CCI decision making and the motivations behind it under the lens of this theory and to this end a conceptual model was built in Chapter 3. By drawing on the literature, three key determinants were identified: stakeholder pressure, the institutional climate and the availability of slack resources. This conceptual model was subsequently empirically tested in Chapter 7. The nature of this model meant that it is universally applicable and, hence, could be used in the first systematic analysis of CCI behaviours in Turkey. The investigation allowed for the second part of the first research question pertaining to: 'How do the variables influence CCI decisions and the choice of CCI behaviours?' Testable hypotheses were developed based on the conceptual framework and these were tested empirically using primary data. After identifying the dependent and independent variables the data was subjected to regression analysis. During this process several new measures were introduced, in particular, that for slack resources.

The findings revealed that the pressures from shareholder/investors and community groups positively affect companies' decisions to engage in CCI. Moreover, it emerged that government and customer stakeholder pressures have a negative significant impact on this, which is in contrast to the research outcomes in relation to developed countries. Further, normative institutional pressure was found to have a positive significant impact on total CCI. In addition, local Turkish companies contribute more to corporate giving than foreign ones, which is consistent with other studies (Committee Encouraging Corporate Philanthropy, 2008) as was the strongly positive significant influence found between size and CCI (Johnson, 1966; Levy and Shatto, 1978; Brammer and Millington, 2004b). Further, the firms engaged in CCI were investigated so as to establish the determinants of the kind of CCI activities that they chose to undertake. However, no significant relation was found in this respect.

9.3 The Way Corporate Community Involvement Activities are Carried Out

In Chapter 5, the scale and variety of forms of CCI in Turkey was probed by first considering the institutional environment. That is, a comprehensive set of social, economic and demographic secondary data was provided, some in a comparative form, for Turkey and selected Western nations, in order to identify the former's particularities that could help explain its corporate giving behaviour. For instance, it was elicited that leading philanthropists from business families play a major role in CCI activities, which are very heavily concentrated among the largest givers. It was also found that there is a high rate of giving amongst producers of consumer goods, thus providing some evidence of there being a strategic rationale. Moreover, as with other studies (Committee Encouraging Corporate Philathropy, 2008), it emerged that foreign-owned and controlled companies are poor givers and that there is a strong orientation of Turkish companies towards education, healthcare and the arts. In addition, as in some other countries, notably Germany, the majority of CCI expenditures in Turkey take the form of sponsorships.

Prior research has devoted limited attention to analysing who the recipients of donations from private companies are, and how companies develop preferences when they have to decide upon the areas to donate to. In order to address this, in the study in Chapter 6, how companies manage their CCI activities was explored by identifying the department from which they arranged their CCI activities. Secondly, the areas of priorities and exclusions were probed. Regarding the departmental issue, the findings suggest that there is no systematic pattern for Turkish companies in relation to the type of giving depending upon who is responsible for CCI. Moreover, it emerged that undertaking CCI activities within a corporate social responsibility (CSR) department is rare, although where this is the case the amount of giving is strikingly high. That is, it was found that most usually the companies placed their CCI activities under other business functions, which is consistent with research outcomes from Lebanon (Jamali and Mirsak, 2007), where such giving is not seen as a main function but as being an add-on benevolent function. Moreover, in both of the aforementioned chapters and in Chapter 8, there was evidence of giving to projects that would normally be the responsibility of the government in Western contexts, but cannot be supported by the state owing to the shortage of revenue. The ranking of the popular priorities and exclusions show similarities with the studies conducted in the UK and US where, overall, education, the environment and the arts and culture were found to be the most preferred areas for CCI and politics along with religion represent the highest exclusion categories.

9.4 The Process of Corporate Community Involvement Decisions

From the existing studies in the CCI field, it was observed that most of them have been quantitative (for example, Wang and Coffey, 1992; Clarke, 1997; Bennett, 1998; Besser, 1999; Dennis et al., 2007; Zhang et al., 2009), but it has been noted that qualitative studies can provide better understanding of the process of CCI decision making inside the firm. To this end, the outcomes of four qualitative case studies were presented Chapter 8. Here, the responses regarding CCI were examined under five categories: motivation, managerial structure, budget, slack resources and the criteria for decision making. The findings show that the companies generally separate philanthropic and sponsorship activities from each other. Moreover, other types of CCI, such as employee volunteerism, cash resources or gifts-in-kind, are undertaken within these two distinct types, if sponsorship is present. Further, it emerged that the investor/owner stakeholder has the biggest influence on managerial CCI decisions, with only a minor role being played by customer and community groups. In addition, industry and ownership type were found to be important determinants regarding which stakeholders had the greatest influence on CCI decisions. For instance, in relation to institutional types of motivation in the case companies, it was found that for Turkish companies there are strong cognitive motives.

However, by contrast, the respondents from the multinational company suggested that strategic normative pressures from the parent company was the driver behind their CCI activities. With regards to managerial structure, in all the case study companies, middle-level managers work on CCI projects, with the general manager/owner having the final say. In relation to the budgeting procedure, all the companies expressed their goal of having sustainability in their CCI projects. However, it was noticed that for local projects carried out by INTENT, these are reviewed by headquarters on a quarterly basis, unlike the Turkish firms where there are annual reviews, which suggests much tighter control and possibly greater strategic motivation for CCI behind the multinational's actions. Initial findings from the survey results presented in Chapter 7 found no positive effect between slack resources and CCI activities. However, the case study respondents all stated that when there were enough financial resources this would affect the budget in a positive manner. Moreover, they pointed out that if there was a decline in financial resources, they would seek alternative options, such as using their employees or gifts-in-kind for philanthropic projects to protect their sustainable projects, rather than setting up new ones. Further, a dramatic fall in the company's budget, all agreed, would result in the existing CCI activities being terminated or frozen. In sum, all four companies identified the same criteria for engaging in CCI activities – areas that are invested in, commercial gain from the CCI projects and their sustainability – but there were differences in the level of commitment to the local environment observed between the Turkish companies and the foreign multinational.

9.5 Theoretical Contributions

In the literature review chapter, two theoretical limitations were brought to light. Firstly, it was noted that the theories/perspectives adopted were only able to explain one type of CCI behaviour, and usually were not transferable to other types. Consequently, a general theory for CCI giving as a whole has yet to emerge. Secondly, the extant theories used to shed light on CCI decision making can only do so for a restricted aspect of it. For instance, stakeholder theory only allows for the examination of stakeholder pressure, institutional theory is limited to explaining institutional pressure and so on. The main theoretical contribution of this research endeavour has been to suggest that the behavioural theory of the firm provides a much more comprehensive perspective as it allows for investigation into all the different forms of CCI as well as eliciting the determinants behind total and particular CCI giving. To this end, a conceptual model was developed within the confines of the behavioural theory of the firm, which covers stakeholder pressures, the institutional climate and the availability of slack resources and was subsequently tested. Moreover, it is posited that this behavioural theory of the firm perspective can be applied in any context, so as to identify the influences of institutional, cultural and socio-political factors in the different settings, which would provide deeper understanding of the various configurations regarding these across the globe in terms of their CCI behaviour. Further, the conceptual model, by adopting the tenets of the behavioural theory, takes into account the complexity of managerial decision making in CCI recognised by many scholars in relation to the multiple internal/external pressures that drive the allocation of the available resources. Another theoretical contribution was provided in Chapter 8 when an exercise in the interpretation of the managerial decision-making responses regarding CCI was undertaken, by matching the reality with the predictions expected according to the core concepts of the theory. That is, applying reported behaviour to the core concepts helped to explain the process of firms' CCI activities and therefore extended the utility of the behavioural theory of the firm.

9.6 Practical Contributions

As explained earlier, this book is the first study that has investigated CCI in Turkey and its outcomes contain some information which may be beneficial for managerial practice in that country. Firstly, the study in Chapter 5 presented descriptive information about the concentration of giving, the average expenditure on CCI per company, which sectors prefer to engage in what type of CCI, and how ownership status influences the choice of CCI type. In relation to this, managers of Turkish companies wishing to engage in CCI or seek out new areas for giving can see what other companies in their sector have donated to successfully in terms of firm strategic behaviour and, hence, use their CCI to position themselves favourably within the market. Secondly, in Chapters 7 and 8 the findings underlined that the investor/owner is the dominant stakeholder in Turkey and knowledge of this would help foreign companies wanting to participate in the Turkish market understand how it works. In addition, knowing that a lot of CCI is viewed as philanthropy could prove useful to them. Moreover, newcomers to the Turkish market, both domestic and international, need to be appraised of the fact that industry is leading the way on CCI/CSR legislation rather than the government and, therefore, they may well need to be very proactive on such matters, finding allies in the business community if they see the need for change.

Thirdly, the data in this book shows that CCI in Turkey is in a transition stage and, thus, it is important that Turkish companies wanting to operate in developed countries need to be aware that practices in those countries are at a mature stage. For instance, they have to publish a CSR report every year based on one or more of the frameworks that have been developed according to various reporting guidelines, such as Global Reporting Initiatives (GRI), The Fair Labour Association, GoodCorporation's Standard and the United Nations Global Compact. Moreover, they need to be cognisant of the fact that in these countries customer activist groups are one of the biggest stakeholders that put pressure on companies, who consequently strive to be members of CSR indices such as the FTSE4GOOD, the Dow Jones Sustainability Group, AccountAbility and so on, so as to have positive visibility in the market, thereby protecting their legitimacy. Regarding these, most of the biggest companies in Turkey have started to act in this way, becoming members of GRIs or the United Nations Global Compact, but very few publish reports on CCI/CSR and, even if they do, most do not do so every year. In sum, the outcomes in this book could prove helpful to Turkish companies wishing to engage in developed country markets by explaining the underpinning environment prevalent regarding these practices.

Finally, the data in this book show that the companies surveyed mostly see their CCI activities as a part of their CSR strategies. Moreover, in the case studies in Chapter 8 it became evident that companies see their CCI decisions as a part of their core strategic business decisions. That is, although there is a debate as to whether CSR and corporate financial performance are linked in the academic literature (McWilliams and Siegel, 2001), the case companies see their CCI activities as potentially providing commercial gain, increased reputation, a long-term loyal relationship with their customers, increased employee motivation and so on.

9.7 Limitations and Directions for Future Research

This book has limitations which point to avenues for improvement when building on the outcomes in future research. Firstly, the number of observations is small when compared with previous studies, because time and resources for collecting the data from the survey questionnaires were restricted by the planned trajectory for the book. Regarding this, prior to the empirical work this researcher underestimated the effort required to collect a sufficient number of responses, in particular, owing to her being somewhat unaware of the gatekeeper procedures needing to be surmounted. Further, the small sample size probably led to the very limited results regarding the determinants of different types of giving, which may have been overcome were the sample size substantially larger. Moreover, Turkey's closed system with regard to the sharing of a company's financial resources information prevented the collection of data about profitability or availability of cash resources as a measurement of slack resources, resulting in a proxy having to be identified, which probably did not produce the robustness desired that would have been possible to achieve were this situation otherwise. Future research will need to take the above into account when designing research frameworks in non-Western contexts. Secondly, the data used in this book only covers a single accounting period and therefore can only reflect time-specific effects, which do not capture the dynamics of CCI in Turkey today nor changes in the country's economic fortunes, that is, which way things are moving, and a longitudinal study is needed to redress this.

The conceptual model employed in this book and the empirical outcomes could act as the basis for researchers wishing to investigate CCI activities in their entirety in different institutional environments. That is, these provide new insights into the determinants of CCI from a holistic perspective, thus, overcoming the partial approach in the described extant literature. Finally, it is posited that the questionnaire approach adopted for this book would prove useful for researchers looking at the relationship between companies and their communities through CCI in non-Western contexts, where the weak institutional environment means that centrally collected data is of poor quality or does not exist.

References

Adams, G.L. and Lamont, B.T. (2003). 'Knowledge management systems and developing sustainable competitive advantage', *Journal of Knowledge Management*, Vol.7, No.2, pp.142–154.

Adams, M. and Hardwick, P. (1998). 'An analysis of corporate donations: United Kingdom Evidence', *Journal of Management Studies*, Vol.35, No.5.

Agle, B.R., Mitchell, R.K. and Sonnenfeld, J.A. (1999). 'Who matters to CEOS? An investigation of stakeholder attributes and salience, corporate performance, and CEO values', *Academy of Management Journal*, Vol.42, No.5, pp.507–525.

Aktaş, A.Z. (2005). 'Turkish private/Public Universities and Information Society in Europe', available at http://www.intconfhighered.org/Aktas,%20Ziya.doc (accessed 3.03.2010).

Akyüz, Y. and Boratav, K. (2003). 'The Making of the Turkish Financial Crisis', *World Development*, Vol.31, No.9, September, pp.1549–66.

Amato, L.H. and Amato, C.H. (2007). 'The effects of firm size and industry on corporate giving', *Journal of Business Ethics*, Vol.72, No.3, pp.229–241.

Anderson, P.F. (1982). 'Marketing, strategic planning and the theory of the firm', *Journal of Marketing*, Vol.46, No.2, Spring, pp.15–26.

Apostolopoulou, A. and Papadimitriou, D. (2004). 'Welcome home: Motivations and objectives of the 2004 Grand National Olympic sponsors', *Sport Marketing Quarterly*, Vol.13, No.4, pp.180–192.

Ararat, M. and Ugur, M. (2003). 'Corporate governance in Turkey: An overview and some policy recommendations', *Corporate Governance*, Vol.3, No.1, pp.58–75.

Arber, S. (2005). 'Secondary Analysis of Survey Data', in Gilbert, N. (ed.) *Researching Social Life*, pp.269–287, Sage Publications: London.

Arupalam, W. and Stoneman, P. (1995). 'An investigation into the giving by large corporate donors to UK charities 1979–86', *Applied Economic*, Vol.27, pp.935–45.

Atkinson, L. and Galaskiewicz, J. (1988). 'Stock ownership and company contributions to charity', *Administrative Science Quarterly*, Vol.33, pp.82–100.

Aupperle, K.E., Carroll, A.B. and Hatfield, J.D. (1985). 'An empirical examination of the relationship between corporate social responsibility and profitability', *Academy of Management Journal*, Vol.28, No.2, pp.446–463.

Austin, J.E. (2003). 'Marketing's role in cross-sector collaboration', *Journal of Nonprofit and Business Sector Collaboration*, Vol.11, No.1, pp.23–39.

Australian Government Statistical, Clearing House, (2005). 'Business Community Involvement Survey', McNair Ingenuity Research Pty Ltd., www.mcnairingenuity.com (accessed 10. 06.2006).

Baghi, I., Rubaltelli, E. and Tedeschi, M. (2009). 'A strategy to communicate corporate social responsibility: Cause related marketing and its dark side', *Corporate Social Responsibility and Environmental Management*, Vol.16, No.1, pp.15–16.

Barney, J.B. (1991). 'Firm resources and sustained competitive advantage', *Journal of Management*, Vol.17, No.1, pp.99–120.

Barone, M.J., Miyazaki, A.D. and Taylor, K.Λ. (2000). 'The influence of cause-related marketing on consumer choice: Does one good turn deserve another?', *Journal of Academy of Marketing Sciences*, Vol.28, No.2, pp.248–262.

Bartkus, B.R., Morris, S.A. and Seifert, B. (2002). 'Governance and corporate philanthropy: Restraining Robin Hood?', *Business & Society*, Vol.41, No.3, pp.319–344.

Basil, D.Z. and Herr, P.M. (2003). 'Dangerous donations? The effects of cause-related marketing on charity attitude', *Journal of Nonprofits & Public Sector Marketing*, Vol.11, No.1, pp.59–76.

Baum, J.A.C., Rowley, T.J., Shipilov, A.V. and Chuang, Y.T. (2005). 'Dancing with strangers: Aspiration performance and the search for underwriting syndicate partners', *Administrative Science Quarterly*, Vol.50, pp.536–575.

Bennett, G., Ferreria, M., Lee, J. and Polite, F. (2009). 'The role of involvement in sports and sport spectatorship in sponsor's brand use: The case of Mountain Dew and action sports sponsorship', *Sport Marketing Quarterly*, Vol.18, No.1, pp.14–24.

Bennett, R. (1998). 'Corporate philanthropy in France, Germany, and the UK', *International Marketing Review*, Vol.15, No.6, pp.458–475.

Berglind, M. and Nakata, C. (2005). 'Cause-related marketing. More buck than bang?', *Business Horizons*, Vol.48, No.5, pp.443–453.

Besser, T.L. (1999). 'Community involvement and the perception of success among small business operators in small towns', *Journal of Small Business Operators in Small Towns*, Vol.37, No.6, pp.16–29.

Bikmen, F. (2003). 'Corporate philanthropy in Turkey: Building on tradition, adapting to change', *SEAL – Social Economy and Law Project Journal*, Autumn, p.2.

Black, L.D. (2006). 'Corporate social responsibility as capability: The case of BHP BILLITON', *Journal of Corporate Citizenship*, Vol.23, No.14, pp.25–38.

Boatsman, J.R. and Gupta, S. (2001). 'Taxes and corporate charity empirical evidence from micro-level panel data', *National Tax Journal*, Vol.XIIX, No.2, pp.193–213.

Boland, L.A. (1991). 'Current Views on Economic Positivism', in Greenaway, D., Bleaney, M. and Stewart, I. (eds) *Companion to Contemporary Economic Thought*, pp.88–104., Routledge: London and New York.

Bourgeois, L.J. (1981). 'On the measurement of organizational slack', *Academy of Management Review*, Vol.6, No.1, pp.29–39.

Bowen, F. (2007). 'Corporate social strategy: Competing views from two theories of the firm', *Journal of Business Ethics*, Vol.75, pp.97–113.

Brace, N., Kemp, R. and Snelgar, R. (2009). *SPSS for Psycologists*, Palgrave Macmillan, Basingstoke.

Brammer, S. and Millington, A. (2003). 'The effect of stakeholder preferences, organizational structure and industry type on corporate community involvement', *Journal of Business Ethics*, Vol.45, No.3, pp.213–226.

Brammer, S. and Millington, A. (2004a). 'Stakeholder pressure, organizational size, and the allocation of departmental responsibility for the management of corporate charitable giving', *Business & Society*, Vol.43, No.3, pp.268–295.

Brammer, S. and Millington, A. (2004b). 'The development of corporate charitable contributions in the UK: A stakeholder analysis', *Journal of Management Studies*, Vol.41, No.8, pp.1412–1434.

Brammer, S. and Millington, A. (2005). 'Profit maximisation vs. agency: An analysis of charitable giving by UK firms', *Cambridge Journal of Economic*, Vol.29, No.4, pp.517–534.

Brammer, S. and Pavelin, S. (2005). 'Corporate community contributions in the United Kingdom and the United States', *Journal of Business Ethics*, Vol.56, No.1, pp.15–26.

Brammer, S., Pavelin, S. and Porter, L.A. (2009). 'Corporate charitable giving, multinational companies and countries of concern', *Journal of Management Studies*, Vol.46, No.4, pp.575–596.

Brammer, S., Williams, G. and Zinkin, J. (2007). 'Religion and attitudes to corporate social responsibility in a large cross-country sample', *Journal of Business Ethics*, Vol.71, No.3, pp.229–243.

Bright, D. (2006). 'Dialogue, virtuousness is necessary for genuineness in corporate philanthropy', *Academy of Management Review*, Vol.31, No.3, pp.752–754.

Broderick, A., Jogi, A. and Garry, T. (2003). 'Tickled pink: The personal meaning of cause related marketing for customers', *Journal of Marketing Management*, Vol.19, Nos 5–6, pp.583–610.

Bromiley, P. (2005). *The Behavioral Foundations of Strategic Management*. Blackwell Publishing, Malden, MA.

Brønn, P.S. (2006). 'Building corporate brands through community involvement: Is it exportable? The case of the Ronald McDonald House in Norway', *Journal of Marketing Communications*, Vol.12, No.4, pp.309–320.

Brown, W.O., Helland, E. and Smith, J.K. (2006). 'Corporate philanthropic practices', *Journal of Corporate Finance*, Vol.12, No.1, pp.855–877.

Bryman, A. (2001). *Social Research Methods*. Oxford University Press: New York.

Bryman, A. (2004). *Social Research Methods*. Oxford University Press: New York, 2nd Edition.

Buchholtz, A.K., Amason, A.C. and Rutherford, M.A. (1999). 'Beyond resources', *Business & Society*, Vol.38, No.2, pp.167–187.

Bugra, A. (1994). *State and Business in Modern Turkey, A Comparative Study*. State University of New York Press, New York.

Burke, L. and Logsdon, J.M. (2006). 'How social responsibility pays off', *Long Range Planning*, Vol.29, No.4, pp.495–502.

Burke, L., Logsdon, J.M., Mitchell, W., Reiner, M. and Vogel, D. (1986). 'Corporate community involvement in the San Francisco Bay Area', *California Management Review*, Vol.XXVIII, No.3, pp.122–141.

Burlingame, F.D. and Frishkoff, P.A. (1996). 'How Does Firm Size Affect Corporate Philanthropy?' in Burlingame, F.D and Young, D.R. (eds), *Corporate Philanthropy at the Crossroads*, pp.86–105, Indiana University Press.

Bush, T. (2002). 'Slack in public administration: Conceptual and methodological issues', *Managerial Auditing Journal*, Vol.17, No.3, pp.153–159.

Bussell, H. and Forbes, D. (2001). 'Understanding the volunteer market: The what, where, who, and why of volunteering', *International Journal of Nonprofit and Voluntary Sector Marketing*, Vol.7, No.3, pp.244–257.

Butler, R. (1991). *Designing Organizations: A Decision-Making Perspective*. Routledge, New York.

Calderón-Martínez, A., Más-Ruiz, F.J. and Nicolau-Gonzálbez, J.L. (2005). 'Commercial and philanthropic sponsorship', *International Journal of Market Research*, Vol.47, No.1, pp.75–99.

Campbell, D. and Craig, T. (2005). *Organisations and the Business Environment*, 2nd Edition. Elsevier Butterworth-Heinemann, Oxford.

Campbell, D., Moore, G. and Metzger, M. (2002). 'Corporate philanthropy in the UK 1985–2000: Some empirical findings', *Journal of Business Ethics*, Vol.39, No.1–2, pp.29–41. Campbell, J.L. (2006). 'Institutional analysis and the paradox of corporate social responsibility', *American Behavioral Scientist*, Vol.49, No.7, pp.925–938.

Campbell, J.L. (2007). 'Why would corporations behave in socially responsible ways? An institutional theory of corporate social responsibility', *Academy of Management Review*, Vol.32, No.3, pp.946–967.

Campbell, L., Gulas, C.S., and Gruca, T.S. (1999). 'Corporate giving behavior and decision-maker social consciousness', *Journal of Business Ethics*, Vol.19, No.4, pp.375–383.

Capital magazine (2008). 'Capital magazine's 500 Biggest Private Companies index'.

Carroll, A.B. (1979). 'A three-dimensional conceptual model of corporate performance', *Academy of Management Review*, Vol.4, No.4, pp.497–505.

Carroll, A.B. (1991). 'The pyramid of corporate social responsibility: Toward the moral management of organizational stakeholder', *Business Horizons*, July–August, pp.39–48.

Cathell, R.B. and Baggaley, A.R. (1960). 'The salient variable similarity index for factor matching', *British Journal of Statistics in Psychology*, Vol.13, pp.33–46.

Celik, O. and Ecer, A. (2009). 'Efficiency in accounting education: Evidence from Turkish Universities', *Critical Perspectives on Accounting*, Vol.20, No.5, pp.614–634.

Chadwick, S. and Thwaites, D. (2005). 'Managing sport sponsorship programs: Lessons from a critical assessment of English soccer', *Journal of Advertising Research*, September, pp.328–338.

Chang, G.A. (2007). 'Multiple Regression, An Introduction to Multiple Regression Prforming a Multiple Regression on SPSS', http://www.palgrave.com/PDFs/0333734718.Pdf (accessed 09.07.2009).

Chang, T. and Chen, S. (1998). 'Market orientation, service quality and business profitability: A conceptual model and empirical evidence', *The Journal of Services Marketing*, Vol.12, No.4, pp.246–264.

Charities Aid Foundation (CAF) website, http://www.cafonline.org/ (accessed 03.10.2007).

Charities Aid Foundation (CAF) website, http://www.cafonline.org/ (accessed 07.05.2009).

Chen, W. and Miller, K.D. (2007). 'Situational and institutional determinants of firms' R&D search intensity', *Strategic Management Journal*, Vol.28, No.4, pp.369–381.

Chong, D. (2003). 'Revisiting business and the arts', *Nonprofit and Business Sector Collaboration*, Vol.11, No.1, pp.151–165.

Christensen, S.R. (2006). 'Measuring consumer reactions to sponsoring partnerships based upon emotional and attitudinal responses', *International Journal of Market Research*, Vol.48, No.1, pp.61–80.

Clarke, J. (1997). 'Shareholders and corporate community involvement in Britain', *Business Ethics: A European Review*, Vol.6, No.4, pp.201–207.

Clarkson, M.B.E. (1995). 'A stakeholder framework for analyzing and evaluating corporate social performance', *The Academy of Management Review*, Vol.20, No.1, pp.92–117.

Cliffe, S.J. and Motion, J. (2005). 'Building contemporary brands: A sponsorship-based strategy', *Journal of Business Research*, Vol.58, No.8, pp.1068–1077.

Committee Encouraging Corporate Philantropy (2009). 'Giving in Numbers', www.CorporatePhilanthropy.org/resources (accessed 12.10.2010).

Coppetti, C., Wentzel, D., Tomczak, T. and Henkel, S. (2009). 'Improving incongurent sponsorships through articulation of the sponsorship and audience participation', *Journal of Marketing Communications*, Vol.15, No.1, pp.17–34.

Cornwell, T.B. and Maignan, I. (1998). 'An international review of sponsorship research', *Journal of Advertising*, Vol.27, No.1, pp.1–21.

Craig, W. (2002). 'Business ethics and stakeholder theory', *Business Ethics Quaterly*, Vol.12, No.2, pp.113–143.

Creswell, J.W. (2007). *Qualitative Inquiry & Research Design*, 2nd Edition. Sage Publications, Inc.

Creswell, J.W. and Clark, V.L. (2007). *Designing and Conducting Mixed Methods Research*. Sage Publications, Inc.

Cyert, R.M. and March, J.G. (1963). *A Behavioral Theory of the Firm*. Prentice Hall, Englewood Cliffs, NJ.

Cyert, R.M. and March, J.G. (1992). *A Behavioral Theory of the Firm*, 2nd Edition. Prentice Hall, Englewood Cliffs, NJ.

Dale, A., Arber, S. and Procter, M. (1988). *Doing Secondary Analysis*. Unwin Hyman, London.

Data Monitor (2009), http://www.datamonitor.com/ (accessed 20.02.2010).

Davis, J.H. Schoorman, F.D. and Donaldson, L. (1997). 'Toward a stewardship theory of management', *Academy of Management Review*, Vol.22, No.1, pp.20–47.

De George, R.T. (1993). *Competing with Integrity in International Business*. Oxford University Press, New York.

De Jongh, D. (2004). 'A stakeholder perspective on managing social risk in South Africa: Responsibility or accountability?', *Journal of Corporate Citizenship*, Vol.15, Autumn, pp.27–31.

Deloitte Recruiting Policy Example (2007). Deloitte website, www.deloitte.com/us/asb (accessed 29.04.2009).

Déniz, M.C. and Oberty, C.Z. (2004). 'The assessment of the stakeholders' environment in the new age of knowledge: An empirical study of the influence of the organisational structure', *Business Ethics: A European Review*, Vol.13, No.4, pp.372–388.

Dennis, B.S., Buchholtz, A.K. and Butts, M.M. (2007). 'The nature of giving: A theory of planned behavior examination of corporate philanthropy', *Business & Society*, Vol.48, pp.360–384.

Denzin, N.K. and Lincoln, Y.S. (1994). *Handbook of Qualitative Research*. Sage Publications, London.

Denzin, N.K. and Lincoln, Y.S. (2003). 'Introduction, The Discipline and Practice of Qualitative Research', in Denzin, N.K. and Lincoln, Y.S. (eds), *Collecting and Interpreting Qualitative Materials*, pp.1–47, Sage Publications.

DiMaggio, P. (1988). 'Interest and Agency in Institutional Theory', in Zucker, L.G. (ed.), *Institutional Patterns and Organisations: Culture and Environment*, pp.3–21, Ballinger, Cambridge.

DiMaggio, P., and Powell, W.W. (1983). 'The iron cage revisited: Institutional isomorphism and collective rationality in organizational fields', *American Sociological Review*, Vol.48, No.2, pp.147–160.

DiMaggio, P.J. and Powell, W.W. (1991). 'Introduction', in Powell, W.W. and DiMaggio, P.J. (eds), *The New Institutionalism in Organisational Analysis*, pp.1–38, University of Chicago Press, Chicago.

Dimmick, D.E. and Murray, V.V. (1978). 'Correlates of substantive policy decisions in organizations: The case of human resource management', *Academy of Management Journal*, Vol.21, No.4, pp.611–623.

Donaldson, L. and Davis, J.H. (1991). 'Stewardship theory or agency theory: CEO governance and shareholder', *Australian Journal of Management*, Vol.16, No.1, pp.49–64.

Donaldson, T. and Preston, L.E. (1995). 'The stakeholder theory of the corporation: Concepts, evidence and implications', *Academy of Management Review*, Vol.20, No.1, pp.65–91.

Drennan, J.C. and Cornwell, T.B. (2004). 'Emerging strategies for sponsorship on the Internet', *Journal of Marketing Management*, Vol.20, No.9/10, pp.1123–1146.

Drucker, F.P. (1984). 'The new meaning of corporate social responsibility', *California Management Review*, Vol.XXVI, No.2, pp.53–63.

Drumwright, M.E. (1996). 'Company advertising with a social dimension: The role of noneconomic criteria', *Journal of Marketing*, Vol.60, No.4, pp.71–87.

Economist Intelligence Unit (1980). *Sponsorship*, Special Report No.86, quoted in Meenaghan, J.A. (1983). 'Commercial sponsorship', *European Journal of Marketing*, Vol.17, No.7, pp.5–73.

Economist Inteligence Unit Report (2008), Country Profile : Turkey.

Eilbirt, H. and Parket, R.G. (1973). 'The corporate responsibility officer: A new position on the organization chart', *Business Horizons*, Vol.16, pp.45–51.

Eisenhardt, K.M. (1989). 'Agency theory: An assessment and review', *Academy of Management Review*, Vol.14, No.4, pp.57–74.

Etang, J. (1994). 'Public relations and corporate social responsibility: Some issues arising', *Journal of Business Ethics*, Vol.13, No.2, pp.111–123.

Etzioni, A. 2010). 'Behavioral economics: A methodological note', *Journal of Economic Psycology*, Vol.31, No.1, pp.51–54.

European Commission website, http://ec.europa.eu/enterprise/csr/index_en.htm (accessed 21.02.2007).

Fama, E.F. (1980). 'Agency problems and the theory of the firm', *Journal of Political Economy*, Vol.88, No.2, pp.288–307.

Farrelly, F. and Quester, P.G. (2003). 'What drives renewal of sponsorship principal/agent relationship?', *Journal of Advertising Research*, Vol.43, No.4, pp.353–360.

Farrelly, F., Quester, P. and Burton, R. (2006). 'Changes in sponsorship value: Competencies and capabilities of successful sponsorship relationships', *Industrial Marketing Management*, Vol.35, No.8, pp.1016–1026.

Farrelly, F.J. and Quester, P.G. (2005). 'Examining important relationship quality constructs of the focal sponsorship exchange', *Industrial Marketing Management*, Vol.34, No.3, pp.211–219.

Field, A. (2005). *Discovering Statistics Using SPSS*, 2nd Edition. SAGE Publications, London.

File, K.M. and Prince, R.A. (1998). 'Cause related marketing and corporate philanthropy in the privately held enterprise', *Journal of Business Ethics*, Vol.17, No.14, pp.1529–1539.

Fletcher, K. (2007). 'Turkey Taking Growth to Next Level', *IMF Survey Magazine: Countries & Regions*, http://www.imf.org/external/pubs/ft/survey/so/2007/CAR0726B.htm (accessed 04.10.2011).

Flick, U. (2006). *An Introduction to Qualitative Research*. Sage Publications, London.

Forbes list of 'Billionaire Cities' in *The Sunday Times* article 'Turkey's new rich find the Midas touch' (accessed 09.03.2008).

Freeman, R.E. (1984). *Strategic Management: A Stakeholder Approach*. Pitman, Boston.

Frooman, J. (1999). 'Stakeholder influence strategies', *Academy of Management Review*, Vol.24, No.2, pp.191–205.

Fry, L.W., Reim, G.D. and Meiners, R.E. (1982). 'Corporate contributions: Altruistic or for-profit?' *Academy of Management Journal*, Vol.25, No.1, pp.94–106.

Frynas, J.G. (2001). 'The false development promise of Corporate Social Responsibility: Evidence from multinational oil companies', *International Affairs*, Vol.81, No.3, pp.581–598.

Fülöp, G., Hisrich, R.D. and Szegedi, K. (1999). 'Business ethics and social responsibility in transition economies', *Journal of Management Development*, Vol.19, No.1, pp.5–31.

Galaskiewicz, J. (1997) 'An urban grants economy revisited: Corporate charitable contributions in the Twin Cities, 1979–81,1987–89' *Administrative Science Quarterly*, Vol.42, No.3, pp.445–471.

Gan, A. (2006). 'The impact of public scrutiny on corporate philanthropy', *Journal of Business Ethics*, Vol.69, No.3, pp.217–236.

García, I., Gibaja, J.J. and Mijuka, A. (2003). 'A study on the effect of cause-related marketing on the attitude towards the brand: The case of Pepsi in Spain', *Nonprofit and Business Sector Collaboration*, Vol.11, No.1, pp.111–135.

Gardner, M.P. and Shuman, P.J. (1987). 'Sponsorship: An important component of the promotions mix', *Journal of Advertising*, Vol.16, No.1, pp.11–17.

Garry, T., Broderick, A.J. and Lahiffe, K. (2008). 'Tribal motivation in sponsorship and its influence on sponsor relationship development and corporate identity', *Journal of Marketing Management*, Vol.24, No.9–10, pp.959–977.

Geert Hofstede Cultural Dimensions, http://geert-hofstede.com/turkey.html (accessed 07.08.2009).

Geiger, S.W. and Cashen, L.H. (2002) 'A multidimensional examination of slack and its impact on innovation', *Journal of Managerial Issues*, Vol.14, No.1, pp.68–54.

Gigerenzer, G. and Selten, R. (2002). *Bounded Rationality Adaptive Toolbox*. MIT Press.

Gilder, de D., Schuyt, T.N.M. and Breedijk, M. (2005). 'Effects of an employee volunteering program on the work force: The ABN-Amro case', *Journal of Business Ethics*, Vol.61, No.2, pp.143–152.

Gnyawali, D.R. (1996). 'Corporate Social Performance: An International Perspective', in Prasad, S.B. and Boyd, B.K. (eds), *Advances in International Comparative Management*, pp.251–273, JAI Press, Greenwich, CT.

Göcenoğlu, C. and Onan, I. (2009). 'Turkey Corporate Social Responsibility Baseline Report', http://www.undp.org.tr/publicationsDocuments/CSR_Report_en.pdf (accessed 24.10.2008).

Gorsuch, R.L. (1974). *Factor Analysis*. Saunders, PA.

Grau, S.L., Garretson, J.A. and Pirsch, J. (2007). 'Cause related marketing: An exploratory study of campaign donation structures issues', *Journal of Nonprofit & Public Sector Marketing*, Vol.10, No.2, pp.60–91.

Greenwood, R. and Hinings, C.R. (1996). 'Understanding radical organisational change: Bringing together the old and the new institutionalism', *Academy of Management Review*, Vol.21, No.4, pp.1022–1054.

Griffin, J.J. and Mahon, J.G. (1997). 'The corporate social performance and corporate financial performance debate', *Business & Society*, Vol.36, No.1, pp.5–31.

Grohs, R., Wagner, U. and Vsetecka, S. (2004). 'Assessing the effectiveness of sport sponsorships – an empirical examination', *Schmalenbach Business Review*, Vol.56, April, pp.119–138.

Guion, L.A. (2006). 'Conductiong an In-Depth Interview', This document is FCS6012, one of a series of the Family Youth and Community Sciences Department, Florida Cooperative Extension Service, Institute of Food and Agricultural Sciences, University of Florida.

Guth, W.D. and Tagiuri, R. (1965). 'Personal values and corporate strategy', *Harvard Business Review*, September–October, pp.123–132.

Hajjat, M.M. (2003). 'Effect of cause-related marketing on attitudes and purchase intensions: The moderating role of cause involvement and donation size', *NonProfit and Business Sector Collabouration*, Vol.11, No.1, p.93–109.

Hakim, C. (1982). *Secondary Analysis in Social Research*. Allen and Unwin, London.

Haley, U.C.V. (1991). 'Corporate contributions as managerial masques: Reframing corporate contributions as strategies to influence society', *Journal of Management Studies*, Vol.28, No.5, pp.485–510.

Hamil, S. (1999). 'Corporate community involvement: A case for regulatory reform', *Business Ethics: A European Review*, Vol.8, No.1, pp.14–25.

Hamlin, R.P. and Wilson, T. (2004). 'The impact of cause branding on consumer reactions to products: Does product/cause 'fit' really matter?', *Journal of Marketing Management*, Vol.20, No.7–8, pp.663–681.

Harris, R. (2005). 'When giving means talking: Public relations, sponsorship, and morally marginal donors', *Public Relations Review*, Vol.31, No.4, pp.486–491.

Harrison, J.S. and Freeman, R.E. (1999). 'Stakeholders, social responsibility, and performance: Empirical evidence and theoretical perspectives', *Academy of Management Journal*, Vol.42, No.5, pp.479–485.

Harvey, B. (2001). 'Measuring the effects of sponsorships', *Journal of Advertising Research*, Vol.41, December, pp.59–65.

Henriques, I. and Sadorsky, P. (1996). 'The determinants of an environmentally responsive firm: An empirical approach', *Journal of Environmental Economics and Management*, Vol.30, No.3, pp.381–395.

Hess, D., Rogovsky, N. and Dunfee, T.W. (2002). 'The next wave of corporate community involvement: Corporate social initiatives', *California Management Review*, Vol.44, No.2, pp.110–125.

Hickman, T.M., Katherine, E.L. and James, C.W. (2005). 'A social identities perspective on the effects of corporate sport sponsorship on employees', *Sport Marketing Quarterly*, Vol.14, No.3, pp.148–157.

Himmelstein, J.L. (1997). *Looking Good & Doing Good*. Indiana University Press, Bloomington and Indianapolis.

Hinings, B. and Greenwood, R. (1988). 'The Normative Prescription of Organisations', in Zucker, L.G. (ed)., *Institutional Patterns and Organisations: Culture and Environment*, pp.53–70, Ballinger, Cambridge.

Hoek, J. and Gendall, P. (2008). 'An analysis of consumers' responses to cause related marketing', *Journal of Nonprofit & Public Sector Marketing*, Vol.20, No.2, pp.283–297.

Hoffman, A.J. (2001). 'Linking organizational and field-level analyses: The diffusion of corporate environmental practice', *Organization & Environment*, Vol.14, No.2, pp.133–156.

Hofstede, G. (1983), 'Dimensions of National Cultures in Fifty Countries and Three Regions', in Deregowski, J.B., Dziurawiec, S., Annis, R.C. (eds), *Explications in Cross-cultural Psychology*, pp.335–355, Swets & Zeitlinger, Lisse.

Holmes, J.H. and Kilbane, C.J. (1993). 'Cause-related marketing: Selected effects of price and charitable donations', *Journal of Nonprofit & Public Sector Marketing*, Vol.1, No.4, pp.67–83.

Howell. D.C. (2002). *Statictical Methods for Psychology*, 5th Edition. Pacific Grove, Duxbury.

Husted, B. (2003). 'Governance choices for corporate social responsibility: To contribute, collaborate or internalize?', *Long Range Planning*, Vol.36, No.5, pp.481–498.

Husted, B. and Allen, D. (2006). 'Corporate social responsibility in the multinational enterprise: strategic and institutional approaches', *Journal of International Business Studies*, Vol.37, pp.838–849.

ICCA CSR Report (2008), published by International Congress and Convention Association, http://www.iccaworld.com/cnt/docs/ICCA-CSR-Report-2008.pdf (accessed 23.10.2010).

Inselbag, I. (1973), 'Financing decisions and the theory of the firm', *Journal of Financial and Quantitative Analysis*, Vol.8, December, pp.763–776.

Jamali, D. and Mirsak J. (2007). 'Corporate social responsibility (CSR) theory and practice in a developing country context', *Journal of Business Ethics*, Vol.72, pp.243–262.

Jennings, P.D. and Zandbergen, P.A. (1995). 'Ecologically sustainable organizations: An institutional approach', *Academy of Management Review*, Vol.20, No.4, pp.1015–1052

Jensen, M.C. and Meckling, W.H. (1976). 'Theory of the firm: Managerial behavior, agency costs, and ownership structure', *Journal of Financial Economic*, Vol.3, No.4, pp.305–360.

Jepperson, R.L. (1991). 'Institutions, Institutional Effects, and Institutionalism', in Powell, W.W. and DiMaggio, P.J. (eds), *The New Institutionalism in Organizational Analysis*, pp.143–163, University of Chicago Press, Chicago.

Johnson, O. (1966). 'Corporate philanthropy: An analysis of corporate contribution', *The Journal of Business*, Vol.39, No.4, pp.489–504.

Johnson, R.A. and Greening, D.W. (1999). 'The effects of corporate governance and institutional ownership types on corporate social performance', *Academy of Management Journal*, Vol.42, No.5, pp.564–576.

Jones, A. (2010). 'Making Sense of Corporate Social Responsibility', http://www.iaf.gov/grants/downloads/csr_eng.pdf (accessed 15.01.2011).

Jones, T.M. (1995). 'Instrumental stakeholder theory: A synbook of ethics and economics', *Academy of Management Review*, Vol.20, No.2, pp.404–437.

Juholin, E. (2004). 'For business for the good of all? A Finnish approach to corporate social responsibility', *Corporate Governance*, Vol.4, No.3, pp.20–31.

Kaler, J. (2006). 'Evaluating stakeholder theory', *Journal of Business Ethics*, Vol.69, pp.249–268.

Kapopoulos, P. and Lazaretou, S. (2007). 'Corporate ownership structure and firm performance: Evidence from Greek firms,' *Corporate Governance: An International Review*, Vol.15, No.2, pp.144–158.

Keller, K.L. and Aaker, D.A. (1998). 'The impact of corporate marketing on a company's brand extensions', *Corporate Reputation Review*, Vol.1, No.4, pp.356–378.

Kelley K. and Maxwell S.E. (2003). 'Sample size for multiple regression: Obtaining regression coefficients that are accurate, not simply significant', *Psychology Methods*, Vol.8, No.3, pp.305–321.

Keskin, T. (2009). 'Spor Turizmi', http://sponsorluk.gov.tr/tamer.htm (accessed 27.09.2009).

Klein, N. (1999). *No Logo: Taking Aim at the Brand Bullies*. St. Martins/Picador, New York.

Kloppenborg, T.J., Tesch, D., Manolis, C. and Heitkamp, M. (2006). 'An empirical investigation of the sponsor's role in project initiation', *Project Management Journal*, Vol.37, No.3, pp.16–25.

Knox, S., Maklan, S. and French, P. (2005). 'Corporate social responsibility: Exploring stakeholder relationships and programme reporting across leading FTSE companies', *Journal of Business Ethics*, Vol.61, pp.7–28.

Korngold, A. and Voudouris, E.H. (1996). 'Corporate Volunteerism: Strategic Community Involvement', in Burlingame, D.F. and Young, D.R. (eds), *Corporate Philanthropy at the Crossroads*, pp.23–40, Indiana University Press, Bloomington.

Kotter, J. and Heskett, J. (1992). *Corporate Culture and Performance*. Free Press, New York.

Kvale, S. (1996). *Interviews: An Introduction to Qualitative Research Interviewing*. Sage Publication, CA.

Lachowetz, T., McDonald, M., Sutton, A.W. and Hedrick, D.G. (2003). 'Corporate sales activities and the retention of sponsors in the National Basketball Association (NBA)', *Sport Marketing Quarterly*, Vol.12, No.1, pp.18–26.

Ladik, D.M., Carrillat, F.A. and Solomon, P.J. (2007). 'The effectiveness of university Sponsorship in increasing survey response rate', *Journal of Marketing Theory and Practice*, Vol.15, No.3, pp.162–171.

Levinthal, D.A. and March, J.G. (1981). 'A model of adaptive organizational search', *Journal of Economic Behavior and Organization*, Vol.2, No.4, pp.307–333.

Levy, F.K. and Shatto, G.M. (1978). 'The evaluation of corporate contributions', *Public Choice*, Vol.33, No.1, pp.19–28.

Lin, Z.J. and Hunter A. (1992). 'Accounting education for the 21st century: A Canadian experiment', *Journal of Education for Business*, Vol.68, No.1, pp.38–44.

Lincoln, D.J., Pressley, M.M. and Little, T. (1982). 'Ethical beliefs and personal values of top level executives', *Journal of Business Research*, Vol.10, No.4, pp.475–487.

Liu, G., Liston-Heyes, C. and Ko., W. (2010). 'Employee participation in cause-related marketing strategies: A study of management perceptions from British consumer service industries', *Journal of Business Ethics*, Vol.92, pp.195–210.

Locke, P.R., Sarkar, A. and Wu, L. (1999). 'Market liquidity and trader welfare in multiple dealer markets: Evidence from dual trading restrictions', *Journal of Financial and Quantitative Analysis*, Vol.34, No.1, pp.57–88.

Longsdon, J.M., Reiner, M. and Burke, L. (1990). 'Corporate philanthropy: Strategic responses to the firm's stakeholders', *Nonprofit and Voluntary Sector Quarterly*, Vol.19, No.2, pp.93–109.

Luca, L.M. and Atuahene-Gima, K. (2007). 'Market knowledge dimensions and cross-functional collaboration: Examining the different routes to product innovation performance', *Journal of Marketing*, Vol.71, No.1, pp.95–112.

Madariaga J.G. and Valor. C. (2004). 'Analysis of Implementation of the Socioeconomic Model of Business among Spanish MNCs,' *Proceedings of the Academy of Marketing Conference Virtue in Marketing*, Cheltenham.

Madden, K., Scaife, W. and Crissman, K. (2006). 'How and why small to medium size enterprises (SMEs) engage with their communities: An Australian study', *International Journal Nonprofit & Voluntary Sector*, Vol.11, No.1, pp.49–60.

Madill, J. and O'Reilly, N. (2010). 'Investigating social marketing sponsorships: Terminology, stakeholders, and objectives', *Journal of Business Research*, Vol.63, No.2, pp.133–139.

Maignan, I. (2001) 'Consumers' perceptions of corporate social responsibilities: A cross-cultural comparison', *Journal of Business Ethics*, Vol.30, No.1, pp.57–72.

Maital, S., and Maital, S. L. (1984). *Economic Games People Play.* Basic Books, New York.

March, J.G. and Simon, H.A. (1963). *Organizations.* John Wiley & Sons, Inc., New York.

Marquis, C., Glynn, M.A. and Davis, G. (2007). 'Community isomorphism and corporate social action', *Academy of Management Review,* Vol.32, No.3, pp.925–945.

Masterson, R. (2005). 'The importance of creative match in television sponsorship', *International Journal of Advertising,* Vol.24, No.4, pp.505–526.

Matten, D. and Moon, J. (2004) 'A Conceptual Framework for Understanding CSR', in Habisch, A., Jonker, J., Wegner, M. and Schmidpeter, R. (eds), *Corporate Social Responsibility across Europe,* pp.335–356, Springer Verlag, Berlin.

McDonald, C. (1991). 'Sponsorsphip and the image of the sponsor', *European Journal of Marketing,* Vol.25, No.11, pp.31–38.

McElroy, K.M. and Siegfried, J.J. (1985), 'The effect of firm size on corporate philanthropy', *Quarterly Review of Economics and Business,* Vol.25, pp.18–24.

McGuire, J.B., Sundgren, A. and Schneeweis, T. (1988). 'Corporate social responsibility and firm financial performance'. *Academy of Management Journal,* Vol.31, No.4, pp.854–872.

McWilliams, A. and Siegel, D. (2000). 'Research notes and communications corporate social responsibility and financial performance: Correlation or misspecification', *Strategic Management Journal,* Vol.21, No.5, pp.603–609.

McWilliams, A. and Siegel, D. (2001). 'Corporate social responsibility: A theory of the firm perspective', *Academy of Management Review,* Vol.26, No.1, pp.117–127.

McWilliams, A., Siegel, D. and Teoh, S.H. (1999). 'Issues in the use of the event study methodology: A critical analysis of corporate social responsibility studies', *Organizational Research Methods,* Vol.2, No.4, pp.340–365.

Meenaghan, J.A. (1983). 'Commercial sponsorship', *European Journal of Marketing,* Vol.17, No.7, pp.5–73.

Meijer, M, Bakker, F.G.A., Smit, J.H. and Schuyt, T. (2006). 'Corporate giving in the Netherlands 1995–2003: Exploring the amounts involved and the motivations for donating', *International Journal Nonprofit Volunteer Sector Marketing,* Vol.11, No.1, pp.13–28.

Menon, S. and Kahn, B.E. (2003), 'Corporate sponsorship of philanthropic activities: When do they impact perception of sponsor brand?', *Journal of Consumer Psychology,* Vol.13, No.3, pp.316–327.

Meyer, J.W. and Rowan, B. (1977). 'Institutional organizations: Formal structure as myth and ceremony', *American Journal of Sociology,* Vol.83, No.2, pp.340–363.

Miller, J.I. and Guthrie, D. (2007). 'The Rise of Corporate Social Responsibility: An Institutional Response to Labor, Legal, and Shareholder Environments', *Social Science Research Council*, http://pages.stern.nyu.edu/~dguthrie/papers/csr/2007-institutionalresponse.pdf (accessed 12.10.2009).

Miloch, K.S. and Lambrecht, K.W. (2006). 'Consumer awareness of sponsorship at grassroots sports events', *Sports Marketing Quarterly*, Vol.15, No.3, pp.147–154.

Mitchell, K.R., Agle, B.R. and Wood D.J. (1997). 'Toward a theory of stakeholder identification and salience: Defining the principle of who and what really counts', *Academy of Management Review*, Vol.22, No.4, pp.853–886.

Moir, L. and Taffler, R.J. (2004). 'Does corporate philanthropy exist?: Business giving to the arts in the UK.', *Journal of Business Ethics*, Vol.54, pp.149–161.

Moore, B. (1995). 'Corporate community involvement in the UK – investment or atonement?', *Business Ethics: A European Review*, Vol.4, No.3, pp.171–178.

Moreno, A.R., Fernandez, L.M.M and Montes, F.J.L. (2009). 'The moderating eEffect of slack resources on the relation between quality management and organisational learning', *International Journal of Production Research*, Vol.47, No.19, pp.5501–5523.

Museum Association (2009). www.museumassociation.org (accessed 12.12.2009).

Myers, P. (1990). *Classical and Modern Regression with Applications*, 2nd Edition. Duxbury, Boston, MA.

Navarro, P. (1988). 'Why do corporations give to charity?' *Journal of Business*, Vol.6, No.1, pp.65–93.

Neale, J.M. and Liebert, R.M. (1980). *Science and Behavior: An Introduction to Methods of Research*. Prentice-Hall, NJ.

Nohria, N. and Gulati, R. (1996). 'Is slack good or bad for innovation?', *The Academy of Management Journal*, Vol.39, No.5, pp.1245–1264.

Nohria, N. and Gulati, R. (1997). 'What is the optimum amount of organisational slack?', *European Management Journal*, Vol.15, No.6, pp.603–611.

Nowak, L.I., and Clarke, T.K. (2003). 'Cause-related marketing: Keys to successful relationships with corporate sponsors and their customers', *Journal of Nonprofit & Public Sector Marketing*, Vol.11, No.1, pp.137–149.

OECD Economic Survey (2008). Vol.14, July, http://www.turkey-now.org/db/Docs/OECD_TR_outlook.pdf (accessed 12.10.2009).

OECD Environmental Outlook (2008). http://www.oecd.org/document/24/0,3343,en_21571361_44315115_40224088_1_1_1_1,00.html (accessed 10.11.2008).

OECD Health Data (2009). November, http://www.oecd.org/document/44/0,3343,en_2649_34631_2085228_1_1_1_37407,00.html (accessed 05.11.2009).

OECD Key Environmental Indicators (2004). http://www.oecd.org/dataoecd/32/20/31558547.pdf (accessed 11.10.2009).

O'Hagan, J. and Harvey, D. (2000). 'Why do companies sponsor arts events? Some evidence and a proposed classification', *Journal of Cultural Economies*, Vol.24, No.3, pp.205–224.

Okumuş, K. (2002). *Turkey's Environment. A Review and Evaluation of Turkey's Environment and its Stakeholders*. Szentendre, Hungary: The Regional Environmental Center for Central and Eastern Europe.

Oliver, C. (1991). 'Strategic responses to institutional processes', *Academy of Management Review*, Vol.15, No.1, pp.145–179.

Oliver, C. (1992). 'The antecedents of deinstitutionalization', *Organisation Studies*, Vol.13, No.4, pp.563–588.

Olsen, G.D., Pracejus, J.W. and Brown, N.R. (2003). 'When profit equals price: Consumer confusion about donation amounts in cause-related marketing', *Journal of Public Policy & Marketing*, Vol.22, No.2, pp.170–180.

Panayiotou, N.A., Aravossis, K.G. and Moschou, P. (2009). 'Greece: A Comparative Study of CSR Reports', in Idowu, S.O. and Filho, W.L. (eds), *Global Practices of Corporate Social Responsibility*, pp.149–164, Springer Verlag, Berlin Heidelberg

Papadimitriou, D., Apostolopoulou, A. and Dounis, T. (2008). 'Event sponsorship as a value creating strategy for brands', *Journal of Product & Brand Management*, Vol.17, No.4, pp.212–222.

Peterson, D.K. (2004). 'Recruitment strategies for encouraging participation in corporate volunteer programs', *Journal of Business Ethics*, Vol.49, pp.371–386.

Pfeffer, J. and Salancik, G.R. (1978). *The External Control of Organisations: A Resource Dependence Perspective*, pp.258–262, Harper & Row Publishers, New York.

Pitts, B.G. and Slattery, J. (2004). 'An examination of the effects of time on sponsorship awareness levels', *Sport Marketing Quarterly*, Vol.13, No.1, pp.43–54.

Polonsky, M.J. and Wood, G. (2001). 'Can overcommercialization of cause-related marketing harm society?' *Journal of Macromarketing*, Vol.21, No.1, pp.8–22.

Poon, D.T.Y. and Prendergast, G. (2006). 'A new framework for evaluating sponsorship opportunities', *International Journal of Advertising*, Vol.25, No.4, pp.471–488.

Pope, N.K.L., and Voges, K.E. (1999). 'Sponsorship and image: A replication and extension', *Journal of Marketing Communications*, Vol.5, No.1, pp.17–28.

Porter, M.E. and Kramer, M.R. (1999). 'Philanthropy's new agenda: Creating value', *Harvard Business Review*, November–December, pp.121–130.

Porter, M.E. and Kramer, M.R. (2002). 'The competitive advantage of corporate philanthropy', *Harvard Business Review*, Vol.80, No.12, pp.56–68.

Powell, W.W. (1988). 'Institutional Effects on Organisational Structure and Performance', in Zucker, L.G. (ed.) *Institutional Patterns and Organisations: Culture and Environment*, pp.115–136, Ballinger, Cambridge.

Pracejus, J.W. and Olsen, G.D. (2004). 'The role of brand/cause fit in the effectiveness of cause-related marketing campaigns', *Journal of Business Research*, Vol.57, No.6, pp.635–640.

Pracejus, J.W., Olsen, G.D. and Brown, N.R. (2004). 'On the prevalence and impact of vague quantifiers in the advertising of cause-related marketing (CRM))', *Journal of Advertising*, Vol.32, No.4, pp.19–28.

Prietula, M.J. and Watson, H.S. (2006). 'When behavior matters: Games and computation in A Behavioral Theory of the Firm', *Journal of Economic Behaviour and Organization*, Vol.66, No.1, pp.74–94.

Pruitt, S.W., Cornwell, T.B. and Clark, J.M. (2004). 'The NASCAR phenomenon: Auto racing sponsorship and shareholder wealth', *Journal of Advertising Research*, Vol.44, No.3, pp.281–296.

Quester, P.G. and Thompson, B. (2001). 'Advertising and promotion leverage on arts sponsorship effectiveness', *Journal of Advertising Research*, Vol.41, Issue 1, pp.33–47.

Ragin, C. (1989). *The Comparative Method: Moving beyond Qualitative and Quantitative Strategies*, University of California Press, CA.

Rigaud, J. (1991). 'Company Giving in France: An Overview', in Dabson, B. (ed.), *Company Giving in Europe*, pp.57–60, Directory of Social Change, London.

Rodgers, S. (2004). 'The effects of sponsor relevance on consumer reactions to internet sponsorships', *Journal of Advertising*, Vol.54, No.4, pp.67–76.

Rosner, M.M. (1968). 'Economic determinants of organizational innovation', *Administrative Science Quarterly*, Vol.12, No.4, pp.614–625.

Ross, J.K., Patterson, L.T. and Stutts, M.A. (1992). 'Consumer perceptions of organizations that use cause-related marketing', *Journal of the Academy of Marketing Science*, Vol.20, No.1, pp.93–97.

Ross, J.K., Stutts, M.A. and Patterson, L. (1991). 'Tactical considerations for the effective use of cause-related marketing', *The Journal of Applied Business Research*, Vol.7, No.2, pp.58–65.

Royal Philharmonic Orchestra (1974). *The Case for Sponsorship*, London, quoted in Meenaghan, J.A. (1983). 'Commercial sponsorship', *European Journal of Marketing*, Vol.17, No.7, pp.5–73.

Saiia, D.H., Carroll, A.B. and Buchholtz, A.K. (2003). 'Philanthrophy as strategy: When corporate charity "begins at home"', *Business & Society*, Vol.42, No.2, pp.169–201.

Scott, W.R. (1992). *Organizations: Rational, Natural, and Open Systems*, 3rd Edition. Prentice-Hall, Englewood Cliffs, NJ.

Scott, W.R. (2001). *Institutions and Organizations*, 2nd edition. Sage Publications, Thousand Oaks, CA.

Seifert, B., Morris, S.A. and Bartkus, B.R. (2003). 'Comparing big givers and small givers: Financial correlates of corporate philanthropy', *Journal of Business Ethics*, Vol.45, No.3, pp.195–211.

Seifert, B., Morris, S.A. and Bartkus, B.R. (2004), 'Having, giving and getting: Slack resources, corporate philanthropy, and firm financial performance', *Business & Society*, Vol.43 No.2, pp.135–161.

Selznick, P. (1957). *Leadership in Administration*. Harper & Row, New York.

Sharfman, M. (1994). 'Changing institutional rules', *Business & Society*, Vol.33, No.3, pp.236–269.

Sharfman, P.M., Wolf, G., Chase, R.B. and Tansik, D.A. (1988). 'The antecedents of organizational slack', *Academy of Management Review*, Vol.13, No.4, pp.601–614.

Shaw S. and Amis J. (2001), 'Image and Investment: Sponsorship and women's sport', Journal of Sports Management, Vol.15, No.3, pp.219–246.

Shen, W. (2004). 'A comparative study on corporate sponsorships in Asia and Europe', *Asia Europe Journal*, Vol.2, No.2, pp.283–295.

Shen, W. and Chen, L. (2009). 'Firm profitability, State Ownership, and Top Management Turnover at the Listed Firms in China: A Behavioral Perspective', working paper, http://warrington.ufl.edu/purc/purcdocs/PAPERS/0820_Shen_Firm_Profitability_State.pdf (accessed 23.06.2009).

Shtatland, E.S., Cain E. and Barton, M.B. (2001). 'The perils of stepwise logistic regression and how to escape them using information criteria and the Output Delivery System'. Vol 222, No.26, Harvard Pilgrim Health Care, Harvard Medical School, Boston, MA.

Siefert, B., Morris, S.A. and Bartkus, B.R. (2003), 'Comparing big givers and small givers: Financial correlates of corporate philanthropy', *Journal of Business Ethics*, Vol.45, No.17, pp.195–211.

Siefert, B., Morris, S.A. and Bartkus, B.R. (2004), 'Having, giving and getting: Slack resources, corporate philanthropy, and firm financial performance', *Business & Society*, Vol.43, No.2, pp.135–161.

Siegfried, J.J., McElroy, K.M. and Bientot-Fawkes, D. (1983). 'The management of corporate contributions', *Research in Corporate Performance and Policy*, No.5, pp.87–102.

Sirgy, M.J., Lee, D., Johar, J.S. and Tidwell, J. (2008). 'Effect on self-congruity with sponsorship on brand loyalty', *Journal of Business Research*, Vol.61, pp.1091–1097.

Smith, C. (1994). 'The new corporate philanthropy', *Harvard Business Review*, May–June, pp.105–116.

Smith, C. (1996). 'Desperately Seeking Data: Why Research Is Crucial to the New Corporate Philanthropy', in Burlingame, D.F. and Young, D.R. (eds), *Corporate Philanthropy at the Crossroads*, pp.1–6, Indiana University Press, Bloomington.

Smith, C. (2003). 'Corporate social responsibility: Whether or how?', *California Management Review*, Vol.45, No.4, pp.52–76.

Smith, J. D. and Locke, M. (2007). 'Beyond Social Capital: What Next for Voluntary Action Research?', in *Volunteering and The Test of Time*, Institute for Volunteering Research, London.

Smith, S.M. and Alcorn, D.S. (1991). 'Cause marketing: A new direction in the marketing of corporate responsibility', *The Journal of Consumer Marketing*, Vol.8, No.3, pp.19–35.

Smyth, J. (2007). *Guide to UK Company Giving*, 6th Edition. Directory of Social Change.

Sneath, J.Z., Finney, R.Z and Close, A.G. (2005). 'An IMC approach to event marketing: The effects of sponsorship and experience on customer attitudes', *Journal of Advertising Research*, Vol.45, No.4, pp.373–380.

Stake, R.E. (2006). *The Art of Case Study Research*. Sage Publiations, Thousand Oaks, CA.

Stout, D.E. and Schweikart, J.A. (1989). 'The relevance of international accounting to the accounting curriculum: A comparison of practitioner and educator opinions', *Accounting Education*, Vol.4, No.1, pp.126–143.

Strahilevitz, M. (2003). 'The effects of prior impressions of a firm's ethics on the success of a cause-related marketing campaign: Do the good look better while the bad look worse?', *Nonprofit and Business Sector Collaboration*, Vol.11, No.1, pp.77–91.

Strahilevitz, M. and Myers, J.G. (1998). 'Donations to charity as purchase incentives: How well they work may depend on what you are trying to sell', *Journal of Consumer Research*, Vol.24, No.4, pp.434–445.

Strauss, A.L. (1987). *Qualitative Analysis for Social Scientists*. Press Syndicate of the University of Cambridge, New York.

Tansel, A. and Bircan, F. (2006). 'Demand for education in Turkey: A tobit analysis of private tutoring expenditures', *Economics of Education Review*, Vol.25, No.3, pp.303–313.

Tapper, R. (1991). *Islam in Modern Turkey: Religion, Politics and Literature in a Secular State*. Tauris, London.

Taylor, J.C., Webb, C. and Cameron, D. (2007). 'Charitable Giving by Wealthy People' HM Revenue and Customs, London, Ipsos MORI.

Tencati, A., Perrini, F. and Pogutz, S. (2004). 'New tools to foster corporate social responsible behavior', *Journal of Business Ethics*, Vol.53, pp.173–190.

Teo, T.T., Wei, K.K. and Benbasat, I. (2003). 'Predicting intention to adopt interorganisational linkage: An institutional perspective', *MIS Quarterly*, Vol.27, No.1, pp.19–49.

The McKinsey Quarterly (2007). 'The State of Corporate Philanthropy: A McKinsey Global Survey', http://www.mckinseyquarterly.com/ (accessed 29.04.2009).

Timmerman, C. (1995). 'Cultural practices and ethnicity: Diversifications among Turkish young women' *International Journal of Educational Research*, Vol.23, No.1, pp.23–32.

Trimble, C.S. and Rifon, N.J. (2006). 'Consumer perceptions of compatibility in cause-related marketing messages', *International Journal of Volunteer Sector Marketing*, Vol.11, No.1, pp.29–47.

Tripodi, J.A., Hirons, M., Bednall, D. and Sutherland, M. (2003). 'Cognitive evaluation: Prompts used to measure sponsorship awareness', *International Journal of Market Research*, Vol.45, Quarter 4, pp.435–455.

Tsiotsou, R. and Alexandris, K. (2009). 'Delineating the outcomes of sponsorship', *International Journal of Retail & Distribution Management*, Vol.37, No.4, pp.358–369.

TUIK Statistical Data (2008). http://www.tuik.gov.tr/Start.do (accessed 12.08.2008).

Turan, I. (1991). 'Religion and Political Culture in Turkey', in R. Tapper (ed.), *Islam in Modern Turkey; Religion, Politics and Literature in a Secular State*, pp.31–55, I.B. Tauris, London.

Turkish–US Business Council of DEİK. (2006). Sector Briefs for Foreign Companies in UNDP: 2008, Turkey Corporate Social Responsibility Baseline Report.

Useem, M. (1988). 'Market and institutional factors in corporate charitable contributions', *California Management Review*, Vol.30, No.2, pp.77–88.

Vaidyanathan, R. and Aggarwal, P. (2005). 'Using commitments to drive consistency: Enhancing the effectiveness of cause-related marketing communications', *Journal of Marketing Communications*, Vol.11, No.4, pp.231–246.

Van der Voort, J.M., Glac, K. and Meijs, L.C.P.M. (2009). 'Managing corporate community involvement', *Journal of Business Ethics*, Vol.90, pp.311–329.

Varadarajan, P.R. and Menon, A. (1988). 'Cause-related marketing: A coalignment of marketing strategy and corporate philanthropy', *Journal of Marketing*, Vol.52, No.3, pp.58–74.

Venkataramani, J.G., Tuan, P.M. and Kirk, W.L. (2006). 'How event sponsors are really identified: A (baseball) field analysis', *Journal of Advertising Research*, Vol.46, No.2, pp.183–198.

Waddock, S. and Graves S. (1997). 'The corporate social performance–financial performance link', *Strategic Management Journal*, Vol.18, No.4, pp.303–319.

Walliser, B. (2003). 'An international review of sponsorship research: Extension and update', *International Journal of Advertising*, Vol.22, No.1, pp.5–40.

Wang, J and Coffey, B.S. (1992). 'Board composition and corporate philanthropy', *Journal of Business Ethics*, Vol.11, No.10, pp.771–778.

Watkins, M. (2000). 'The Internal Stakeholder: Management Factors in the Implementation of an Environmental Management System in a Multi-Site Organisation', *PhD Book*, University of Bath, England, UK.

Watts, R.L. and Zimmerman, J.L. (1978). 'Towards a positive theory of the determination of accounting standards', *The Accounting Review*, Vol.53, No.1, pp.112–134.

Webb, D.J. and Mohr, L.A. (1998). 'A typology of consumer responses to cause-related marketing: From skeptics to socially concerned', *Journal of Public Policy & Marketing*, Vol.17, No.2, pp.226–238.

Wei, S. and Chen, L. (2009). 'Firm profitability, state ownership, and top management turnover at the listed firms in China: A behavioral perspective', *Corporate Governance: An International Review*, Vol.17, No.4, pp.443–456.

Weintraub, E.R. (2002). *How Economics Became A Mathematical Science*, Duke University Press, Chapel Hill.

Wei-Skillern, J. (2004). 'The evolution of Shell's stakeholder approach: A case study', *Business Ethics Quarterly*, Vol.14, No.4, pp.713–728.

Welford, R. (2004). Corporate Social Responsibility in Europe, North America and Asia: 2004 Survey Results, Corporate Environmental Governance Programme, University of Hong Kong, http://web.hku.hk/~cegp/image/publications/report11.pdf (accessed 26.08.2009).

Werber, J.D. and Carter, S.M. (2002). 'The CEO's influence on corporate foundation giving', *Journal of Business Ethics*, Vol.40, pp.47–60.

White, J.B. (2002). *Islamist Mobilization in Turkey*, University of Washington Press, Washington.

Wild, C. (1993). 'Corporate Volunteer Programs: Benefits to Business', *The Conference Board Report*, No.1029, New York.

William, R. and Endacott, J. (2004). 'Consumers and CRM: A national and global perspective', *Journal of Consumer Marketing*, Vol.21, No.3, pp.183–189.

Williamson, B. (1987). *Education and Social Change in Egypt and Turkey*. MacMillan Press, London.

Wokutch, R. E. and Spencer, B.A. (1987). 'Corporate saints and sinners: The effects of philanthropic and illegal activity on organisational performance', *California Management Review*, Volume XXIX, No.2, Winter, pp. 62–77.

Wulfson, M. (2001). 'The ethics of corporate social responsibility and philanthropic ventures', *Journal of Business Ethics*, Vol.29, Issue.1/2, pp.135–145.

Wymer, W.W. and Samu, J.S. (2003). 'Dimensions of business and nonprofit collaborative relationship', *Journal of Nonprofit & Public Sector Marketing*, Vol.11, No.1, pp.3–19.

Yankey, J.A. (1996). 'Corporate Support of Nonprofit Organisations', in Burlingame, D.F. and Young, D.R. (eds), *Corporate Philanthropy at the Crossroads*, pp.7–22, Indiana University Press, Bloomington.

Youn, S. and Kim, H. (2008). 'Antecedents of consumer attitudes toward cause-related marketing', *Journal of Advertising Research*, March, pp.123–137.

Yurtoğlu, B. (2003). 'Corporate governance and implications for minority shareholders in Turkey', *Corporate Ownership & Control*, Vol.1, No.1, pp.72–86.

Zhang, R., Rezaee, Z. and Zhu, J. (2009). 'Corporate philanthropic disaster response and ownership type: Evidence from Chinese firms: Response to the Sichuan earthquake', *Journal of Business Ethics*, Vol.91, No.1, pp.51–63.

Zucker, L.G. (1988), *Institutional Patterns and Organisations: Culture and Environment*. Ballinger, Cambridge.

Zwetsloot, G.I.J.M. (2003). 'From management systems to corporate social responsibility', *Journal of Business Ethics*, Vol.44, No.2/3, pp.201–207.

Index

For Product Safety Concerns and Information please contact our EU representative GPSR@taylorandfrancis.com Taylor & Francis Verlag GmbH, Kaufingerstraße 24, 80331 München, Germany

Printed and bound by CPI Group (UK) Ltd, Croydon, CR0 4YY

04/05/2025

01860547-0001